Predators

Wild Dogs & Cats

An Altitude SuperGuide

Predators

Wild Dogs & Cats

by Kevin Van Tighem

Altitude Publishing
The Canadian Rockies/Vancouver/Denver

Publication Information

Altitude Publishing Canada Ltd.
The Canadian Rockies / Vancouver / Denver

Head Office: 1500 Railway Avenue
Canmore, Alberta T1W 1P6

Copyright 1999 © Kevin Van Tighem

Canadian Cataloguing in Publication Data

Van Tighem, Kevin J.
Predators, Wild Dogs & Cats
(An Altitude SuperGuide)
Includes index.
ISBN 1-55153-804-0
1. Predatory animals--Rocky Mountains, Canadian (B.C. and Alta.) 2. Predatory animals--Rocky Mountains, Canadian (B.C. and Alta.)--Pictorial works. . I. Title. II. Series.
Ql758.V36 1999   591.5'3'09711   C98-910914-3

Printed and bound in Western Canada by Friesen Printers, Altona, Manitoba.

Altitude GreenTree Program

Altitude Publishing will plant twice as many trees as were used in the manufacturing of this product.

We acknowledge the financial support of the Government of Canada through the Book Publishing Industry Development Program (BPIDP) for our publishing activities.

Photographs

Front cover: Wolf
Frontispiece: Cougar
Back cover: Lynx
Back cover inset: Bobcat kitten

Project Development

Publisher	Stephen Hutchings
Associate Publishers	Dan Klinglesmith
	Patrick Soran
Concept/art direction	Stephen Hutchings
Design/layout	Dan Klinglesmith
Editor	Sabrina Grobler
	Dan Klinglesmith
Index	Elizabeth Bell
Financial management	Laurie Smith

A Note from the Publisher

The world described in *Altitude SuperGuides* is a unique and fascinating place. It is a world filled with surprise and discovery, beauty and enjoyment, questions and answers. It is a world of people, cities, landscape, animals and wilderness as seen through the eyes of those who live in, work with, and care for this world. The process of describing this world is also a means of defining ourselves.

It is also a world of relationship, where people derive their meaning from a deep and abiding contact with the land—as well as from each other. And it is this sense of relationship that guides all of us at Altitude to ensure that these places continue to survive and evolve in the decades ahead.

Altitude SuperGuides are books intended to be used, as much as read. Like the world they describe, *Altitude SuperGuides* are evolving, adapting and growing. Please write to us with your comments and observations, and we will do our best to incorporate your ideas into future editions of these books.

Stephen Hutchings
Publisher

Contents

Acknowledgements

T his book owes its existence to the many people who contributed their knowledge, skills and energies to help me pull it together. Bill Dolan, Rob Watt and my other colleagues generously filled in for me during the months that I took off work to write the book.

Gail Van Tighem, my wife and the best field companion and hiking partner I've ever met, put up with my long hours and piles of paper long after anyone else would have booted me out to the garage. She also proofread and critiqued the text.

Information for this book came from a great variety of sources—both individuals and published materials. Thanks go, in particular, to Clayton Apps, Wendy Arjo, Diane Boyd, Keith Everts, Waneeta Fisher, Stephen Herrero, Ron Larsen, Toni Ruth, Paul Paquet, Steve Pozzanghera, Andy Russell, John Seidel, David Spalding, Rob Watt and John Weaver, as well as the staff of various state and provincial wildlife agencies who responded promptly to information requests.

My thanks to those who commented on parts of the text: Clayton Apps, Diane Boyd, Ron Larsen, Paul Paquet, Gail Van Tighem and John Weaver. I take responsibility for any errors that may have survived the edits or that crept in during the final rewrites.

I dedicate this book to two people whose faith, love, wisdom and support opened so much of the richness of this world to an aspiring young naturalist: my mother, Eileen Van Tighem and my father, the late Jack Van Tighem.

How To Use This Book

This is more than a book about wolves, cougars, bobcats, foxes and other wild hunters which range western North America's mountains and plains. It's a book about people—people who study wild hunters, who live in places where predators are common and who work to protect or manage them. You can use this book to develop an in-depth understanding of the featured species, and you can also use the book to explore how we perceive, and live with, animals that hunt and kill other animals.

The West is home to several kinds of wild carnivores. The bear family (*Ursidae*) forms the focus of another title in this series. The dog family (*Canidae*), which includes coyotes, wolves and foxes, and the cat family (*Felidae*), including cougars, bobcats and lynx, form the focus of this book. Two other kinds of carnivore occur in western North America: the weasel family (*Mustelidae*)—ferrets, fishers, mink, marten, weasels and wolverines—and the raccoon family (*Procyonidae*).

If you want to learn about predators in general and some of the conservation issues that affect most of North America's wild dogs and cats, the introduction chapter including "Who are Predators?," "What Are Predators?" and "Where are Predators?" are good places to start.

If specific topics interest you, such as the historical use of poisons to control predators, or research, or certain people or places that you come across in the book, check the index.

Because of the way we present information in these *Altitude SuperGuides*, you may encounter the same subject, from a different angle, in different places. The index will help you tie the bits together.

Each species of wild dog or cat which lives in western North America has a chapter of its own. These chapters begin with basic biology information: where to find the species, what the species eat, how it breeds and so forth, and concludes with a discussion of conservation issues affecting that species.

Finally, the section entitled Reference provides conservation resource contacts and addresses for more information about predators, and where to find ways to better live with the animals you will meet in this *Altitude SuperGuide*.

Predators, Wild Dogs & Cats is organized according to the following color scheme:

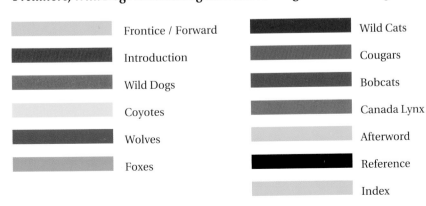

Frontice / Forward	Wild Cats
Introduction	Cougars
Wild Dogs	Bobcats
Coyotes	Canada Lynx
Wolves	Afterword
Foxes	Reference
	Index

Forward

It was late April and I was utterly exhausted. All day I had struggled up the Cascade Valley in the Canadian Rockies through wet, granular snow that soaked through my snowshoe webbing and drenched me to the waist. At length I gave up, discouraged and worn out.

I was too tired to set up the tent or even to worry about the grizzly tracks on the trail. I rolled out my sleeping bag, crawled in and fell asleep.

Somewhere in the darkest part of the night, six lean shapes emerged from the timber. As they drew near, two separated from the others to investigate the strange lump beside the trail. Curiosity satisfied, the two wolves halted a few feet away and howled to the rest of the pack.

I woke in blind terror, their deep resonating wails pulsing through the forest beside me. I sat bolt upright, staring wide-eyed into the blackness. I was only nineteen years old. I had never really considered that I might not be at the top of the food chain.

But all was still—I could hear only the faint, distant chatter of the Cascade River. I lay awake the rest of that eternal night, staring up at the icy cold stars, listening, waiting and feeling very small, very humble and more vulnerable than I had ever felt before.

In the morning, the tracks told me the story of my first wolf encounter. I followed them up the valley all the rest of that day. By the time their footprints veered off into the trees, I felt I had formed some kind of bond with these creatures who had spared me in the night and shared their lonely valley with me through the following day.

That winter, I heard that problem wildlife officers had poisoned a pack of six wolves with strychnine a few miles away.

Wolves were rare in the Rockies in those days. Certainly my parents had never seen one, nor had my grandfather. For all that, they didn't strike us as exotic. It felt like they belonged.

Mountain lions, however, seemed the stuff of myth and fable. I was 24 and working in Kootenay National Park the summer that cougars first became

real to me. One afternoon, I heard a hysterical, high-pitched shrieking just outside the bunkhouse. Peering through the window, Jim Mulchinock and I spotted a small coyote, every hair standing on end, pacing back and forth as it peered into the trees, barking and howling. We pushed the door open and stepped out so that we could see around the corner. There, emerging from forest gloom into the bright May sunlight, was an immense, tawny cougar. He paused in mid step and turned his head, fixing us in a cold, yellow-eyed gaze. Then, unhurried and deliberate, he turned, eased his way back into the shadows and was gone. He left behind a nerve-shattered coyote and two thunderstruck young naturalists.

Since that time, I've been privileged to spend most of my adult life in the wild country where wild hunters raise their families, pursue their prey, mate, give birth and die. I've enjoyed many glimpses into the world in which they live. I know them well enough, now, to realize that I barely know them at all.

This book reflects the beginning of understanding.

Predators

Introduction

Eyes and ears alert, a curious bobcat kitten stalks a mystery.

Western North America, from Alaska and Yukon south to Mexico's Sierra Madre, is filled with natural wonders. In the north, glacier-gouged valleys, dark with forests of spruce and fir, filled with the noise of water and wind, separate upthrust mountains of limestone and granite. Farther south, blue-gray sagelands and tawny prairie finger uphill into dwarf forests of pinyon and juniper, aspen thickets and ponderosa pine. Rivers snake their way out of the high country through broad, fertile valleys or deep-cut canyons. Yellowstone's thermal basins, Banff's Columbia Icefield, Arizona's Grand Canyon, Wyoming's high plains and the great wilderness valleys of northern British Columbia's Liard drainage are among only a few of the natural wonders that draw visitors to this region.

Those fortunate enough to live here year-round know that these famous places are only the tip of the iceberg. And just as visitors and residents alike find themselves humbled and inspired by the West's spectacular landscapes, so do we find our imaginations captured by the diversity and abundance of its wildlife. Among the most spectacular and special of these are the wild dogs and cats which still range the open spaces of the West.

North America's giant cat, the cougar, slides silently through the shadows of the forest edges, hunting mule deer and elk. Their tracks appear from time to time at the near edges of our settlements, reminding us that our familiar world is nonetheless a place of mystery and power. Coyotes shiver the night with near-maniacal shrilling. Wolves—among the most controversial and compelling of the region's wild hunters—leave their tracks along an ever-expanding network of game trails and river flats as they re-colonize their ancient homeland.

Wild cats and dogs—lynx, bobcats, cougars, foxes, coyotes and wolves—give depth and texture to our living West. Elk and deer, rabbits and rodents are rarely placid for long; their need to watch for and avoid predators keeps them wild and wary. Where history has deprived parts of the west of healthy predator populations, like north-central Colorado and parts of Wyoming, elk populations damage their ranges and sicknesses such as chronic wasting disease and brucellosis flourish in prey populations. The land needs the dogs and cats its evolution has produced—and, unlike too much of North America, those wild hunters persist throughout most of the West. These are superb creatures, crafted by countless generations of natural selection into intelligent, socially complex and highly adapted animals. Their natures fascinate, and often trouble, the humans with whom they share the landscape. Our relationship with wild cats and dogs is complex and ambivalent. Many people keep dogs and cats as pets because we admire the very attributes that make us fearful or uncertain of their wild relatives. If we can come to know the wild ones better, perhaps we can learn to live with them more comfortably. These remarkable animals, after all, are among the natural wonders which give the West its unique character, fill its mythology, and help to make us who we are.

Who are Predators?

Across North America this century, people have killed millions of wolves, coyotes, foxes, cougars, lynx and bobcats. The arsenal of weapons used in the war against predators fills a long and lethal list: strychnine, bullets, snares, traps, cyanide gas. Governments at every level have devoted entire bureaucracies to killing predators. Taxpayers have generated hundreds of millions of dollars to finance this war.

But the war, for the most part, has been lost. Foxes and coyotes are more widespread than ever. Wolves have started to spread south into areas where, a half century ago, predator control programs eradicated them. Cougar populations have reached all-time highs in many parts of western North America.

A century ago, society had no popular understanding of ecology and few people could imagine any legitimate role for predators in the modern world. Most people wanted predator control to protect livestock for farmers, big game for hunting, and the security of people generally. Many people still think that way, but a growing number believe that large predators— including North America's native members of the dog and cat families—should continue to play dynamic and productive roles in the continent's diverse ecosystems. Biologists have learned enough about wild dogs and cats to make it possible for people to coexist with these predators peacefully. It turns out that many of the fears that people have about predators are unfounded.

Nonetheless, the war against the West's wild dogs and cats continues today, though clothed in softer rhetoric and conducted with more restraint. Even supposedly protected national parks, wild predators face an uncertain future: too many die on highways and railroads, and too many die when, as they must, they cross

What Children Learn About Predators

Even magic rings are not much use against wolves, especially against the evil packs that lived under the shadow of the goblin-infested mountains, over the Edge of the Wild on the borders of the unknown. Wolves of that sort smell keener than goblins, and do not need to see you to catch you!

J.R.R. Tolkien, *The Hobbit*

The Wolfe pull'd the bobbin, and the door open'd; upon which he fell upon the good woman and eat her up in the tenth part of a moment. After that he shut the doors and went into the grandmother's bed, expecting the Little Red Riding Hood.

"Little Red Riding Hood" in
I. and P. Opie,
The Classic Fairy Tales

It was a huge black panther, leaping through the air like Black Susan leaping on a mouse. It was many, many times bigger than Black Susan. It was so big that if it leaped on Grandpa it could kill him with its enormous, slashing claws and its long, sharp teeth.

Laura Ingalls Wilder,
Little House in the Big Woods

Then along came the wolf and said 'Little Pig, Little Pig, let me come in!' 'No, no, by the hair of my chinny chin chin.' 'Then I'll huff and I'll puff and I'll blow your house in.' So he huffed and he puffed, and he huffed and he puffed, and at last he blew the house down and he ate up the little pig.

Joseph Jacobs,
The Three Little Pigs

Predators such as the red fox have highly developed senses of vision, hearing and scent.

park boundaries and people aggressively hunt them down.

What motivates the deep antipathy many people feel toward wolves, coyotes, cougars and other animals that rely on sharp teeth and sharp wits to make a living? What makes it possible for good people to rationalize the cruelty of leg-hold traps and strychnine to kill predators when we would never dream of using such weapons against other animals? Why does killing remain our instinctive response when the needs of wild hunters collide with human ambitions?

Our species has devoted considerable energy over the years to eliminating the risks we face in the real world. We try to control floods with dams, and drought with irrigation. We put out the fires which once to swept the prairies and forests. Our clothing and houses protect us from exposure. We engineer new medical technology to control disease. No investment seems too great to ensure certainty, security and safety.

The control or eradication of large predators flows from the same impulse. Predators pose a long-standing double threat to people. They hunt the animals we hunt or raise for food, and occasionally, they even kill us.

Predators represent chaos and uncertainty in a world where we seek security. Killing predators reasserts our dominance, our ability to control nature's risks and free ourselves from fear.

Many cultural traditions reinforce human fear of predators: tales about the big bad wolf, werewolves, cougars sneaking up in the night and sinking their fangs into unwary throats, foxes outwitting shepherds and slaughtering sheep. Generations of children have grown up with stories linking predatory animals to childhood fears, creating a sense that there is no safe way to live with wild hunters. Most of North America's first peoples, of course, knew differently. For the most part, they saw large predators as hunters of great spiritual power. But Europeans brought their own beliefs when they invaded this continent.

It is easy to fear what we do not know or understand. Our instincts tell us to strike out blindly at things with sharp teeth. A dead animal can't hurt anyone. But we have another way to master our fears that is more difficult but ultimately more human. We can learn to understand wild hunters better.

What Are Predators?

Predators are animals that kill and eat other animals. Most predatory mammals belong to the order *Carnivora*, a specialized group of animals that includes the dog family and the cat family as well as bears, weasels and raccoons. Carnivores have three kinds of specialized teeth allowing them to slice through flesh: long canine teeth, three pairs of sharp incisors and specially adapted molars or carnassial teeth much like self-sharpening kitchen shears. Unlike many other mammals, carnivore jaws can only move up and down. Herbivores need jaw action to grind and pulverize, but meat eaters need to bite and cut.

Carnivores also have highly developed brains. Animals that hunt and kill mobile prey cannot rely on simple pattern recognition or habit. They need their wits to find food. They must learn from experience, solve problems and execute sometimes-complicated hunting strategies.

In nature, species with high intelligence and complex lifestyles usually nurture their young through an extended childhood. Humans are the ultimate example, but many large carnivores, too, spend a long time with their young. Bear cubs may remain with their mothers for up to three years. Cougar families may remain together for a year and a half. Wolf packs consist of related wolves which, in some cases, may remain together for several years.

The less-complicated life of a herbivore, by contrast, requires less preparation. Deer usually separate from their young in a year or less. Mice can have several litters of young each year.

Young carnivores observe, experiment and learn during the time they spend with their parents. Their parents also help them find food, an important function since young carnivores grow fast, need lots of energy, but lack hunting skills. By the time young predators forge out on their own, their bodies are well-developed. They have experienced many successful hunts and learned how to find prey in different seasons and habitats.

Because predators rely on meat for most of their meals, most predator populations are relatively small. Basic high school biology covers the food pyramid: abundant vegetation at the bottom, a small number of predators at the top and a layer of grazing animals in between. A species high on the food pyramid has a smaller population than one lower on the pyramid. Nature doesn't work if predators outnumber prey.

Dogs and Cats

The Canidae (dog family) and Felidae (cat family) hunt the same prey, but they are only distantly related. Dogs are much more closely related to raccoons and bears, cats to hyenas and mongooses.

Since both are carnivores, dogs and cats share some characteristics: canine teeth, carnassial teeth, stereo vision and high intelligence. The molars of dogs, however, are designed for chewing and crushing. They enable dogs to gnaw on or crack bones, and to chew sinew and hide. Cats, by contrast, can only slice their food since they lack chewing molars. A carcass that wolves or coyotes have fed on usually has some crushed bones, while a cougar or lynx kill has intact, well-cleaned bones.

Anyone familiar with domestic dogs and cats will have noticed another important difference between the two kinds of predator: dogs constantly sniff at things while cats study objects intently with their eyes.

Most members of the dog family have long noses. This provides more internal surface area for scent receptors. They also drool, keeping their smelling apparatus moist and sensitive. Scent is an important part of how dogs hunt and communicate. Cats have short faces with jaws capable of gaping widely. They have special muscles that enable them to bite down hard on large objects such as the necks of their prey.

Stairway to Heaven

A Shuswap legend demonstrates the powers that some indigeneous peoples associated with large carnivores. It tells how Grizzly, Black Bear, Wolf and Cougar helped people bring down fish from the upper world to our world.

When the animal people grew hungry, they decided they had to go to the upper world to search for food. Grizzly, Black Bear, Wolf and Cougar shot arrows into the sky to form a ladder for the animal people to climb. When all the animals had climbed up, Black Bear remained at the bottom to guard the ladder.

Black Bear had a beautiful long white-tipped tail in those days. Fox, who hadn't gone to the upper world with the other animals, liked it so much that he asked Black Bear if he could try it on. Black Bear agreed. Once Fox had the tail, he refused to return it. He still has it.

Cats have larger eyes than dogs, relative to the size of their head. They also have special adaptations inside their eyes enabling them to see six times better after dark than humans. Because cats rely on their eyes to locate prey, and then stalk to within close attack range, they also have a highly developed sense of touch. Long, brittle whiskers in their paws, toes and faces allow them to feel obstacles before blundering into them and foiling their stalk.

Cats have razor-sharp, hooked claws which they can extend suddenly to grip and tear at prey. When running or bounding, the alignment of bones and ligaments in their feet keeps their claws retracted inside their toes. Dogs, by contrast, always show the marks of claws in their tracks since they rely on their claws only for traction, not for grasping or tearing.

North America's wildcats are usually solitary animals. Males accompany females only during the short breeding season. Males may breed with several females. North American dogs, however, are more sociable and have more monogamous breeding habits.

Fast Deer, Alert Elk

What would deer, elk, rabbits and other animals be like without predators to hunt them? They would likely be similar to domestic cows and sheep: slow and dull-witted, plagued by diseases and para-

sites. Domestic animals have been spared the selective pressure of constant predation; as a result, they require constant baby-sitting.

A clumsy deer will almost certainly die young. Absent-minded elk, unhealthy rabbits and slow mice have little hope of a long life. Wild predators quickly dispatch the slow, the sick or the stupid, leaving only the healthiest to survive and reproduce.

Through millennia of natural selection, wild predators have honed hunting skills in parallel with the fine-tuned escape skills of their prey. This ongoing predator-prey arms race has shaped, over thousands of years, the attributes that many human hunters admire in deer, mountain sheep, game birds and other prey animals.

Biologists note, in virtually every in-depth study of predator-prey relationships, that most attacks end in failure. The deer outruns the cougar. The elk stands off the wolves. The hare sprints from beneath the reaching claws of the lynx. Predation is not a one-sided game; it's a near-equal match whose outcome can go either way. A weak or unwell prey animal is more likely to get eaten than to escape. A sick or injured predator is far more likely to starve than to capture a meal.

Domestic animals— jealously protected from predators and bred for characteristics which make them tractable; large and delicious— are not fast, alert, sleek or particularly beautiful. Had deer or moose evolved in the absence of wolves, coyotes and cougars, they might very well have ended up looking little different from milk cows. Placid bovines cannot thrill the human spirit in the same way as a flashing glimpse of a bounding white-tail whose ancestors, for centuries beyond number, have managed to elude wolves, cougars and other predators long enough to breed and pass on their superior survival skills.

Sport Hunting

Kittens play at stalking and pouncing. They hide, dash out and land, claws extended, on a littermate, a human foot or eventually, perhaps, on a mouse.

Puppies chase balls, race in joyful circles, play hide and seek, and chew on things—eventually, perhaps, on a young bird.

Young animals play endlessly, practicing skills they will need when they grow up. Later in life, if those kittens or puppies were wild predators, they would re-enact each of those play behaviors again and again in hunting.

Play is fun, but also deadly serious. By the same token, hunting is serious but nevertheless fun. For predators, the line between play and hunting may not really exist except in terms of outcomes.

Idle curiosity can instantly change to an intent hunting gaze if a cougar notices the right signals from its object of interest.

Predators sometimes kill more than they can eat. A wolf or cougar may kill a whole herd of deer trapped in deep snow. If coyotes corner an unprotected flock of domestic sheep, they may leave the ground littered with uneaten carcasses. "Surplus killing" evokes moral outrage among people who claim with some justification that those predators must have killed just

Eyes That Glow In The Dark

A bobcat's dilated pupils let in light that its tapetum then magnifies.

Medieval Europeans thought that the fires of hell shone out of the eyes of wolves and wildcats, one more proof of the relationship between wild predators and the devil. Modern North Americans see the same fires late at night when their headlights pick

out a pair of gleaming eyes in the darkness long before they reveal the form of a fox, lynx or coyote crossing the road.

Animals that hunt or travel by night have larger eyes, relative to their size, than other creatures, and more rod cells (the cells in the retina that detect light). A thin membrane, called the *tapetum lucidum*, lines the back of night hunters' eyes behind the retina. This membrane makes their eyes glow in the dark.

The *tapetum lucidum* acts like a power-booster for rod cells. After light has passed through the rods once, the *tapetum lucidum* reflects it back through them again, doubling their effectiveness.

When an unusually bright light shines through the dilated pupils of a night hunter, the *tapetum lucidum* reflects the light like a mirror, creating the brilliant, glowing eyes that stare out from forest shadows.

Lynx rarely face conflict with human interests.

for the fun of it.

The underlying assumption which supports this kind of moral outrage is that it is wrong for predators to kill for pleasure. Human values, however, apply only to humans. In nature, hunting and playing appear to be flip sides of the same coin: "hunting" is play that ends in a meal, "playing" is a hunt that does not.

From its earliest days, a predator rehearses

constantly. If it didn't enjoy rehearsals, it wouldn't have much of a life. Sometimes a rehearsal turns into the real thing; often the real thing turns into just another rehearsal. Playful hunting only rarely yields more dead prey than the hunters may eat—a good thing, since the food pyramid would otherwise cave in on itself.

Predator Control

Most ranchers and farmers live at peace with wild predators, experiencing few problems and enjoying the chance to see coyotes, cougars and even wolves on their land. Nonetheless, some people in the agricultural community prefer simply to kill predators than go to the trouble of learning how to coexist with them. Many agricultural and livestock organizations continue to lobby governments for predator-control programs.

Wars against predators probably began when humans first took up agriculture. Hunter-gatherer cultures tolerate predators and some even worship them. But once humans had herds of domestic livestock and flocks of chickens or other fowl to protect, they began to see predators as a scourge.

Many modern farmers and ranchers have found alternatives to deadly force. They try to prevent predator problems. Properly designed chicken yards bar foxes, coyotes and cougars. Wolves kill fewer cattle if herds calve and winter in pastures near farm residences instead of out on the range. Shepherds who train and use guard dogs or llamas discourage the interest of the neighborhood coyotes.

But all these measures require a willingness to tolerate wild hunters on what humans consider agricultural land. In some cases, the measures mean costly changes to traditional ways of operating and they do not guarantee that predators will leave livestock alone. Eradicating predators, however, eliminates both that risk

An Extinction Chronicle

In their recent book, *The Last Extinction*, J.D. Williams and R.N. Nowak list the dates when various carnivore subspecies became extinct in North America:

1903	Southern California kit fox
1910	Kenai Peninsula wolf
1911	Newfoundland wolf
1920	Banks Island wolf
1925	Florida red wolf
1925	Wisconsin cougar
1925	California grizzly
1926	Great plains wolf
1935	Southern Rocky Mountains wolf
1940	Cascade Mountains wolf
1940	Northern Rocky Mountains wolf
1942	Mogollon Mountains wolf
1942	Texas gray wolf
1970	Texas red wolf

In the Red

The U.S. Department of Agriculture estimates that in 1990 alone, predators killed $27.4 million worth of sheep and goats and $41 million worth of cattle in the United States. Coyotes did by far the most damage. Under its animal damage control program, the department spent almost $30 million to kill nearly 100,000 predators that year.

and the need for special management measures. Little wonder that 20th century agri-business has made animal-control poisons a growth industry.

Poisons have eradicated some of the smaller predators such as the Swift fox and the black-footed ferret from most of western North America. Still, poisons alone generally cannot eliminate predators. Poisons reduce the number of predators, but leave prey populations untouched. The surviving predators respond to reduced competition for food by raising more young.

Habitat loss has had a larger long-term impact on predators than poisons. Cougars and wolves no longer survive in much of southern Canada and the U.S. east of the Rockies because agriculture, urban development and industry have radically changed their ecosystems. They started to decline in the late 1800s when frontier slaughters wiped out the bison and other large prey animals. Soon after, settlers began converting prairie ecosystems to farmland. Within a few short decades, the large predators had nowhere to live and not much to eat.

Most predator specialists agree that the conflict between agriculture and wild predators has only two long-term solutions: wipe out the whole wild ecosystem or find ways to reduce the risk that predators will prey on domestic animals.

Prehistoric Predators

The world has known many kinds of predators since the dawn of life four billion or more years ago. Mammals—creatures like us with hair or fur, warm blood and the biological ability to produce milk—have only roamed the earth for the past 100 million years or so, not even a third as long as reptiles.

During the Mesozoic era, most of the large animals on earth were reptiles. The predators of the day included remarkable creatures such as *Tyrannosaurus*, *Albertosaurus* and *Velociraptor*. Some weighed more than six tons, an extravagant size made possible by huge prey species, some of which weighed in at 30 tons!

In a world of such giants, the first mammals must have been nervous little things.

With the end of the age of dinosaurs, mammals emerged into the limelight, becoming the dominant group of vertebrate animals.

Mammals have existed in many forms over the centuries. Most of those forms are now extinct. For the first 30 to 40 million years of the age of mammals, the vast majority of the world's mammalian predators belonged to the order *Creodonta*, which like *Carnivora*, began contributing its remains to the fossil record about 70 million years ago. Creodonts included more than 50 genera and hundreds of species of predators that resembled today's weasels, cats, hyenas and civets, including some large saber-toothed creatures that died out 40 million years ago.

For some reason, however, the last creodonts faded away about seven million years ago. Long before then, primitive early carnivores called miacids had started to evolve into subgroups that became the families of carnivores we recognize today. One subgroup, which first appeared about 60 million years ago, became *Ursidae* (bears), *Procyonidae* (raccoons and civets), *Canidae* (dogs) and *Otariidae* (walruses). Another became the *Mustelidae* (weasels) and *Phocidae* (seals). A third subgroup gave rise to the *Felidae* (cats), *Viverridae* (mongooses) and *Hyaenidae* (hyenas).

With the passing of the creodonts, carnivores rose to dominance.

Two or three million years ago, the most recent sorting of the evolutionary deck began with the onset of the Pleistocene ice age. Polar ice caps and mountain glaciers swelled and overran much of North America, Asia and Europe, then melted back, and advanced again. Habitats shrank, grew and changed. Some species became extinct during glacial advances, others during retreats. As recently as 12,000 years ago, giant saber-tooth cats, dire wolves, California lions and other great carnivores ranged across western North America. No scientist has ever figured out why they became extinct. It is probably no coincidence, however, that primitive humans spread across the continent at about the same time as the great predators vanished, along with most of their prey species.

Today, other predators are taking their turn in the earth's great pageant of life: timber wolves, coyotes, foxes, cougars, lynxes and bobcats.

And today, another great extinction event is sweeping the planet—one of the most dramatic ever. It is being caused by growing populations of another recent mammal: *Homo sapiens*.

Predators are difficult to study in forested areas where human persecution has made them shy.

Studying Predators

Many predator populations started to recover during the 1950s, after a long decline that had begun in the 1800s. At the same time, and probably by no coincidence, the population of another wilderness creature—the wildlife biologist—also began to increase.

In 1944, Adolph Murie published one of the first serious predator-ecology studies. His field studies of the wolves of Mt. McKinley (now De-nali) National Park in Alaska broke new ground in seeking to describe predators as part of ecosystems. Earlier studies had focused on management questions about how much livestock predators killed, the best way to get rid of predators and so forth. Ironically, some of the best studies of predator food habits came out of the ambitious predator-eradication campaigns of the U.S. Biological Survey. In one 1941 study, for example, biologists examined the stomach

Responsible Research

"You have to weigh the benefits and the costs of research. Research has an impact on animals and we don't know to what degree in a lot of respects. But we can get some valuable solutions from research.

I think as we continue down that road—research on cougars and bears has been going on for 30 years now—we need to start being really picky about what constitutes necessary research and whether collaring animals is the way to go about things.

Glacier National Park has asked that sort of question a lot: when we're out there trying to get information, what kind of influence are we having by being in there among all these predators and ungulates? Because we're bound to be affecting the way ungulates move through the landscape and their vulnerability to predators. At the same time, we're *also disturbing predators from their kills.*

[Glacier National Park] has been more restrictive than most of the places I've been, which I think in a lot of respects is good. They're at least watching what's going on.

There are some species like bears that you can observe visually—just sit and watch and spend a lot of time without ever putting a radio collar on an animal. But there are also certain species that you can't observe that way. The majority of information we've got on cougars has come from radio-collared individuals.

The knowledge base is much more advanced on coyotes, wolves and bears compared to animals like wolverines and cougars. We're way back with some of these secretive animals."

Toni Ruth,
Cougar Researcher, Hornocker Institute

contents of more than 14,000 coyotes killed by officers.

Murie spent many months in the field tracking wolves, watching them with binoculars and recording countless hunting forays and pack interactions. During the 1960s and 1970s, a small but growing number of biologists followed his example, producing numerous studies on the ecology of predators and other species in North America and around the world. They worked without portable computers, radio telemetry, satellite-based global positioning systems and other modern tools. These early biologists, many of them "lone wolves," spent endless hours in the field, striving to accumulate enough observation time to draw conclusions about the animals they studied.

Early ecology studies also relied on snow tracking to interpret the cross-country movements and hunting behavior of predators, and scat analysis to discover predators' food habits.

Scat analysis involves collecting feces, heating them to kill parasites and bacteria, and then painstakingly dissecting them under a microscope to identify the kinds of hairs or bone fragments in them. Scat analysis does not reveal everything: predators digest some foods so completely that they do not turn up in scats, and scats need the corroboration of tracks or other evidence to link them with certainty to the species that deposited them.

With direct observation, early researchers could learn about open-country animals such as northern wolves, coyotes and bears. They needed other techniques, however, to learn about the secret lives of cougars, bobcats, lynx and many predators living in forested areas.

Maurice Hornocker, who studied cougars in Idaho's Big Creek country in the 1960s, was among the first biologists to experiment with radio signals as a way to keep track of wide-ranging predators. To put a radio collar on an

Protecting National Parks From Predators

It was 1886. The West was filling with prospectors, ranchers and speculators. Once-numberless bison herds had already vanished from the prairies and foothills. The reckless greed of the newcomers had decimated elk and deer herds. A melancholy stillness had settled over the once-great game ranges of the West.

Canada's Minister of the Interior wanted Banff, that country's first national park, to provide tourists with readily viewed herds of large animals. He sent W.F. Whitcher west on the new Canadian Pacific Railway to figure out what to do. Whitcher's report confirmed the scarcity of big game and advised the government to destroy all the predatory animals in the park.

In response, the government passed a regulation stating: "The shooting at, wounding, capturing, killing or in any manner injuring wild animals or birds within the park is hereby prohibited excepting, however, mountain lions, bears, wolves, lynxes, wolverines, coyotes, wild cats and hawks."

Elk, squirrels and mountain sheep were welcome in Canada's national parks; animals that ate them were not. And that, with little change, remained the working policy on predators in Canadian national parks for the next 75 years.

James Harkin, Canada's first national parks

commissioner, though in many ways visionary, did not escape the prejudices of the day. He scolded park wardens in the early 1930s for not killing enough coyotes. Public pressure to get rid of predators became so intense that park authorities hired professional hunters to kill cougars and grizzly bears in Banff and Jasper.

A rabies outbreak in foxes during the 1950s added more justification for the war against predators. The mountain national parks unleashed strychnine, a cruel and nonselective poison, on their predators in the name of rabies control, as did communities across the West. It devastated predator populations so badly that some have yet to recover.

An explosion of public environmental awareness in the late 1960s finally forced national park managers in both Canada and the U.S. to stop killing predators in national parks. By then, however, the wolf was gone from Yellowstone, Rocky Mountain and other U.S. parks, and mountain lions were rare. Today's national park managers rigorously protect predators—sometimes even closing areas to protect denning animals from disturbance. In 1995, proving how far attitudes had changed, American biologists used wolves from Canada to restock the oldest national park in the world—Yellowstone, which had been wolfless for half a century.

Voles and small rodents are important coyote prey.

animal, researchers first must capture it in a trap modified to reduce injuries. They then give the animal a drug which induces unconsciousness or at least immobilizes it. Some researchers do not bother with the trapping and simply shoot the target animal with a tranquilizer dart or net gun, often from a hovering helicopter. Once the animal is incapacitated, researchers usually take a blood sample, pull a tooth, give the animal a tattoo or some other kind of mark, and then fit it with a leather collar containing a radio transmitter and long-life battery pack. They then release the animal in a safe place where it can recover from the drugs and return to its everyday life.

COSEWIC Risk Categories

Vulnerable: A native species at risk because of low or declining numbers, or because it occurs in Canada at the edge of its natural range or in only a limited area, but which is not threatened.

Threatened: A native species likely to become endangered in Canada if the conditions making it vulnerable persist.

Endangered: A native species threatened with imminent extinction or extirpation throughout all or most of its range in Canada because of human activities.

Extirpated: A species once native to Canada that no longer survives here.

Extinct: A species lost for all time.

Researchers use the blood sample to check for parasites and other health indicators, as well as for DNA analysis. When lab technicians shave thin sections out of the tooth and examine them under a microscope, they can tell the age of the animal by counting the layers of cementum—one layer for each summer of the animal's life.

Field biologists use directional antennae to find radio-collared animals and track their movements. This can be difficult from the ground if collared animals go behind hills or cover long distances. Researchers with enough money, track wide-ranging predators from the air in helicopters or airplanes. Some new collars allow satellite monitoring.

A radio collar transmits continuously for one to three years. Some contain special monitors which tell researchers whether the animal is moving, lying down or dead.

In its early days, radio telemetry was frustrating and failure-prone. The original radios had limited range, short-lived batteries and collars which often broke. By the 1980s, however, radio collars had revolutionized research on predators and other animals previously too uncommon, wide-ranging or nocturnal to observe directly.

The benefits of predator-ecology research are obvious: more people know more about predators than ever before. Informed understanding has started to replace old prejudices. Predator management has moved from "shoot, shovel and shut up," to more sophisticated techniques based on applied predator ecology.

A growing number of biologists and wildlife conservationists worry that radio collars and helicopters harass wild predators. Bear specialist Charlie Russell argues that trapping, drugging and mutilating wild animals comes from a wrong-headed relationship with the natural world that infects 20th century society. Many national parks now restrict the degree to which researchers may handle wild animals or use aircraft to monitor them.

Researchers have now answered many basic questions about large predators, according to Dr. Paul Paquet and other carnivore biologists. We need to dig deeper to answer others and that will take money for long-term studies. But Paquet says we already know enough to build predator conservation into land-use planning, resource management, and agricultural and economic policy. Too often, however, governments and industries resist hard but necessary decisions such as restricting industrial development. Instead, they fund more short-term studies and call it mitigation.

Endangered Species

Predators are sensitive indicators of environmental health: where wild predators thrive, it is usually a good sign of healthy populations of prey species, good-quality habitat and either enough wild country or a sufficiently enlightened human population to ensure their survival.

Many predator populations are doing surprisingly well. Others have become extinct. Some predator populations may yet disappear without special measures to protect them from persecution and loss of habitat.

Tools Of The Trade

The predator-prey arms race has produced an array of physical weaponry and tactical skills to make western North America's wildcats and wild dogs formidable hunters.

Millions of years of evolution have equipped these creatures with senses far more acute than humans possess. They have developed specialized bodies and a range of behaviors and physical adaptations which help them kill just-as-well-adapted prey. Wild predators live in the same world as we do, but it looks and feels very different to them.

At night, when humans stumble awkwardly through darkness, coyotes and bobcats see mice scurrying about beneath flickering leaves. Human movements are clumsy and loud, whereas cougars place each paw silently, alerted to any loose leaves or twigs by sensitive whiskers which protrude be-

Cats' whiskers are sensory organs enabling them to feel obstacles in the dark and avoid blundering into them. Like all carnivores, bobcats have long, pointed canine teeth for puncturing and tearing flesh.

tween their toes. We tire quickly, but need to eat frequently. Wolves travel for days on empty stomachs, then eat half their weight in a few hours.

Cat eyes have large pupils to let in lots of light, and larger lenses to accommodate it. Because the larger opening in their eyes means that light coming in must be refracted (bent) more for the image to come into focus on the retina, cats have thick eye lenses and a more curved cornea. The retina—a thin pink layer of cells at the the back of the eye which captures the image of what an animal is looking at— is made of two kinds of cells described by their shapes: rods and cones. Cat eyes have more rod cells than cone cells, because rods are most effective in low light levels. Cone cells, however, are what give color richness and crisp detail to the visual image, so cats probably see less color than we do. Most of what colors they do see are probably in the blue and green range.

Long-legged and lean, wolves are designed for long, tireless journeys and short, high-speed dashes. Unimaginably sensitive noses help them, like other members of the dog family, to locate prey. Their vision and hearing, too, are highly acute. Large jaws and powerful canines allow wolves to attack animals much larger than themselves and rip at exposed flanks or throats.

The United States Endangered Species Act (ESA) became law in 1973. It had become obvious that, without legal protection, many U.S. plants and animals would slide into extinction. The act defines an endangered species as any species which is in danger of extinction throughout all or a significant portion of its range. It defines a threatened species as one likely to become endangered.

Many predators that remain relatively common in Canada are endangered or threatened south of the 49th parallel. Wolves, for example, barely range into the northern U.S. Rockies. Lynx occur in very small, patchy populations in the mountainous West.

Because of this, the U.S. government has listed wolves as an endangered species and may soon list lynx. The ESA requires the U.S. Fish and Wildlife Service to determine recovery plans for species formally listed as endangered

Tools Of The Trade

Foxes have oversized ears and elongated snouts—evidence of the importance that hearing and scent play in their lives. The wet muzzle comes from copious mucus and saliva production, keeping nose membranes sensitive to odors.

Vision is important to wild hunters, and hearing is no less important. Humans can hear sounds only at frequencies up to 20 khz; cats can hear at least up to 70 khz and in some cases up to 200 khz. Most of the sounds rodents make are too high to even register in human hearing—between 20 to 70 khz—but are fully audible to cats. However, these kinds of high frequency sounds are also low intensity. To pick up the faint, high-pitched noises of their prey, lynxes, bobcats, foxes, coyotes and other predators which eat rodents have large, magnifying ears.

Scent is more important to members of the dog family than to cats. The olfactory bulb—the part of the brain that processes smells—occupies about 5 percent of a dog's brain. Only about 3 percent of a cat's brain deals with scents. This is still more of a scent-processing portion than we humans possess, and although cats have shorter noses and therefore less area for scent receptor cells, their receptor cells are packed more densely inside their noses.

Night-hunting predators such as cats and foxes rely on mystacial (moustache) whiskers and other bristly hairs in their feet to detect objects in the dark. Nerves from these whiskers are connected directly to the brain, making touch no less important than vision for night hunters. When a cat uses its nose to smell things, its moustache whiskers lie back against its face. When walking, they extend forward. When biting prey, the whiskers form a kind of net helping the cat choose accurately where to bite.

Clumsy wolves, night-blind lynx, soft-muscled cougars and uncoordinated coyotes do not last long. Their prey—whose reflexes, alertness and speed these wild hunters have helped develop over the centuries—make sure of that. Predators and their prey are partners in evolution. Each continually selects for the best qualities in the other. Only the best survive. And the best are indeed exceptional creatures.

A cougar's jaws, like those of other cats, can be opened extremely wide. Powerful cheek muscles, the temporalis and masseter, give the cat a vise-like grip when it closes its jaws on muscle and bone. Behind the long canines, razor-like carnassial teeth function to slice and dice meat while the cougar feeds.

A Predator-Killing Arsenal

Wire Snares

To snare predators, trappers often leave a carcass where wolves or coyotes will find it. Once the trapper finds evidence that predators are feeding on the carcass, he sets snares at all access points. When the pack returns that night, the snares are waiting. Trappers may kill as many as five or more wolves or coyotes in a single night using this technique. The victims choke to death slowly. Snares can accidentally kill eagles, deer and other nontarget species.

Leg-hold Traps

Trappers set leg-hold traps on the ground, usually near a bait, and cover them with sand or leaf litter. They do their best to eliminate all traces of unnatural odor from the trap site. Bears, wolves, coyotes and foxes caught in leg-hold traps struggle desperately, often injuring themselves. Wildcats usually lie quietly until trappers return to shoot or club them.

Hounds

Where it is legal to hunt coyotes and foxes with hounds, hunters usually do this for sport more than for predator control. Hounds can track and tree cougars, a very effective way to locate and kill individual cats preying on domestic stock.

Guns

Guns are selective weapons. They enable hunters to target individual predators. Guns work best on species that range in open country, such as coyotes during winter. Because of the small size of the target and the long range of many shots, hunters prefer to shoot coyotes with small-calibre rifles (.22, .243, .25) whose bullets follow a flat trajectory.

Poisons

Predator-control officers put strychnine, Compound 1080 and other poisons either in "drop baits," small pieces of poisoned meat simply dropped on the ground for animals to find, or in the meat of bait animals. They usually only use poison baits in winter and cover them with logs to reduce the risk of killing eagles, bears and other nontarget species, but poison baits often kill other species nonetheless.

Gas

Predator-control officers use cyanide gas to kill fox and coyote puppies in their dens. Flooding dens with water also works. But neither technique has much impact on predator populations. They rarely kill breeding adults or even many pups. Most dens are too well hidden.

A Predator-Killing Arsenal

"Coyote-getter"

The getter is a miniature cannon buried in the soil with its trigger wired to bait. It is a highly selective and effective weapon for predator control. When a coyote, wolf or fox tugs at the bait, the getter shoots a charge of cyanide into the animal's mouth. Eagles, ravens and other scavengers cannot tug at baits the same way as members of the dog family, so the getter rarely kills them. The getter does, however, sometimes kill domestic dogs.

Chemical Warfare

The war against wolves, coyotes and foxes took a lethal turn in the 1940s with the advent of sodium monfluoroacetate or Compound 1080, a chemical particularly deadly to members of the dog family. Compound 1080 has all the attributes of the perfect poison: water-soluble, odorless, tasteless and easy to handle. It has, however, no antidote.

Compound 1080 quickly became the weapon of choice for predator-control officers in Canada's western provinces and in the U.S. Department of Agriculture's animal damage control program. They could load it into coyote-getters to selectively kill target animals, but they usually chose an easier and cheaper method. Officers would kill an old horse or other animal, cut the carcass into chunks, and inject the still-warm chunks with 1080. They allowed the chunks to freeze and then just dropped them around the countryside.

Animals poisoned by 1080 die a horrible death. The poison accelerates their metabolic systems. They run around in circles, fall on their sides kicking their legs and eventually die in convulsions. Many victims die a considerable distance from the poisoned baits, making it impossible to tally the actual death toll and putting other scavenging animals at risk from secondary poisoning.

Compound 1080 resulted in the near extermination of Swift foxes from many parts of their already diminished range. Some predator-control officers argue that the government should never have restricted its use, because no other poison is as effective. But public revulsion has resulted in a near-total ban of its use in most of North America.

Want More Predators? Try Poison!

Programs to eradicate predators often backfire. Sometimes they result in an explosion of other "pests." Erwin Bauer describes an example in his 1994 book, *Wild Dogs*. In 1962, the U.S. government killed more than 200,000 predators. That same year, it spread 700 tons of rodent poison and used 350,000 poison-gas cartridges to kill rodents those predators would have eaten!

Sometimes, predator control even results in more predators. The biology of predators often regulates the density of their populations. Wolves and coyotes live in packs with one pair of dominant, or alpha, animals, which prevents other pack members from breeding. Male cougars and lynx seek out and kill kittens. When prey becomes scarce, the home ranges of wolf packs, cougars and other predators expand as the predators travel more widely in search of food. Lower population densities are the result.

Predator control throws these natural population checks out of whack. Killing adult male cougars, for example, can result in higher kitten survival—more cougars, in other words. Setting out poison for wolves and coyotes often kills the dominant animals because they feed first. This frees up other pack members to mate and produce offspring—more wolves and coyotes. Many studies have shown that killing predators leads the survivors to breed at a younger age and allows them to raise more of each litter to maturity. This only makes sense: the survivors benefit from more prey and easier hunting.

According to Chuck Cadieux, a former U.S. predator-control officer, the state of North Dakota introduced a coyote bounty in 1898. In the first year, people killed almost 6,000 coyotes. The state offered the bounty continuously for almost half a century; it would be reasonable to think few coyotes would survive. But in 1946, the last year of the program, bounty hunters killed 11,867 coyotes—twice as many as in the first year!

and it prohibits federal agencies from taking actions which put those species at further risk. Most of the western U.S. is public land and falls under the control of federal agencies such as the U.S. Forest Service, the Bureau of Land Management and the National Parks Service. This means that protection under the ESA can lead to restrictions on how Westerners harvest trees, graze cattle or recreate.

As a result, right-wing politicians and states-rights advocates have attacked the ESA. They resent the influence of federal agencies and Eastern voters on rural Westerners whose livelihoods depend on exploitation of public lands. They see the ESA as a symbol of "uncaring outsiders who put animals before people."

The ESA does have sharp teeth. In 1996, the courts sentenced a poacher who killed a wolf near Yellowstone National Park to six months in jail. Legal rulings forced wide-reaching changes in logging practices to protect the northern spotted owl.

But endangered animals clearly need laws with bite not bark. Without the ESA, no wolves would survive at all in the northern Rockies. Of the more than 900 species which the U.S. government has listed under the ESA, more than 40 percent now have stable or increasing populations. The bald eagle and American alligator have recovered almost completely, and peregrine falcons, sea otters, black-footed ferrets and many other species are far more secure than in 1974.

Critics of the ESA want it eliminated or made toothless. Conservationists want the ESA to receive more funding. They argue that it just needs to balance its regulatory clout with positive incentives.

In Canada, different controversies define the endangered species debate. Canada provides no legal protection for endangered species outside national parks. The provinces control most of the land and wildlife in Canada, while in the western U.S., it is under the legislation of the federal government. The Natural Resources Transfer Act ceded federal control to the provinces in 1930.

Since Canada has few federal powers to protect endangered species, it relies on moral leverage and voluntary cooperation. A national committee, the Committee on the Status of Endangered Species in Canada (COSEWIC), reviews all available information on species at risk

Coyotes are one of the most visible of predators.

and issues an annual status report which lists them under five risk categories. Another national program, the Recovery of Nationally Endangered Wildlife (RENEW), develops recovery plans for the highest-profile species. The plans, however, rely on voluntary cooperation from provincial, territorial and other governments.

COSEWIC lists the Swift fox as extirpated and the eastern cougar as endangered. It considers other Canadian predators to be safe, even though some local populations face serious

Predation In Perspective

Causes of death among cows and calves in the U.S. in 1992; U.S. Dept. of Agriculture:

Respiratory ailments:	30%
Digestive failures:	21%
Unknown:	16%
Calving problems:	14%
Weather:	7%
Predators:	2%
Other:	10%

Open areas are favorite hunting areas for coyotes.

threats to their survival.

The Canadian approach to endangered species has shown some successes. For example, the recovery of the American white pelican, improvement in the status of the whooping crane and the reintroduction of the Swift fox have been major breakthroughs. More and more Canadians, however, want clear legal pro-

tection for endangered species and habitats, as human population and industrial activity continue to grow across the country. Such legislation, if it is to be effective, must protect habitat for endangered species on both federal and provincial lands. Many feel that it must also provide financial rewards and incentives to private landowners whose good stewardship helps protect or restore endangered animals.

Where Are Predators?

The large national, state and provincial parks are the best places to see most large predators. They usually have good concentrations of the major prey species. Both prey and predators tolerate humans better in protected areas than where hunting is allowed.

You are more likely to see coyotes and foxes than the larger, or scarcer, predators, but serious naturalists spot wolves quite often in some areas and, occasionally, cougars and lynx. The more time you spend in the field, the better your odds. Winter is always the best time to look for large predators, for a number of reasons: predators are more active in daylight, range over larger areas and are more visible against snow. It also helps that their prey is concentrated onto winter ranges rather than widely dispersed across the landscape.

Here are some of the best places for spotting large predators in the West:

Yellowstone National Park

Introduced wolves are now well established in packs that range the Lamar and Hayden valleys, as well as more remote parts of the park. Visi-

Breeding Better Predators

Natural selection gives each species its particular strengths and characteristics. Only the fittest animals survive. Birds too weak to migrate, for example, die when winter comes. Strong flyers survive, and pass their strength on to their offspring.

Predators, whether human or wild, select for the survival of animals that manage to avoid them. Coyotes that stand still when pickup trucks stop often end up with bullet holes in them. Warier coyotes survive and eventually, wariness becomes a characteristic of coyotes. Cougars that hunt by day get shot. Wolves that fail to study strange foods get poisoned. Eventually, most cougars are nocturnal and

most wolves avoid poison baits. The rest are dead.

Researchers in and around Yellowstone have found that predator-control programs produce animals better able to avoid poisons, bullets and traps than their ancestors. The surviving predators—used to being harried by humans—also hunt more aggressively, feed for shorter periods and breed more prolifically than similar animals in populations not subjected to predator control.

Predator-control programs, rather than solving predation problems, often breed and train more elusive, more prolific, tougher and hungrier predators.

A coyote rests between explorations.

tors in winter have the best wolf-watching opportunities anywhere in North America in the Lamar valley, where wolves often hunt elk in broad daylight. Check with the park before visiting during the off-season, as some park roads close in winter.

Coyotes are also present in Yellowstone, although they are less common than they were before the return of the wolves. Mountain lion sightings are rare. You are most likely to see them at low elevations near Gardiner.

Jasper National Park

Several packs of wolves range this large park. The lower Athabasca Valley between the towns of Jasper and Hinton supports good numbers of cougars and foxes. Coyotes often turn up near the town of Jasper and sometimes den in the Highway 16 right-of-way.

In winter, wolves use the frozen Athabasca River and Jasper Lake as travel corridors, putting them within sight of the major park highways. In fact, they even use the highways, especially the Icefields Parkway. The Yellowhead Highway north of the town of Jasper has several vantage points worth visiting in the early morning or evening. Use binoculars or a spotting scope to scan for wolves, foxes and cougars along the far side of Jasper Lake and the Athabasca River. People have spotted cougars lying in the sun on rock outcrops above Jasper Lake on several occasions.

Teaming With Wildlife

Early in this century, hunters across the U.S. asked their federal government to tax them harder. The resulting 1930s-era Pittman-Roberts Act has bankrolled half a century of wildlife conservation through a tax on hunting gear. Unlikely as the idea of citizens asking for more taxes may seem, it's happening again. This time it's called "Teaming With Wildlife." An initiative supported by more than 2,900 groups and businesses across the U.S. aims to raise even more money for wildlife programs by adding a user fee to a wider range of outdoor recreation equipment. Most state fish and wildlife agencies—

faced with declining revenues from hunting—strongly support Teaming With Wildlife. So do state parks and many conservation groups who want to see more funding go to endangered and non-game wildlife species. Teaming With Wildlife may provide funds for predator conservation—organized hunting groups have traditionally opposed their state wildlife agencies, spending Pittman-Roberts funds on animals that compete for the same prey.

For more information consult their website at www.teaming.com/

Banff National Park

Wolves and coyotes frequent the lower Bow Valley between Lake Louise and the town of Banff. The Bow Valley Parkway provides a low-speed route through high-quality habitat for deer, elk and moose, and the frozen Bow River becomes a popular travel corridor for wild canids in winter.

Rocky Mountain National Park

Rocky Mountain Park no longer has wolves or lynx, but coyotes are abundant. You can hear them howling in the evenings around Moraine Park and Glacier Basin, as well as the Colorado River valley on the west side of the park. Coyotes hunt the open parks along main park roads and are easy to spot in winter when most park wildlife is concentrated in the lower valleys.

Mountain lion sightings are more common in Rocky Mountain Park than many other parts of the West, partly because of the abundant elk, mule deer and other prey. Watch for them in ponderosa pine areas at lower elevations in the park; the best times to spot a mountain lion are right at dawn and dusk, but they are shy animals, so don't count on seeing one.

Waterton Lakes National Park

More cougars inhabit this park than parks further north in the Canadian Rockies because frequent, intense chinook winds ensure shallow snow and good winter range for deer and elk. People regularly see cougars right in and around the village of Waterton. In winter, cougars leave tracks between ornamental spruce trees and the uncovered crawl spaces of vacant summer cottages.

You can spot coyotes and rarely wolves

Predator-friendly Products

Becky Weed raises sheep in northern Montana, but she doesn't kill coyotes. Instead, she owns a llama.

"We have coyotes regularly in our pasture area," she says, "but we haven t had any losses since we got into guard animals."

Weed and her husband decided against a guard dog because they worried about conflicts with the many dogs that already lived in their vicinity. Guard dogs defend their territories jealously. Instead, Weed bought a young llama and raised it as a companion for her sheep.

"Llamas have some kind of instinctive dislike for canine animals and they're very territorial," she says. "I've never seen the llama interacting with the coyotes, but our neighbors have watched her run them off. But most of the time, there isn't any conflict because the coyotes seem to know to avoid her."

It costs more to run a predator-friendly ranch than a conventional one: guard animals such as llamas are expensive to buy and keep, and coyotes still take the occasional sheep. But Weed thinks consumers will pay more for her wool, once they know about it. Several years ago, she founded Predator Friendly Growers Cooperative for wool products from progressive ranches.

The organization started small, distributing sweaters and hats and building a certification program for predator-friendly producers. "We didn't want to put too much effort into recruiting new growers," Weed says, "until we could get the market developed."

That wasn't easy: predator-friendly wool costs more and the small-scale cooperative lacked the capital to build profile in the marketplace. Nevertheless, the demand for predator-friendly wool has grown, and Weed and her partners may soon start looking for more producers.

From her quiet place under the big sky of Montana, Weed remains convinced that people who care about wildlife and good stewardship will pay fair prices for wool from ranchers who adopt a live-and-let-live relationship with coyotes and other predators.

"Guard animals aren't a sure thing," she says. "There's still risks involved. That's the whole idea—to get the consumer involved in making it possible to grow sheep without killing predators."

Some ranchers living near Yellowstone National Park have recently joined the move to enlist consumers in sharing the risks of raising livestock in predator country. "Wolf-friendly beef" is now available from ranches in the recovery zone of the recently reintroduced Yellowstone wolf population.

Where to Buy It:
Predator Friendly Growers Cooperative
13000 Springhill Road
Belgrade, Montana 59714

Predator dens are usually well hidden and, in any case, best left alone.

along the main highways into the park, particularly from roadside lookouts on Knight's Hill, about two kilometers (1.25 miles) south of the park gates.

Elk Island National Park

Elk Island has the highest density of bison, elk, white-tailed deer and moose of any national park in Canada—mostly because it has no wolves, cougars or bears (which sometimes prey on calves and fawns). People eradicated these predators from the area many years ago and none have succeeded in dispersing back into the park across the expanse of agricultural land and city that separates the park from other wild areas. Without predators to pick them off, ungulates die from disease or starvation, which makes the park a rich source of carrion and a great place to watch for coyotes.

Pacific Rim National Park

Wolves (considered endangered on Vancouver Island until only a decade or so ago) and cougars inhabit Clayoquot Sound and sometimes turn up along the Pacific Rim Highway or along the forested edges of Long Beach late in the evening or early in the morning. Generally, however, the dense vegetation of the Pacific rain coast makes it hard to spot predators.

Who Killed That Animal?

Predators leave evidence at the scene: each species has different hunting techniques and tools. Wolves and coyotes, for example, chew on bones but cougars do not. Cougars have no crushing teeth. They pick bones thoroughly clean, but leave them intact.

Wolves have large, powerful jaws compared to coyotes or foxes. They can chew ribs down to the backbone. Coyotes usually only eat the cartilaginous ends of ribs and leave the rest intact.

Cougars cover their kills with grass and leaves. But so do bears, so this only helps identify the predator reliably in winter. Bears cover their kills with logs and boulders—much larger objects than cougars use. With their strength and powerful jaws, bears pull the remains apart and crush bones. These clues can help distinguish between cougar and bear kills, but most biologists recommend against trying to find out. If there is a chance it may be a bear kill, leave immediately by the same route you followed in and make a lot of noise.

Wild canids don't cover their kills, but they like to carry parts away and hide them. A carcass missing one or more legs is likely the work of coyotes or wolves. I once watched a wolf carrying the entire hind leg of a deer as it trotted with the rest of its pack across the frozen surface of Jasper Lake.

Writing-On-Stone Provincial Park

Writing-on-Stone is among the few parks in Canada where bobcats occur with any regularity. It supports a healthy population of cottontail rabbits—you can often spot rabbits in the campground and among the sandstone hoodoos that line the Milk River valley. Bobcat-spotting may prove easiest in winter when the snow reveals their tracks. Police Coulee contains extensive shrubby habitat used by both rabbits and bobcats. The area has many coyotes too. The Milk River Natural Area and Kennedy Coulee Ecological Reserve, east of the park, contain similar habitat, but they are remote and difficult to access.

Finding Predators

Wildlife is seen by those who look. The key to finding relatively rare creatures like predators is to spend a lot of time in the field, much of it sitting still with binoculars or a spotting scope.

Some questions to ask before deciding where to search are the following:

- What do predators usually eat at time of year you plan to look?
- What time of day do they become active?
- Where is the best habitat?

Most people take their holidays in summer, the worst time to look for predators. In summer, lush vegetation obscures wildlife from view,

Clues From Other Creatures

The behavior of other animals often gives away the presence of predators on the hunt. If you see any of the following prey behaviors, quickly find a sheltered spot to hide—downwind if at all possible—and settle in to watch.

• Deer, elk or moose standing in knee-deep or deeper water, or on the ice of a frozen lake. Large ungulates often retreat to open water to escape wolves, coyotes and cougars. Ungulates have longer legs than predators and deep water gives them an advantage. Wolves and coyotes often lie down and wait nearby, especially during cold winter weather. Cold water soon begins to sap the energy of the besieged ungulate, and eventually it will try to move up to dry land. Then its pursuers press their attack again. If you see a large animal standing in deep water, carefully search the shore with binoculars. You might see one or more predators lying or pacing about nearby.

• An animal running for no apparent reason. Sometimes predators pursue prospective prey for a considerable distance. If a predator has managed to draw blood, or if the animal it is chasing is obviously weak or vulnerable, a wolf, coyote or lynx may choose to follow it and try for a final attack. Wolves and coyotes also use a chase-and-ambush strategy: While one chases a deer or rabbit, another lies in wait and dashes out unexpectedly. Watch not only behind a fleeing animal but in front, too.

• A herd of deer or elk, or other potential prey animals, standing alertly and staring in one direction. Prey animals do not automatically run away when a predator comes near. They usually find a secure spot near shelter or in a clearing and wait to see what the approaching predator does next. In some cases, they may not even know where the danger lies, perhaps because they can smell it but not see it. When you see deer, elk, sheep or other animals acting agitated or watchful, find a good vantage point downwind from them and wait. You may be rewarded, eventually, with a chase.

• Fussing by chickadees, magpies, jays or squirrels. Many species of animals have a mobbing or fussing behavior when large predators are near. Their incessant scolding or calling alerts potential prey to the movements of predators. It is a useful clue for hopeful human observers too. Chickadees and other small birds do not just scold large predators. Their calls may betray the presence of a mink, marten, weasel or owl.

• Ravens, crows, magpies. Ravens feed on the carrion of large-predator kills. These highly intelligent birds adopt a number of behaviors that can give away the presence of wolves, coyotes or cougars. Some ravens make a habit of shadowing wolf and coyote packs on the hunt. Watch for ravens circling in a small area or repeatedly flying across the same place. A squabble of magpies or crows may also indicate a carcass worth bickering over and predators nearby.

Muscular legs and large paws: cougars grip and bite their prey.

predators become nocturnal to avoid the day-time heat and prey populations have dispersed over the landscape. Many people spend the bright hours of the day outside and retreat home well before dark. But wildlife becomes most active around dawn and dusk. That's when to look for predators.

Look for wolves and coyotes on the frozen surfaces of winter rivers or lakes, or along open south-facing slopes where snow remains shallow and large animals tend to congregate. Watch for foxes in similar places and along the edges of forests and shrubby areas around streams, wetlands and lakes.

Watch for lynx in dense young spruce or pine forests, muskegs, or along the edges of extensive willow thickets. Look for hare tracks or, better yet, the well-trampled runways that mark concentrations of hares. Road-killed hares may indicate good places to revisit just after dark to see if a lynx turns up in your headlights.

Bobcats are most likely to turn up in rocky, broken areas such as the outcroppings along the Columbia and Kootenay river valleys, or coulee slopes in southern Alberta and Saskatchewan.

The snowy season is the best time to look for wild hunters. Find a good vantage point, make yourself inconspicuous and examine every inch of visible countryside with good binoculars or a spotting scope. Do it often enough and something will turn up.

Tracks and Signs

At the end of every set of tracks there stands an animal. Following those tracks makes one of the

Calling All Predators

Predator-call devices, available in most hunting and sporting goods stores, exploit both the natural curiosity of most predators and the importance of their sense of hearing. Predators such as coyotes, foxes and even cougars will often travel a considerable distance to investigate the high-pitched wail of a predator call. Most calls imitate the sound of a rabbit or other small mammal in distress.

You can make a predator call with your knuckle. It doesn't carry as well over large distances but it is free. Wet a knuckle thoroughly with saliva, make a

fist and kiss it noisily. It doesn't take long to develop the ability to make high-pitched mouselike squeaking sounds that coyotes, in particular, find fascinating.

One small word of caution: When using a predator call, you can expect predators to approach you as prey. Do not wait until they are too close before disillusioning them. Coyotes have actually pounced on some people, fooled by their calls. Too much success at predator calls can lead to injury and rabies shots.

Between hunts, predators such as cougars conserve their energy.

most enjoyable ways to learn about and, if you are lucky, observe large predators. Follow the tracks in reverse to keep from disturbing the animal that made them. Seasoned biologists almost always backtrack animals to avoid inadvertently harassing them during the hungry season. Along the way, the tracks record part of the story of the animal: their scent-marking behavior, hunting strategy, attempted kills and, occasionally, successful attacks. In late winter, patches of blood in tracks may reveal that coyotes, wolves or foxes have come into heat. At kill sites, the tracks of other animals show the im-

portance of predator kills to the ecology of martens, squirrels, ravens and other creatures.

Droppings contain clues about predators' diets. A word of caution about wolf, coyote and fox scats: Never handle them or poke at them. Most wild canids carry a tapeworm species that is often fatal to humans, though not to its usual hosts. The tapeworm spreads through tiny dust-like eggs in scats. The eggs survive drying and are easy to inhale by accident.

Safety When Tracking

Following animal tracks will take you well away from trails and into hazardous terrain. Prepare for each field trip as if you know you will sprain an ankle, because you just might. Tell someone where you're going and when you expect to get back, so they'll know where to search if you fail to return. Carry spare clothing, especially warm hats and dry socks. Take some candles and matches, lots of extra food, orange (visible) plastic garbage bags or other emergency shelter and, if possible, a flare or other signalling device.

Be realistic about when to turn back. Winter days are short, and you'll be a lot more tired and clumsy on the return trip than when you started out. Common sense is the most important tool in anyone's winter-survival kit.

CAUTION

Ravens and other animals rely on predator kills for food. A gathering of scavengers can indicate a carcass nearby. The smell of decomposition can also betray the presence of a kill. NEVER approach a place where you may find a predator kill. Your presence may displace animals which need the food. You may also surprise a bear claiming the carcass. Bears defend kills aggressively.

If a bear attacks, either you or the bear may end up injured or dead. Those of us who observe nature have an ethical obligation to avoid behavior that may bring hardship or danger to predators, bears and other wildlife. We have freedom of choice in most matters, but with choice comes responsibility. Wild animals depend on us to make the right choices.

Wild Dogs

Wild Dogs

Exceptionally acute noses, radar-like ears and intelligent eyes; wild canids are highly-tuned hunters.

Few western game trails lack the tracks of wild dogs. In national parks such as Jasper and Yellowstone as many as three kinds of dog tracks may interweave along the same snowy slope—red foxes, coyotes and wolves. Foxes rarely wander far from home.

Wolves, on the other hand, may undergo journeys of several hundred miles. Although related, each of the west's wild dogs is a distinctly different creature. While their ranges may overlap, their lifestyles seldom do.Wolf distribution aligns itself with the patterns of their favored prey—elk, moose and deer. Timber wolves live and range through the broad valleys separating western mountain ranges, seldom straying far from forest cover. Wolves would disperse eastward into the prairies and south to the fringes of desert country if we would let them; someday, almost surely, they will.

Coyotes, the most adaptable and intelligent

of the west's wild dogs live there already. In the absence of wolves they often adopt wolf-like life styles, teaming up to hunt large prey. Like their larger relatives, coyotes are most at home between the high mountain ranges, not amid them. Unlike wolves, however, they have no difficulty surviving in open prairie, sagelands and even the outskirts of large towns and cities.Generations of coyotes have spurned the most ambitious of predator control campaigns, making mockery of human bull-headedness.

Foxes are the least dog-like of wild dogs. East of the Rockies, tiny Swift foxes trace secretive trails through the prairie night as they hunt for

Rogue Wolves In American Folklore

Big-game hunters, wolves have blockier, more powerful bodies than foxes or coyotes.

The violent conquest of the American West in the late 1800s took only three decades, but it gave rise to a remarkable body of folklore and legend. The stories tell of great native defenders such as Geronimo and Chief Joseph, larger-than-life heroes and bad guys, epic war and conquest, and mythical wolves.

The great frontier wolves of legend always loomed larger than other wolves. They had missing toes or scars that recorded narrow escapes and gave them distinctive tracks. They outwitted countless humans bent on their destruction and killed vast numbers of sheep and cattle simply for the joy of killing.

Ernest Thompson Seton's tale, "Lobo, King of the Currumpaw," from his famous book *Wild Animals I Have Known*, has thrilled generations of readers with its tale of a great wolf that eludes traps, guns

and poisons, but finally dies of a broken heart when he loses his mate and his freedom.

Other famous rogue wolves include Arizona's Old Aquilla, Oklahoma's Geronimo and Osage Phantom, and Old Three-Toes. The exploits of these wolves have grown in the retelling and have added to the visceral fear and loathing that some people feel toward wolves today.

Just as the last of the frontier's surviving wolves became larger than life in oral tradition, so did the last of the wolfers. In Texas, the legend of Q.T. Stevens, who waged a single-minded war to rid the Texas hill country of its last wolves lives on, told and retold to illustrate the exceptional qualities of the men who tamed the West.

A fox's large ears help it zero in on the high-intensity, low-frequency sounds of mice.

rabbits and rodents. West of the Rockies, the closely related kit fox lives a similar lifestyle in its desert environs. Tree-climbing gray foxes haunt the deciduous woodlands of riverbottoms and canyons which penetrate the southern Rockies. Most widespread of all, red foxes range from sub-Arctic Canada through most of the west.

Foxes hunt small prey and watch out constantly for opportunities to scavenge meals from the remains of animals killed by other predators. Wild dogs rely on exceptionally acute noses to find their prey by scent, and radar-like ears to accurately locate it in darkness or beneath snow. The larger wild dogs—wolves and

coyotes—are what biologists call coursing predators. As such, they play uniquely important roles in nature. They constantly test and challenge prey animals like elk, deer, bighorn sheep and pronghorns. At the faintest sign of weakness, idle testing becomes deadly serious. Wild herds exposed to constant hunting pressure from wolves and coyotes rarely contain sick or ill-adapted animals.

The west's wild dogs are not only compelling animals in their own right—they continue to play an ancient and vital role in keeping other animals alert, healthy and wild.

Coyotes

Tricksters of myth, coyotes thrive in spite of persecution.

Coyotes, *Canis latrans,* have always figured prominently in the myths of North America's indigenous peoples, often as a semi-divine trickster who both helps and deceives humans. "Coyote" probably comes from "*coyotl,*" the name that Aztecs gave to the species.

The Navajo term for coyote means "little brother." The original people of western North America knew the coyote well. The grinning-faced, little wolves ranged from the arctic coasts of what are now Alaska and Yukon, south through the mountains and plains of North America to central Mexico, and east to the Mississippi basin. Coyotes are opportunistic scavengers who no doubt stole many meals from camps and kill sites.

White Europeans arrived in North America in the 1500s, and by the late 1800s had spread across the continent. The arrival of this new variety of human brought unprecedented changes to the landscape and, consequently, to the distribution of native wildlife such as coyotes.

Most native predators retreated before the flood of European settlement, but coyotes prospered. The clearings created by settlers and timber barons cutting into the great eastern forests made good coyote habitat. By the early 20th-century, the coyote had expanded east into southwest Ontario, Minnesota and Michigan, hybridizing with the scattered remains of the

Coyote Facts

Size: 1-1.5 meters / 3-4.5 feet
Weight: 10-14 kilograms / 22-32 pounds
Description: Gray and brown, with large, pointed ears, a pointed muzzle and bushy tail, carried low
Reproduction: Normally breeds first at age two
Gestation: 63 days
Litter size: 1-10 pups; average 6
Life span: 10-15 years
Food: Rodents, hares, birds, insects and other animals
Distribution: All of North America south of the Arctic barrens

43

dwindling wolf population. The eastern coyote, as a result, is bigger than the western coyote (up to to 25 percent larger) and looks more wolflike. The coyote continued to spread east until, by the 1960s, its range included New Brunswick and Nova Scotia south to West Virginia.

Farther south, coyotes colonized the Ozark Mountains, the lower Mississippi basin and the coastal plain of Texas, where the red wolf had once thrived. Settlers waged a fierce war against predators in this region: by the middle of the 20th-century, red wolves were nearly extinct. Coyotes hybridized with the surviving red wolves and now occupy most of the southeastern U.S.

Coyotes are more widespread today than ever, despite more than a century of determined efforts by farmers, ranchers and government wildlife officers to eradicate them.

Coyote Country

Western singer Ian Tyson describes the coyote's diverse taste in habitat in his popular song about the four-legged western songster, *The Coyote and the Cowboy.* "He lives in the snow at 40 below, or in Malibu by the sea." Given the chance, coyotes will live just about anywhere, just so long as there is food to eat and the snow doesn't get too deep in winter. Coyotes are scarce at high elevations, and in the snowbelt mountains of northern Idaho and Washington, and of neighboring British Columbia.

Elsewhere, coyotes range the badlands and canyons of Saskatchewan and the Dakotas, the rolling wheat and barley landscapes of the plains, the foothills and the sagelands of the intermontane West. Coyotes are just as likely to be at home in the suburbs of large cities, where they subsist on stray pets and garbage, as in remote wilderness canyons and windswept prairie.

Unlike wolves, coyotes don't need wooded cover to keep them safe. Heavy woods, in fact, are unfriendly terrain for an animal that relies on sharp eyes and its ability to put distance between itself and a potential adversary. A patch of tall grass is hiding cover enough for most coyotes. In open country, coyotes take advantage of the slightest hollows or dips in the landscape to vanish from sight when curious humans touch the brake pedal.

Like wolves, coyotes benefit from frozen

Grassland is ideal coyote habitat.

lakes and rivers, snowmobile tracks and ploughed roads in the winter. Thanks to snowmobile trails, hunting coyotes now regularly chase snowshoe hares and other prey once inaccessible to them because of deep snow. Most coyotes, however, winter at low elevations where their short legs and small feet don't put them at a disadvantage.

Coyote Society

Coyotes are adaptable animals: they live in a wide range of landscapes and adjust their social life to fit their hunting needs.

Coyotes living in farm country or surviving in patches of wild prairie eat mostly mice, voles and other small animals. These coyotes generally live alone or in small family groups: hunting small creatures does not require much help and rarely produces enough meat to share.

Where populations of small animals are more patchy, but ungulates such as elk and deer occur in abundance, coyotes form packs, as wolves do. Before wolves were reintroduced to Yellowstone National Park, biologist Eric Gese observed packs of six to 10 coyotes which hunted and killed full-grown elk. Packs can

A young coyote, tail raised, asserts dominace over its littermate.

more efficiently kill big animals than lone coyotes and each kill provides enough protein to feed several coyotes.

Coyotes in Banff and Jasper national parks mix the two hunting styles. During the summer, when food is abundant, the coyotes remain alone or in family groups. As winter blankets the landscape with snow and large animals begin to congregate on winter ranges, the coyotes group together and put more energy into hunting big game or scavenging on winter-killed deer and elk.

The social life of coyote packs resembles that of other dog species such as wolves. Coyote packs have a dominant, or alpha, male and female pair who do all the breeding. They do not permit subdominant animals, generally younger, to mate.

Coyotes establish rank through a wide range of postures and threat displays. Dominant coyotes show their status by carrying their tails high, raising their ears and approaching other pack members aggressively. Subordinate coyotes tuck their tails between their legs, lower their ears and cower or roll onto their backs. Domestic dogs show many of the same behaviors toward humans. A large part of obedience training involves asserting dominance over dogs and getting them to show submission.

When coyotes who don't know each other

Having carefully stalked the rustling of a small rodent, a coyote pounces with forepaws and nose extended.

meet, perhaps at a carcass, the first order of business is to establish social rank. If one animal does not submit to the other, they may settle the matter with a brief fight. Once rank is established, the two coyotes tend to get along.

Coyotes living in packs mark and defend their core home ranges from other coyotes. Solitary coyotes do not exhibit as much territorial behavior and the home ranges of several coyotes may overlap.

Coyote Families

Coyotes, like wolves, go into heat in midwinter. Females begin to leave patches of blood in their tracks and emit odors signaling to males they are ready to breed.

Within well-defined packs, only the alpha pair mate. Where coyotes are more dispersed or predator control programs break up established packs, a female coyote may breed with several males.

Research in the western U.S. shows that coyotes in stable populations with low mortality usually produce small litters from which an average of 1.6 pups survive. By contrast, aggressively hunted coyotes produce much larger litters—from eight to 10 pups—and more pups survive. Females in heavily hunted populations may begin to breed before they are a year old. In unhunted populations, they seldom start breeding until they reach two to four years.

Coyotes will dig their own dens, but they are just as likely to adopt a badger, ground squirrel or other animal's den and adjust it for their own purposes. In the Rocky Mountain national parks, coyotes like to den near highways, even within a few meters of the pavement, because of the abundance of food from roadkills and from ground-squirrel colonies along the grassy highway margins.

Coyote Food

In 1941, the U.S. National Parks Service published a study of what coyotes eat. Researchers had analyzed the stomach contents of more than 14,000 coyotes killed in government-funded coyote-control programs throughout the western U.S. The results showed that coyotes eat meat and prefer easily gotten meat: small mammals, carrion or domestic sheep.

Food Item	Percent
Rabbits and hares	43
Carrion	12
Mice, squirrels and other rodents	17.5
Domestic sheep and goats	13
Deer	3.5
Vegetable matter	2
Domestic calves and swine	1
Other mammals	1
Domestic poultry	1
Grouse, quail and other game birds	1
Non-game birds	1
Insects	1
Other	3

The payback: a tasty vole snack.

The pups, blind, helpless and little bigger than a hot dog, are born in April or May. The mother nurses them for the six weeks of their life. Pups begin to eat solid food, regurgitated for them by their parents, when they are less than a month old.

Coyote pups greet returning adults joyfully, wagging their tails and jumping up at them. The pups bite at the adults' lips, triggering a gagging reflex which makes the adult regurgitate partially-digested food.

Coyotes often move their pups from one den to another, either because of disturbance by other animals or because too many fleas, worms and other parasites have made the den unhealthy.

Among coyotes that do not form packs, coyote pups generally remain with their parents for only the first few months of their lives, heading off to seek their own fortunes late in the fall or during their first winter. Dispersing young coyotes may travel more than 100 kilometers / 60 miles before establishing a new home range. In coyote populations that form packs, yearlings often remain with their parents and help to care for the next year's litter.

Coyotes as Hunters

Predators that eat small animals need to work harder than those that eat large prey. It might take a wolf pack several days to finish off one kill, but a coyote may often consume a meal in a single mouse-sized gulp.

Coyotes depend heavily on small mammals in the summer, especially rabbits, hares, voles and ground squirrels. Because small mammals

Don't Feed The Coyotes!

Research in Alberta points to a simple way to control coyotes: stop feeding them. Coyotes thrive where they can find livestock carcasses. In part of a study area, researchers arranged for the clean disposal of all carcasses. The coyote population in that area dropped, but it remained abundant in another part of the study area where farmers continued to leave livestock carcasses on the range. As with most predators, food supply, not death rate, limits coyote numbers.

How Coyote Brought Salmon

A Salish legend credits Coyote with bringing salmon to the Thompson and upper Fraser rivers and teaching the people how to fish for them with spears. In most versions of the myth, women rescue Coyote from drowning but, mischievously, he destroys a dam of stones which they had built across the river. The salmon, blocked from travelling upstream, swim over the ruined dam and spread throughout the valleys of the Thompson and upper Fraser rivers. Coyote teaches the people how to make spears for hunting salmon.

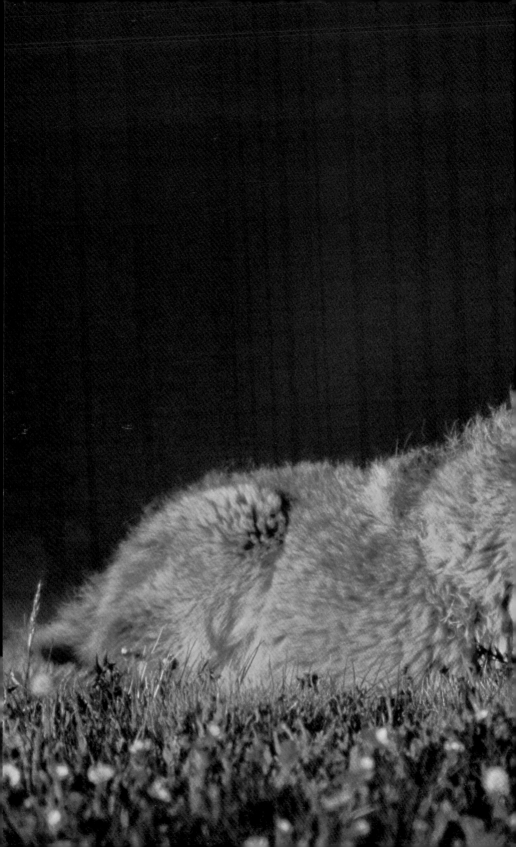

generally occur in large numbers, a coyote's wanderings rarely take it as far in a day as a wolf's. But hunting small prey is still a demanding and active business: coyotes need more successful hunts to get the same amount of energy from small prey as from large.

Coyotes rely on their eyes, ears and noses to locate prey. Once a coyote detects a promising scent or movement, it orients itself to the exact location of the animal, stalks it, and then either rushes or pounces. Coyotes catch voles and mice by pouncing with both forefeet extended and then thrusting their heads into the grass and snapping up their meal. They grab rabbits and ground squirrels with their teeth after a surprise rush.

Coyotes hunt at any time of day, especially in national parks and other places which protect them from hunting. Like many animals, however, coyotes are most active at daybreak and sunset.

In the spring, during calving season, coyotes often keep company with elk, cattle and other large animals. They clean up afterbirths and stillborn young, and sometimes hunt young animals.

Mule deer and bighorn sheep become quite aggressive toward coyotes during this critical season, charging stifflegged, ears forward and head extended, then jumping forward or striking out with their hooves. This protective behavior no doubt saves many of their offspring. Domestic sheep and cattle rarely behave so effectively. Sheep, in particular, seem to have had all their defenses bred out of them. Coyotes that develop a taste for mutton can often kill several sheep in one attack by grabbing the throats of the sheep and asphyxiating them.

Lone coyotes rarely hunt animals the size of deer or larger, though some do search out fawns and the young of bighorn sheep. Coyote packs will, however, hunt large animals in winter. Rarely, they will even kill animals as large as a full-grown elk or domestic cow.

More often, coyotes hunt the same small mammals in winter as in summer. Coyotes listen alertly for voles or mice moving under the snow. They stalk close to accurately locate the little animal, then bound high in the air and land with all four feet, plunging their noses into the snow and grabbing at the startled rodent.

Winter is a hard season for coyotes. They hunt or they eat the remains of animals killed by wolves, cars or other causes. The remainder of the time, coyotes rest, often on sunny slopes, to conserve their energy.

How To Control Coyotes

Generally speaking, coyote control is a myth. Bounties have proven useless. Harmless coyotes end up dying along with problem ones. Hunters kill coyotes near roads but leave more remote populations

Coyotes In Wolf Country

A coyote lays its ears back, snarls, showing its canine teeth in a threat display.

Wendy Arjo laughs a little self-effacingly when she admits that she studies coyotes.

In the famed north fork of the Flathead River, her colleagues track wolves, cougars and grizzlies. But Arjo does not apologize for choosing the less-glamorous coyote.

"I've put in more than a 1,000 trap-nights [one trap set for one night] in the past two years trying to get radio collars on coyotes," she says. "But I've only gotten 14 in two years. They're smart. Compared to coyotes, wolves aren't nearly as bright. It's no accident that coyotes have survived a century of persecution that wiped out wolves from most of the same range."

Arjo wants to find out what happens to coyotes when wolf populations increase. Ten years ago, the Flathead's north fork valley had a lot of coyotes. But wolves have steadily increased: three packs now range different parts of the valley.

"There are two schools of thought," she says. "One says coyotes and wolves can coexist. Another says that when the wolves move in, they force the coyotes out."

Arjo's studies so far suggest that coyotes do persist, but that they avoid wolves. They choose territories between the core home ranges of wolf packs and

hunt at different times of the day. Arjo says coyotes are most active between 7 a.m. and 11 a.m. Wolves become active at nightfall and hunt mostly from 1:00 to 7 a.m.

Wolves, in fact, may even help some coyotes survive. "I've got one five-year-old who is blind in one eye and missing part of his tail. You can tell he's led a rough life. He spent a lot of time following the North Camas wolf pack around and scavenging on their kills. He spent five days on one elk carcass. But it's definitely a dangerous way for a coyote to make a living."

The Flathead Valley's coyotes spend most of their time alone, eating rodents or scavenging on kills made by other predators. Even though the Flathead coyotes aren't pack animals, Arjo and other researchers have found four coyote-killed deer.

During the first two years of Arjo's study, seven of her radio-collared coyotes died. Cougars killed and ate four of them, but that doesn't necessarily mean cougars consistently hunt coyotes.

"The cougar-kills were during winter," she says, "which is the same time that Toni Ruth [a cougar researcher in the same area] was finding cougars that had starved to death."

Bounties, poison, traps and bullets have failed to eradicate the coyote.

untouched. People can abuse and defraud bounties easily while leaving coyote populations undented.

Today, no province or state pays bounties on coyotes because bounties aren't useful, except perhaps for teaching coyotes to avoid humans.

Poison, trapping and aerial shooting, however, remain part of the arsenal of most government agriculture or wildlife agencies.

In 1914, the U.S. Congress created the largest predator-control agency in the world.

Did The Coyotes Get Your Deer?

Bumper stickers, meeting hall rhetoric and newsletter diatribes throughout the West blame the wily coyote for declining mule deer populations. From Arizona to Alberta, few hunters would disagree with the sentiment that fewer coyotes would mean more deer. Mule deer populations peaked in the 1960s when Animal Damage Control also peaked as a coyote poisoning agency. Since then, coyote populations have increased and mule deer have declined.

Colorado game warden Jim Haskins says, "I really think if you look back to the deer we had in the 60s and 70s, it probably was an artifact of predator control...Probably poisoning had something to do it. But we probably had way more deer than the habitat could support." Haskins acknowledges that coyotes kill mule deer fawns. But, he says, under normal circumstances most mule deer does give birth during a two week period in the spring. Coyotes barely have time to make a dent in the supply of easily captured newborns before those fawns are strong enough to avoid them. Mule deer cope with predation by literally flooding the market with fawns.

Coyotes probably do kill more fawns than they used to but if so, it's likely the result of human hunting seasons. Haskins and his colleagues point out that when too many hunters harass or shoot buck mule deer during their November breeding season, many does miss the opportunity to breed. If that happens, females come into heat again a month later. If a buck fails to breed them then, they wait another month and come into heat yet again. Does bred later give birth later—and coyotes get two or more chances to hunt newborn fawns rather than just one. As John Seidel, a southern Colorado wildlife manager, says: "Spreading out the estrous cycles also spreads out the calf crop, so that rather than a lot of animals hitting the ground in a short period of time, they're spread out over a longer period of time."

If there is a problem with coyote predation on mule deer fawns—and biologists are divided on the question—the solution may have nothing to do with reducing the number of coyotes. It may be a simple matter (though controversial with some hunters) of scheduling mule deer hunting seasons before and after the November rut so that deer can mate in peace.

They named it the National Biological Survey, surely a case of Orwellian double-speak, and directed it to take care of "the destruction of wolves, coyotes, and other animals injurious to agriculture."

It used traps, strychnine, guns and any other method that seemed effective to accomplish this objective. Officers tracked down coyote dens and killed the pups. They fished them out with long cables that tangled in their fur, or filled dens with smoke or poison gas and then blocked the entrances. It was all-out war to free the western range for sheep and cattle production, no holds barred.

In 1939, the invention of the "coyote-getter" made coyote control much easier. The coyote-getter is a device buried in the soil and baited with a bit of meat. It works by shooting a dose of cyanide into the mouth of the coyote as it tugs at the bait. It proved to be both effective and selective compared to the older technique of lacing a carcass with strychnine.

The cruelty of poison, and the fact that it puts other scavengers at risk (many poisoned coyotes, especially those poisoned with Compound 1080, die far from bait, unrecovered by officers) led to a 1972 presidential order banning the use of poisons by federal employees and on federal land. In 1975, the Environmental Protection Agency authorized, again, the M-44 cyanide coyote-getter, but federal agencies use the device far more conservatively now because of public concerns.

The B.C. Ministry of Environment still uses Compound 1080 for predator control. Alberta Agriculture uses strychnine. Livestock producers can get coyote-getters and drop-baits—chicken heads laced with poison—on request from most county and municipal agriculture offices.

In the 45 years up to 1981, the U.S. government killed more than 3.5 million coyotes. That total leaves out coyotes which died where officers could not count them. Chuck Cadieux, a former U.S. federal wildlife control officer, estimates the actual tally at closer to 6 million coyotes.

Despite public and private funds pouring into coyote control, new and sophisticated techniques developed over the years, and the suffering they inflicted, North America has at least as many coyotes as it ever did. Indeed, coyotes have expanded their range from coast to coast. Today, they are the most abundant and widely distributed predator in North America.

Perhaps the coyote does have a link to the divine, after all. It may have been sent to keep us humble!

Coydogs

Some of the worst pillaging blamed on coyotes turns out to be the work of "coydogs," hybrid offspring of coyotes and domestic dogs, or even family pets running wild at night. Domestic dogs belong to the genus *Canis* like coyotes, wolves, African jackals and Australian dingoes. All have the same chromosome count and all can interbreed.

Coydogs occur most frequently where lots of dogs wander freely in well-populated rural areas. Coydogs are still fairly rare, however, because dogs and coyotes have different breeding cycles. Dogs come into heat twice a year: coyotes only once, usually in midwinter.

Coydogs are often larger than coyotes and have aggressive hunting instincts. They have been implicated in surplus killing of domestic sheep, white-tailed deer and other species. Some are also aggressive toward people.

Coyote Encounter

One December, I watched four coyotes attack and eventually kill a mule deer in Jasper National Park. The coyotes surprised three does on a steep slope and rushed them from above. Two of the deer lowered their ears and necks and faced the charging coyotes aggressively, but the third, a small yearling, ran. The coyotes quickly closed on her. They jumped at her flanks as she crossed a highway and plunged into the Athabasca River. The coyotes waited until the mule deer had forded the river before following her across. There, in a heavy pine forest, she stopped to fight and they surrounded her.

The end was inevitable: during the first attack, the coyotes managed to rip several bites out of her rump. When she lay down to rest, the coyotes would promptly close in, forcing her to stand again, and then take turns darting in at her. She fought back fiercely, kicking with her forelegs. Even so, it took more than 24 hours for the coyotes to finally kill her.

Wolves

The wolf's unfathomably wild gaze inspires many humans, while filling others with loathing and fear.

The wolf, *Canis lupus*, is not a wilderness animal. Wolves have come to represent wilderness in the minds of most modern North Americans simply because we have never tolerated them anywhere else. In some parts of Europe, wolves forage in back alleys.

In the foothills of Alberta and northern Montana, they sometimes wander past herds of cows. There is virtually no city or farm in North America that was not once wolf habitat. If we could think about them rationally, wolves could probably range across much of this country just as they did in the past.

But people rarely think rationally about wolves. Most hunters see them as unwanted competition for big game. Farmers and ranchers fear for the safety of their herds. Many environmentalists see wolves as a near-sacred symbol of pristine nature. Many urban Canadians value wolves so highly that they ignore the impact that wolf depredations on livestock can have on rural families.

Once in a while, wolves get in the news and extremists on all sides (most with no direct experience of wolves) unleash their rhetoric on one another. In the end, little is resolved and the wolf remains a shadow that haunts the continent's dwindling wilderness and the minds of those who argue so vehemently about its fate.

"Only the mountain," wrote American con-

Wolf Facts

Size: 1.3-1.8 meters / 4-6 feet
Weight: 20-80 kilograms / 45-180 pounds
Description: Black, gray or white, rarely brow; similar to a German shepherd but with longer legs and a straight tail
Reproduction: Breeds at 2 or 3 years of age
Gestation: 63 days
Litter size: 1-10 pups; average 6
Life span: 15 years
Food: Large ungulates, beavers, other mammals
Distribution: All of Canada except major agricultural regions; survives in parts of Montana, Idaho and Wyoming

Wolves have powerful jaws and shoulders to help them bite and hold animals larger than themselves.

servationist Aldo Leopold, "has lived long enough to listen objectively to the howl of a wolf."

Wolves once ranged across most of North America from the islands of the Arctic south to what is now Mexico. They denned in the rain forests of the Pacific slope, the deciduous woodland of the upper Mississippi basin, and from Newfoundland south to Delaware. Wolves hunted white-tailed deer in what is now Washington D.C. and shadowed bison herds where

now the cities of Winnipeg, Minneapolis, Omaha and Fort Worth sprawl across the western plains.

North America has three species of wolf: the timber wolf, the coyote and the red wolf, *Canis rufus*. The endangered red wolf once ranged from what is now North Carolina to eastern Texas.

European settlers arriving in North America brought their hatred and fear of wolves with them. Before the 20th-century, European cul-

The Dire Wolf

"The dire wolf collects his dues, while the boys sing round the fire: Don't murder me, I beg of you don't murder me."

- Dire Wolf,
The Grateful Dead

The dire wolf, *Canis dirus*, was the largest wolf species that ever existed. It was half again the size of the timber wolf and much more powerfully built. This massive carnivore first appears in the North American fossil record about a million years ago. It was an ice age animal, part of a fauna that included huge bison, mastodons, sabre-tooth cats, giant ground sloths and mammoths.

Like most of this Pleistocene mega-fauna, the dire wolf died out 8,000 years ago or so, during the

retreat of the last great glaciers that covered North America. Nobody knows why, but scientists note that the mass extinction coincided with the arrival of primitive humans invading the continent from the northwest. Fossils from Arkansas, however, suggest that some dire wolves may have survived in the Ozark Mountains as recently as 3,000 or 4,000 years ago.

Did the dire wolf hunt down early humans? Probably no more than the timber wolf did. The huge size and powerful build of dire wolves were adaptations for preying on the giant herbivores that lived in North America at the time.

Dire wolves and timber wolves could breed with one another, so dire wolf genes may live on in today's smaller wolf species.

ture had no concept of ecology and recognized no useful role for predators. It associated wolves with evil and the works of the devil. An oral tradition about wolves attacking humans fueled legends of werewolves and folklore stories such as *Peter and the Wolf.*

In Europe and Asia, wolves did sometimes attack and kill people. Between 1764 and 1767, for example, around Gevauden in France, two wolves attacked more than a hundred people and killed and ate several. Biologists, reviewing the records, now suspect that the animals were hybrids between dogs and wolves, but folk tradition just called them wolves. Rabies outbreaks also accounted for several well-documented attacks.

Beyond the often irrational fear of wolves and werewolves lay a more practical matter: wolves compete with humans for food.

When settlers arrived in North America, wolves soon discovered that draught horses and milk cows were easy prey. The settlers saw it as their manifest destiny to civilize the untamed land. They ploughed the soil, cleared the forests, pushed aside aboriginal people and set about ridding North America of its wolves and other predators.

Wolves are highly susceptible to poison. Settlers, spreading west in waves across the conti-

nent, soon eradicated them. By the mid 20th-century, the wolf was virtually extinct south of the 49th parallel and throughout the Canadian prairies.

Since about 1960, however, wolf numbers have slowly increased in some of the areas they formerly occupied. A wolf population that ranges from southern Ontario through northern Minnesota, Wisconsin and Michigan now numbers more than 2,500, after a gradual recovery during the 1970s and 1980s.

In the late 1970s and early 1980s, wolves from northern British Columbia and Alberta dispersed south along the Rocky Mountains, appearing in northern Montana in the mid 1980s. Today, a slowly growing population of nearly 100 wolves occupies Glacier National Park and the region around it in Montana, British Columbia and Alberta. Farther south, wolves transplanted from Canada into parts of Wyoming and Idaho have established healthy breeding populations. Endangered Mexican wolves, released in 1998, wander the wilds of Arizona's Blue Mountains where Aldo Leopold wrote regretfully about helping to eradicate their ancestors. Biologists in Colorado estimate dispersing wolves from the Yellowstone area will recolonize that state within the next 10 years.

Wolf Researcher

"I started working with wolves *in 1988 in Algonquin Provincial Park in Ontario. I was really fortunate, because I got to work* for and learn from [wolf biologist] Dr. John Theberge. I remember that a lot of people used to accuse him of bias. For example, when he took the public position that wolf numbers should not be managed, that was unethical. He always argued right back that his critics were subject to a lot more bias and less objectivity in the positions they were taking.

Since then I've worked in Alberta, mostly in Banff National Park's Bow Valley, under the supervision of Dr. Paul Paquet. I study wolf population dynamics and habitat use as part of the requirements for my Ph.D. from the University of Guelph.

I don't know if I'm looking at a lifetime career of studying wolves, but I'm not tired of wolves by any stretch of the imagination. The questions with wolves are very interesting and I guess you have to be somewhat of a political individual to keep involved with wolves because they evoke controversy and politics one way or another.

I think that when you're looking at wolves you never have the whole picture. They never reveal everything. There's always some mystery left. I think the challenge for us is to strike up a relationship with wolves in a way that will allow them to remain viable."

-Carolyn Callahagn, Central Rockies Wolf Ecology Project.

Although it is against the law in both Canada and the U.S., people still poison wolves from time to time along the southern fringe of their range. In Canada, where shooting wolves is legal, some hunters, ranchers and trappers hunt them aggressively.

During the 20th-century, however, wolves have gradually recovered in areas where human populations remain low. Eventually, wolves will probably range again throughout the U.S. Rocky Mountains and parts of the Great Lakes states and provinces. They have little chance, on the other hand, of recovering their former range on the prairies or in the deciduous forest of eastern North America, both now heavily developed.

Wolf Country

Rolling country with mixed aspen and evergreen woodland is ideal wolf habitat, especially if beaver dams create wetlands and the trails of elk, deer and moose wind through the woods. Wolves will live anywhere, given a chance, but it is probably no accident that many people know them as timber wolves. Where wolves are most common, throughout most of the West, forest covers well over half the landscape. Only in winter do wolves regularly frequent open country and then, it's only because they have little choice but to hunt elk and deer where they congregate on windswept grasslands and open slopes.

When hunting, wolves often follow linear features in the landscape—long ridges, river

Wolfers

Just as the great herds of eastern Africa support predators such as the lion, hyena and jackal, so the unimaginable biological wealth of the pristine North American prairies supported abundant wolves, grizzlies and cougars.

Nobody knows how many bison once roamed the Great Plains of North America, but, from descriptions of the great herds, some estimates say as many as 60 million. Countless pronghorns lived among the bison. Large numbers of elk ranged the river valleys, coulees and isolated hill systems of what is now Manitoba, Saskatchewan, Alberta and the prairie states.

Wolves ranged with the big game, in numbers we find hard to imagine today. Captain Meredith Lewis, exploring the Missouri River country in 1805, described wolves as "shepherds of the buffalo." Artist Paul Kane, near the present-day Alberta-Saskatchewan border, wrote in 1848: "We saw great numbers of wolves busily employed in devouring the carcasses of drowned buffaloes, and had some amusing hunts with our boats after them."

John ("Kootenai") Brown hunted wolves in Montana and southern Alberta in 1865. He reported: "We saw very few coyotes on the open prairie, but hundreds of wolves ran the country in bands."

Like many other frontier exploiters, Brown took advantage of the market for wolf pelts, sold at that time for around $2 to $3 dollars each. He later recalled: "We averaged about 1,000 wolves in a winter." He may have stretched the truth a little, but

records do show that by the late 1860s the peak of the wolfers' trade posts along the Missouri River shipped up to 10,000 wolf and coyote pelts each year.

One Montana historian estimates that wolfers took an average 55,000 wolves each year from 1870 through 1877. That statistic includes some coyotes, but many more wolves.

All a wolfer needed was a rifle and some strychnine. When winter began, wolfers shot and butchered bison every few miles, salting the carcasses liberally with poison. They then tried to keep the wolves away until the carcass froze. If the carcass did not freeze, a few wolves might gulp down most of the poisoned meat, wasting it.

According to Brown, "It was a common thing to get 20 wolves dead the first morning. Instances have been known where 50 to 80 have been poisoned."

The indigeneous peoples of the plains detested wolfers because poisoned carcasses killed their dogs and sometimes even people. The poison baits must have also killed thousands of eagles, Swift foxes, magpies, ravens and other animals that eat carrion.

The repeating rifle, invented in the late 1860s, together with improved rail and steamship access to the West, brought the seemingly inexhaustible bison to virtual extinction within only two decades. The loss of the bison marked the end of the prairie wolf population and of wolfing.

floodplains and even roads. Their travels rarely take them far from cover. Wolves den most frequently at the edge of the timber. Rendezvous sites are commonly in small meadows surrounded with forest—often the edges of beaver ponds or sedge meadows that have grown up on abandoned beaver ponds.

Even though wolves shun open country, they show little reluctance to cross it when they need to. Dispersing wolves from Canada have turned up in Idaho and Wyoming—they would have had to cross large tracts of open high grasslands and sagebrush. When trees and brush aren't available, wolves are likely to use darkness for cover instead.

People eradicated the prairie wolf before biologists really had a chance to describe its lifestyle, but it seems likely that even out on the plains wolves denned and raised their young in the shrubbery and woodlands along rivers and canyons. Deer, beavers and other prey animals were readily available there. The packs that followed wide-ranging herds of bison would have been non-breeding animals or families with young large enough to travel.

Wolves seem to have an instinctive affinity for good habitat, even when colonizing places they have never seen before. After one pack was wiped out in Montana's Nine-Mile Valley, other wolves appeared several months later and began to use the very same areas, even though they had access to a great diversity of unused habitat. Similarly, whenever wolves have taken up residence in Waterton Lakes National Park—in the 1940s, again in 1993 and once again in 1996—they selected the heavily wooded Belly River Valley as the center of their home ranges and ranged only occasionally into other seemingly good habitat nearby.

Wandering Wolves

Wolves are inveterate travellers. They stay on the move except during the denning season. Their long-legged gait both conserves energy and enables them to cover great distances in a short time.

One wolf radio-collared in northern Montana in the late 1980s was killed near Fort St. John, B.C. 840 km (520 miles) north. Wolves often travel long distances, especially two- and three-year-old wolves that have reached sexual maturity and disperse in search of vacant terri-

Werewolves

Unfounded fears persist that wolves kill humans.

The belief that some humans can assume the shape of wolves arose in German-speaking countries more than five centuries ago when wolves were still widespread in central Europe. Rabid wolves periodically terrorized farmers and villagers, who thought evil spirits or the devil had possessed the animals.

Local legends told of outlaws and sorcerers who, by putting on a wolf hide or buckling on a magic belt, transformed themselves into huge wolves that slaughtered sheep and cattle. In some rural areas, an oral tradition of werewolf stories still survives. In the stories, people hunt down werewolves and kill them with dogs or beat them to death with sticks. The werewolves, as they die, return to their human forms.

The brothers Grimm recorded many werewolf stories, including one from the town of Littich where "two sorcerers were executed in 1610 because they had transformed themselves into werewolves and killed many children. Every time they went out on their hunts to tear up and consume their prey they were accompanied by a twelve-year-old boy whom the Devil would transform into a raven."

The original werewolf legends likely came not only from rabid wolves, but from the predation of real wolves and wolf-dog hybrids on livestock. Medieval peasants lived isolated lives that magnified their fear of outsiders and people who behaved unconventionally. As people told the stories again and again, the magical powers and horrific deeds of werewolves became more elaborate and formalized. Modern cartoonists and novelists have taken the werewolf far from its humble origins into the realm of occult fantasy.

Evergreen woodland is ideal wolf habitat.

tory they can colonize.

The record for long-distance travel may go to wolves dispersing into new habitat, but even established wolf packs make long trips. In Canada's Arctic, biologists have observed wolf packs following northern caribou herds for up to 160 kilometers / 100 miles. An old Russian proverb says, "A wolf is fed by its feet." Wolves readily travel more than 50 kilometers / 31 miles a day in winter.

The home ranges of wolves shrink in summer, when young pups are confined to dens or rendezvous areas, and expand in winter. Summer home ranges in high-quality habitat with abundant prey may only cover 50 km² (about 20 square miles). Winter home ranges may cover as much as 5,000 square kilometers / 1,900 square miles in the far north, where caribou, the main prey of northern wolves, trek on long migrations.

Wolf packs wander widely. In winter, the pups have grown and frozen lakes and rivers offer good travel routes. Winter prey often concentrates in small patches across the landscape: deer may congregate where heavy coniferous cover intercepts snow; moose in willow thickets around beaver ponds or avalanche paths; and elk and bighorn sheep on windswept grassy slopes.

The pack commonly travels in single file, each wolf placing its feet exactly in the tracks of the one ahead of it. On more than one occasion I have followed what looked like the tracks of a single wolf, only to have it branch into separate tracks of six to eight individuals.

Incredible Journeys

It was raining when Dr. Paul Paquet found a five-year-old wolf waiting for him in a trap he had set in Alberta's Peter Lougheed Provincial Park. After fitting her with a radio collar, Paquet set the wolf—named Pluie after the French word for rain—free.

Pluie moved north and became a member of the Cascade pack in Banff National Park for a while, but it soon became apparent that she didn't really consider herself an Alberta wolf. She was a citizen of the world.

Within three years, Pluie had journeyed south not once, but twice through British Columbia's Elk and Flathead river valleys, crossed the international boundary into Montana, looped west into Idaho, then found her way back to the Alberta Rockies near Banff. On one of those trips, the satellite that monitored Pluie's radio signal indicated that she had trekked far to the east of Browning, Montana.

Pluie's radio transmitter was found in 1993 on a mountainside north of the Waterton-Glacier International Peace Park. The remains of the collar, and Pluie herself, were missing. Paquet assumed the wandering wolf was dead. She wasn't. Late in 1995, a hunter near Invermere, B.C. shot three wolves from a pack that ranged in and around Kootenay National Park. One—the alpha female—turned out to be Pluie.

Pluie travelled an area of more than 100,000 kilometers / 38,500 square miles.

Opal travelled even farther. Another five-year-old wolf that was radio-collared in Kananaskis Country, Opal made the mistake of dining on Alberta beef in 1993. The rancher who caught her in the act had a rifle handy. When he called Dr. Paquet to report the shooting, he said he hadn't been able to find Opal's carcass.

There was a good reason for that. Four years later, Animal Damage Control wolf specialist Carter Niemeyer responded to a complaint about wolves that were killing cattle north of Yellowstone National Park. Niemeyer found the culprits: a ten-year-old female wolf and her five pups. The mother was none other than Opal—having travelled well over a 1,000 kilometers / 600 miles from her birth den.

Other species confined to fragmented patches of habitat face decline from isolation and inbreeding. Not so with wolves, if Pluie and Opal were at all typical. Paquet says wolves have

Wolves By Airmail

History must have taught wolves by now that the "whup, whup, whup" of a helicopter generally means trouble. Nothing, however, could have prepared west-central Alberta's wolves for what happened during the winter of 1994-95.

Earlier that year, the U.S. Fish and Wildlife Service offered trappers in Alberta $1,000 for each live wolf they captured—an unprecedented windfall. Biologists fitted the trapped wolves with radio collars and then turned them loose to rejoin their packs. A few weeks later, as political and legal battles raged from Wyoming to Washington D.C., the biologists returned. Leaning out the doors of roaring helicopters, they shot tranquilizer darts into wolves innocently betrayed by their radio-collared pack mates. They captured a total of 29 wolves.

The biologists measured, tattooed, poked and prodded the unwilling wolves and fitted them with shiny new radio collars of their own. They then shipped them south to Yellowstone National Park and to the Frank Church/River-of-No-Return Wilderness in northern Idaho. They turned 14 wolves loose in Yellowstone and another 15 in Idaho.

The capture and relocation of Canadian wolves was part of a controversial but highly popular program to remove the wolf from the U.S. endangered species list. The U.S. government will consider wolves recovered in the northern U.S. Rockies when the wolves have established three distinct populations, each with at least 10 breeding pairs or about 100 wolves.

Biologically, the transplant was unnecessary. Wolves had already begun to find their way back to Yellowstone and wilderness areas in Idaho. But ranchers and hunters killed most of them in short order, illegally, out of distaste for both wolves and

the Endangered Species Act (ESA).

The wolves transplanted from Canada, designated an "experimental, non-essential" population, do not qualify for the rigid protection of the ESA. But their radio collars help biologists respond quickly if someone shoots them. By agreement, ranchers can shoot wolves if they see them attacking livestock.

Within the first year of their release, four of the wolves were shot illegally. Wildlife officers killed a fifth—a loner who developed an unfortunate taste for domestic mutton—to honor their commitment to local ranchers. Undeterred by these losses, or by the withdrawal of government funds for the program and the concerns of animal rights advocates, biologists released a second shipment of wolves from British Columbia, this time early in 1996.

By 1998, both populations had increased to more than 100 wolves. The majority of the increase were new pups born in 1997 and 1998, but biologists also found wolves which had dispersed from northern Montana and joined with the new colonists. While the human occupants of what is again wolf country continue to debate the merits of wolf reintroduction, the wolves continue to thrive. Few domestic cows, sheep or dogs have fallen prey to the wolves and where problems have developed, wildlife officials have either trapped or, in some cases, killed the offending wolves.

Hank Fischer, a member of the U.S.-based conservation group, Defenders of Wildlife, played a key role in this controversial reintroduction program and has written a book about it called *Wolf Wars*.

Ralph Maughan, an Idaho-based conservationist, posts regular updates on the status of the reintroduced wolves at http://www.poky.srv.net/~jim-rm/maughan.html

the ability to recolonize former ranges and to find other wolves with which to breed. For wolves to recover, all they require is protection from indiscriminate killing.

Pluie's and Opal's incredible journeys helped inspire the Yellowstone-to-Yukon Conservation Initiative. Hunters, hikers, ranchers, biologists and people from all walks of life are now working to ensure that wilderness-loving creatures can always travel safely up and down the entire Rocky Mountain chain.

Yellowstone to Yukon?—learn more about it at www.rockies.ca

Wolf Society

The wolf pack, rather than the individual wolf, is the basic unit of wolf ecology. The pack is more than the sum of its parts—a complex web of relationships and responsibilities that functions, when hunting, as a sort of super-predator.

Winter wolf packs range in size from four members to as many as 20. A pack of 36 wolves was recorded once, but such a large pack is extremely rare and too inefficient to remain together for long. A typical pack has six to 12 animals consisting of a dominant "alpha" male, an alpha female, their pups from the summer, yearlings born the year before, and one or two unrelated members.

Where's A Wolf Supposed To Go?

Conservation biologists have started to worry that Banff, Canada's oldest and most famous national park, may be a killing field for wolves rather than a place of refuge.

Rampant over-development has laid claim to the Bow River Valley, the site of some of the most productive wildlife habitat in the park. The valley contains a townsite and a resort complex which bars an important movement corridor for wolves. One of the busiest highways in western Canada, the Trans-Canada, slices right through it.

Until the early 1980s, cars and trucks on the Trans-Canada killed up to 200 large animals, mostly elk, every year. When Parks Canada allowed Sunshine Village and Lake Louise ski resorts to expand, the government expanded the two-lane highway into a four-lane divided highway to handle the extra traffic. It built a fence along both sides of the highway to keep elk off.

The fence worked: the number of kills dropped by three-quarters. As elk populations recovered, so did wolf populations.

But wolves have not adapted well to the fenced highway, according to studies by Dr. Paul Paquet and his students in the late 1980s and 1990s. The highway has large culverts and other underpasses to allow animals through. Elk, deer, coyotes and other animals have adapted well to the underpasses. Black bears just climb the fence and run across, often dying in the attempt. Wolves, for some reason, appear reluctant to use underpasses.

"We've seen wolves on the highway, milling about on the shoulder," says Carolyn Callahagn, who conducted research on wolf movements in the central Rockies during the mid 1990s. "They really want to cross, and the more they have to wait, the more nervous things get. Suddenly they put their heads down and go across with no thought to traffic. It's amazing that any survive."

Callahagn has tracked wolves for several seasons, documenting the impacts of human development on Banff National Park.

Callahagn says so many wolves died on the highway during the winter of 1995-96 that two wolf packs west of the town of Banff merged into one. At the time, a third pack, the Cascade pack, ranged the Lake Minnewanka and Cascade valleys north of the highway.

"The Cascade pack should be using the area south of the highway and east of town, because it's high-quality wolf habitat," she says. "We had an incident last November that showed how much of a barrier the highway is in that area. Two wolves from the Cascade pack tunnelled under the fence at a place where the coyotes had gone under. They both approached the road. One crossed it and approached the fence on the other side, turned around and went back, joined the other one and they tunneled back out. Three elk had been killed on the railroad. The wolves were keying in on that but they couldn't get across the fenced highway."

In 1996, work began to twin the highway west to Lake Louise. Park officials decided to install two short overpasses in the hope that wolves and other animals that fear going under the road would be willing to go over it.

posite sex.

Wolf packs are strongly territorial, marking and defending their home ranges against strange wolves or other packs. Wolves avoid direct conflict as much as possible. They spend little time in places where their home ranges overlap with those of adjacent packs. They post their boundaries with scent and howl to warn other wolves to steer clear. It doesn't always work, especially when packs become large and require a larger prey base. In 1995, wolf researcher Kyran Kunkel found two dead wolves at the scene of an encounter between two wolf packs in Montana's Glacier National Park.

Alpha wolves sometimes lose rank if they become injured or weak and as other members of the pack mature. The displaced leader often leaves the pack and becomes a loner. Dispersing young adults may live as loners too.

Where wolves are relatively common, loners survive in the no-wolf's-land between the core home ranges of different packs. Packs avoid these areas because of the risk of a confrontation. Lone wolves keep a low profile: they scent-mark less often than packs and often go off-trail to defecate or urinate.

In areas where wolves are scarce, however, lone wolves advertise their presence in the hope of finding a mate.

Wolves mate in February, unlike domestic dogs, which may come into heat at any time of the year. Their mating resembles mating in dogs; females in heat leave spots of blood in their tracks and mating wolves become stuck together, standing back to back, for up to half an hour at a time.

Usually, only the alpha animals of a pack mate. They aggressively prevent other pack members from breeding, which may contribute to the long-range dispersal of young adults. A young wolf that wants to mate has to leave the pack and travel until he or she finds a territory not already occupied by another pack, and then hope to meet up with an eligible wolf of the op-

Talks With Wolves

It looked like a mountain goat crossing the highway, but as I drew abreast and stopped, I realized I was looking at a large, pure-white wolf. He glanced back at me over his shoulder, then continued up the slope toward the forest.

A friend was only a minute or so behind me in a different vehicle. I wanted him to see the wolf too, but it was almost into the trees. Without too much hope of success, I rolled down my window and howled at him.

My howl sounded pretty pathetic to me, but to my surprise the wolf stopped, turned and howled back. I howled again. He sat down on his haunches and answered.

I never figured out what we were talking about, but the conversation lasted until John pulled up a few moments later. At length, the wolf turned and trotted off into the trees, leaving me bemused and humbled by the encounter.

Dan Strickland, chief naturalist of Ontario's Algonquin Provincial Park, was a pioneer in the art of calling wolves. He thought park visitors might find it rewarding to hear wolves howl, so he advertised an organized car caravan to wolf-howl in the late 1960s. Crowds have been turning out ever since.

Wolves will often respond to any reasonable imitation of a howl, especially in late summer when pups are waiting at rendezvous sites for adults to bring them food and the adult pack members are scattered around the landscape. Sometimes wolves will even reply to the toot of a car horn.

When hopeful humans subject wolves to too much impromptu howling, however, the wolves soon stop replying. Some national and provincial park managers worry that too much recreational howling may cause unnecessary stress and confusion to wolves.

Domestic Dog: *Canis familiaris*

Archaeologists excavating in the Jordan River Valley found a 12,000-year-old human skeleton with its hand resting on the skeleton of a wolflike creature. Dogs and humans have lived in association for a long time, probably for as long as *Homo sapiens*—the younger species—has walked the earth.

Humans no doubt learned early that they could steal meat from wolves, which were far more effective at hunting. Wolves, in turn, learned that they could scavenge for scraps from humans, especially when humans killed large numbers of big game by herding them over cliffs or into swamps and snowdrifts.

The two species must have seen a lot of each other. Wolves, coyotes and similar wild canids had characteristics that made them useful to humans: intelligence and sociability, the capacity to learn from repetitive experience, strength and hunting skills. At some point, humans began to adopt wolf pups and raise them to maturity.

Human selection replaced natural selection in the evolution of the domestic dog. We think of evolution as a natural process in which changes to the physical environment—warmer or cooler climates, new habitat, new competitors—shape the genetic make-up of populations. The animals best suited to survive a change live to breed and pass on their characteristics. Those less well-adapted die and fail. But, thousands of years ago, the relationship between humans and the dog family altered the course of nature and produced today's bewildering variety of domestic-dog breeds.

As far as we can determine, people domesticated wolves in several parts of the world, giving rise to several ancestral stocks of domestic dog. Many of today's breeds seem to have originated in southern Asia, but when European explorers first arrived in the New World, they found that North America's aboriginal people already had dogs. These may have accompanied the people who crossed the Bering land bridge into North America from Asia, but they might also have arisen from the domestication of native North American canids. David Thompson, venturing into the Pacific Northwest in the early 1800s, commented on the similarity of many native dogs to the coyote.

Indigenous peoples relied on dogs mostly as draught animals. Dogs were so entwined with their lives that when the Spanish introduced domestic horses to North America, plains tribes simply called them "big dogs." Plains tribes used dogs to pull lodge poles and travois loaded with supplies and belongings. Farther north, the tribes occupying the northern forests and barren lands employed dogs to pull loaded sleighs. European fur traders continued to use dog teams well into the 20th-century, crossbreeding the small native sled dogs with mastiffs and other big European dogs to produce huskies and other larger, more powerful sled dogs.

Konrad Lorenz and other ecologists argue that some breeds of dog may actually be descended from the jackal, but most biologists believe that most domestic dogs are descended from the same ancestors as modern wolves. Some breeds of dog appear to have more in common with the big timber wolf of northern and temperate regions, while others appear related to species from more southern regions. Biologist Diane Boyd points out that wolves vary greatly in size and color—an indication that wolf populations may have greater genetic diversity than coyote or jackal populations, which show much less variability. With selective breeding, the range of characteristics in wolves could have produced the variety we see today in *Canis familiaris*.

The breeds of domestic dogs found in western North America today—from miniature poodles, dachshunds and Pomeranians to pit bulls, Irish terriers and Afghan hounds—all share similar behavioral traits that link them to wild canids.

When dogs bury bones, they are exhibiting food-caching behavior seen in wolves, coyotes and foxes. Dogs that leap up at people to greet them are behaving like wolves rejoining the pack, or like wolf pups greeting adults at the den. A dog that rolls on its back is displaying submission, while one that raises its tail and hackles is displaying aggression. Dogs and wolves both have that unappealing habit of smelling each others' hind ends when they meet. They are checking each others' anal glands, communicating with one another by scent.

Obedience training aims to establish the dominance of a human over a dog so that the dog will

Domestic Dog: *Canis familiaris*

behave submissively toward the human, just as it would toward the alpha animal of a pack.

Domestic dogs now far outnumber native wolves, coyotes and foxes in North America. Most have little direct impact on the remnant wild ecosystems of the West. But, on the loose, dogs can become deadly predators. They have wolflike hunting instincts and superior physical stamina from a reliable diet of store-bought dog chow. Dogs frequently engage in surplus killing, more often than wild canids. They need not kill to eat and, being well fed, they have energy to waste. Many slaughters of domestic sheep or fowl that were initially blamed on coyotes or wolves have, on investigation, turned out to be the work of dogs.

Many owners refuse to believe that little Fifi or Sport would engage in such uncivilized behavior in the dark of night, but it should come as no surprise. Dogs are pets to us, bred to be friendly and obedient. But they remain members of the *Canidae* and descendants of wild hunters. Their biological programming makes them just as inclined to hunt and kill. Responsible dog ownership means keeping dogs from roaming the countryside.

Wolf Families

Wolves become sexually mature at two years of age, although they may not successfully reproduce until they are older. Generally, only the dominant pair of wolves in a pack breed. In the expanding wolf population of northern Montana, however, researchers have found that more than one female in a pack may produce

Building Tolerance Toward Wolves

Wolf biologist Diane Boyd

Diane Boyd, one of North America's foremost wolf biologists, says successful wolf conservation comes down to building tolerance. In the fragmented landscapes of western North America, she says, conservationists need to work things out with groups that oppose bigger wolf populations. "We need to work with the ranchers, hunters, farmers, fur trappers."

Boyd tells the story of an interpretive presentation she watched one night in Montana's Glacier National Park. The park ranger talked about man's inhumanity to wolves, showed slides of dead and slaughtered wolves, waxed eloquent about the intrinsic value of wolves and said nothing at all about the legitimate fears and concerns of the people living outside the park. Instead, he painted them as the enemy.

"You can't have an island of wolves," says Boyd, "so you shouldn't do things to polarize the situation. We need to work with these interest groups, give them information, listen to them and find ways to deal with their concerns. Inflamed rhetoric is exactly the kind of thing that destroys conservation and recovery efforts."

pups in the same year. The death of alpha pack members, which happens more often in heavily hunted wolf populations, sometimes releases the controls on breeding and several young wolves may produce litters as the pack social system breaks down.

Wolf pups are usually born in April, a little more than two months after the adults mate. Wolves usually give birth in underground dens, although in some cases they use a rough nest under a wind-blown tree or some other form of natural shelter. Biologists have counted as many as 11 pups in a single litter, but the average is six.

The mother nurses the pups for about five weeks. Other members of the pack bring her food. After she weans them, the mother begins hunting again and the other members of the pack share with her the task of bringing food to the pups.

Early in summer, the pups are strong enough to move to a new home. The mother and other pack members relocate them to a "rendezvous" site a few miles from the original den. A rendezvous site is usually a small meadow of a few acres. The adults leave the pups there while they hunt and the pups, lacking the confidence to explore far on their own, stay put. They play and sleep and wait for the adults to return with food.

Pups begin to capture some of their own foods while in the rendezvous sites, as their playful stalking and pouncing starts to produce the occasional mouse or ground squirrel. By fall, the pups have grown large and gangly and start to accompany the rest of the pack on extended hunts. Ten months after birth, the pups are nearly full-grown, but the process of learning to hunt large animals may go on for many more months.

Wolf Communication

Before wolves execute a complicated hunt, they have a nose-sniffing, tail-wagging session during which, evidently, some kind of planning takes place. Wolves rely heavily on this kind of body language to communicate not only hunting strategies but social information, too.

The alpha pair of a pack, for example, carry their tails at or above the horizontal position and their heads high. Other wolves, and human observers, have no trouble picking them out.

The subordinate members of the pack carry their tails low, often between their legs, and their bodies communicate submission. When they interact with each other, subordinate wolves lay their ears back, crouch low or roll onto their backs to show they mean no offense to their superiors.

The best-known form of wolf communication is howling, but it may not be the most important. Howling, whining and barking help wolves keep in touch from a distance, to celebrate kills and other social occasions, and to warn or challenge one another. But other forms of communication play important roles in wolf life too.

Scent, for example, plays a very important role in wolf communication; wolves have much more sensitive noses than people. They also have scent glands on either side of their anus that they use to mark home ranges. Wolves, especially the alpha wolves of a pack, deposit scent from these anal glands on their droppings as they travel through their territory. The scented droppings, as well as strong-smelling urine and scent deposited from glands in the paws, inform other wolves which wolf has passed that way and when.

Wolf packs scent-mark most heavily along their home-range boundaries. This helps to keep packs apart, an important function since wolves from strange packs sometimes wound or kill each other if they meet. Pack separation also serves an ecological function: it ensures that wolves space themselves out across the landscape, reducing the pressure on any single group of elk, deer or other prey animals.

Pioneer Mothers

Biologist Bruce McLellan checked his grizzly bear trap line one day and found a wolf in one of the snares. She was almost pure-white. He fitted her with a spare radio collar and let her go.

This was in the early 1970s. McLellan was studying the impact of industrial activity on grizzly bears in British Columbia, west of the Waterton-Glacier International Peace Park. He had caught a particularly significant wolf, as it was soon revealed.

The researchers who tracked her named her Phyllis. She proved to be the alpha female of a pack that had recolonized the Flathead Valley. The Flathead River has headwaters in British Columbia and flows into Montana. In 1986, Phyllis followed the valley south and became the first wolf known to den in Montana in almost half a century. Researchers dubbed her pack the "Magic Pack" because of its tendency to utterly vanish for weeks at a time, only to reappear just as the researchers were ready to give it up for dead.

The U.S. Endangered Species Act protected Phyllis, her offspring and other wolves that found their way into the Montana's wild Flathead country. They thrived on the valley's abundant white-tailed deer, mule deer, elk and moose. Although hunters shot some wolves in the British Columbia portion of the valley, and a pack was poisoned illegally on B.C.'s Wigwam Flats, the population

Newborn pups stay close to the den.

continued to grow.

By the early 1990s, close to 70 wolves in five packs ranged through the Flathead Valley and ad-

Juvenile pups play at a rendezvous site.

Pioneer Mothers

jacent watersheds. Many wore radio collars, compliments of American researchers eager to learn about the dynamics of an expanding wolf population.

Phyllis, however, was no longer among them. In 1987, another wolf had displaced her as the alpha female of the Magic Pack. Phyllis became a loner. Wolf biologist Diane Boyd knew the battery on her radio collar was due to fail, but she had no luck trying to replace it.

"I tried to catch her again for years," Boyd recalls. "But she was just too smart. Maybe I'd nipped her toes once or something. She would do things like walk right by the traps, then come in from the side and dig them out. Nobody saw her much.

"Another year went by, and by now her radio was dead. One morning, at first light, I had just stepped out of my cabin when I spotted what looked like a light-colored coyote coming from about half a mile away across a long open meadow. I went and got my friends, we got behind the barn to watch, and to my surprise it was Phyllis.

"She walked in a straight line right up to the cabin, stopped, stared at it for a while, and then she just turned and walked right back all the way across that meadow on her own tracks. It was like she was deliberately thumbing her nose at me. I never saw her again."

Phyllis drifted north and crossed the Continental Divide into Alberta, a dangerous place for wolves.

Ironically, once she had arrived in Alberta, a province noted for its lax regulations on wolf killing, she began to show herself regularly. It was only a matter of time before someone shot Phyllis, the pioneer mother of the Flathead wolf population.

Phyllis's legacy continued, however. Three of her descendants, all females which Diane Boyd also radio-collared, wandered northeast into Alberta not long after Phyllis' death. There, just as Phyllis had done in Montana, they joined up with other wolves that had wandered in from British Columiba and Alberta's more northerly foothills.

Salix, the first to establish herself in the prey-rich aspen parkland along the eastern edge of the Rocky Mountains, became the alpha female of the Belly River pack. She denned in 1993 and 1994 on the eastern edge of Waterton Lakes National Park. The other two became the breeding females of the Beauvais and Carbondale packs, which denned west of Pincher Creek in the summer of 1994.

In Alberta, however, wolves rarely live long. Biologists estimated that the population of the Oldman River watershed which included the Belly, Beauvais and Carbondale packs had grown to around 60 wolves by summer of 1994. By the following spring, people had killed at least 44 of them. The dead included all the pioneer mothers and most of their offspring. The population has yet to recover.

Wolves as Hunters

Wolves have evolved over the millennia into social animals superbly adapted for preying on large mammals. An average pack of wolves needs to kill one animal the size of a deer or larger about every two to five days—a total of 70 to 180 animals a year.

Wolves range over the whole landscape—along wildlife corridors, ridges and floodplains, for example—keying in on places where they have found prey before.

As they travel, wolves use all their senses to locate prey. Usually, they smell their prey and then move upwind, sneaking in quietly, but with growing agitation, until they can surprise it with a sudden rush. On other occasions, wolves simply stumble over prey in the course of their travels, spotting it at a distance or surprising it at close range. Less frequently, wolves hunt like bird dogs, picking up a fresh scent and tracking the animal that made it.

For much of the year, deer and moose travel alone or in small family groups. Elk and sheep, by contrast, generally congregate in larger herds. The more solitary the animal, the more random its distribution across the landscape. All things being equal, wolves usually find more

Who Else Dines Here?

Wolves are good at turning large animals into large meals. They sustain not only themselves but a wide range of other animals that have come to depend on the wolf's hunting abilities to help them meet their own needs. When a wolf kills an elk, for example, the carcass may become habitat for more than 400 kinds of insects. In winter, wolf kills may mean the difference between survival and starvation for many animals.
Mammals and birds that feed at wolf kills include:

- Red squirrel, deer mouse
- Coyote
- Marten, weasel, wolverine
- Bobcat
- Arctic fox, red fox
- Black bear, grizzly bear
- Bald eagle, golden eagle
- Herring gull, California gull, ring-billed gull
- Blue jay, Steller's jay, gray jay
- Black-capped, mountain and boreal chickadees

Grizzly bear and carcass

Bald eagle and kill

Wolverine on antlers

moose and deer than elk and sheep.

Once a pack of wolves has located, stalked and rushed its prey, several outcomes are possible and only one ends in a meal. Some moose, elk or even deer face the attacking wolves and fight back, kicking out with their forelegs. When healthy prey fight back, wolves often break off the hunt and go in search of something less dangerous to eat.

Small ungulates stand and fight less often than large—young or weak ungulates nearly always flee. An animal that runs nonetheless stands a good chance of escaping, especially if it can stay ahead of the wolves long enough to get into deep water or onto broken terrain. Sometimes they simply outdistance the pursuers. Wolves rarely chase a fleeing animal more than

a few hundred meters before breaking off the attack and regrouping to seek easier prey.

When wolves close on their prey, they dart in close and bite at the legs, rump or shoulders. The attack may end quickly, with the wolves pulling down their victim and killing it, or it may last for some time. Once the wolves draw blood, however, death inevitably follows as the prey becomes weak from shock and exhaustion.

Wolves chase far more animals than they catch. Their hunting repeatedly tests the vigour and alertness of their prey species. Wolves quickly weed out the unhealthy, weak and unlucky. They often take fawns, calves and yearlings, and animals weakened by disease, injury or old age. Wolves do not appear to select the weak and unfit—they simply kill whatever prey

A Green Fires Burns Again

Pioneer conservationist Aldo Leopold became famous for his eloquent and passionate book, *A Sand County Almanac*. He argued for a more ecological and ethical relationship between people and nature—but his argument was that of a mature man who learned some of his lessons the hard way. In his youth, working for U.S. Forest Service pine forests of Arizona and New Mexico, Aldo Leopold helped eradicate the Mexican wolf.

Leopold's oft-quoted essay *Thinking Like a Mountain* describes a pivotal experience in his life, when he and his partner encountered a family of wolves and wounded two of them with rifle fire. "We reached the old wolf in time to watch a fierce green fire dying in her eyes. I realized then, and have known ever since, that there was something new to me in those eyes—something known only to her and the mountain. I was young then, and full of trigger-itch. I thought that because fewer wolves meant more deer, that no wolves would mean hunters' paradise. But after seeing the green fire die, I sensed that neither the wolf nor the mountain agreed with such a view."

Leopold's regrets were too late to save the lobo wolves of the southwestern mountains. Extirpated from the wild by 1970, for many years Mexican wolves survived only in captivity. Their time was past. The mountains where they once ranged were full of cattle, cottages, hunters and hikers.

More than half a century after Leopold's powerful plea for wisdom, popular beliefs about what

might be possible began to change with the first rumblings of a plan to reintroduce Mexican wolves to their ancestral home. The U.S. Endangered Species Act, after all, mandated it. And captive wolves still survived. Against all odds, the U.S. Fish and Wildlife Service began the process of preparing wolves for release.

In the spring of 1998, three different groups of Mexican wolves—eleven in all—loped away into the ponderosa pine forests of Arizona's Blue Mountains. None had ever had to live in the wild before. None knew the hunting skills they would need to earn their own living. The odds against survival were formidable—but the wolves were back.

Several of the reintroduced wolves, however, died at the hands of poachers. Others vanished—probably victims of the same fate. Secretary of the Interior, Bruce Babbitt swore not to let criminals stop the recovery program of Mexican wolves.

The Mexican wolf will not truly be home again until the released wolves prove they can hunt wild prey, produce healthy pups and keep out of trouble with domestic animals—and until enough humans prove their ability to overcome prejudice against wolves and laws. Even then, they will range a landscape much different from the one their ancestors occupied. But, for now at least, the howl of the lobo wolf rings again in Aldo Leopold's much-loved southwestern mountains. Leopold's mature writings have proved more potent than his youthful bullets. The green fire is flickering back to life.

Does Colorado Need Wolves?

Colorado's last wolf died in 1945. A New Mexico state trooper shot the lone animal in the southern San Juan Mountains. Few residents of the mile-high state mourned its passing. High country sheepmen and ranchers along the foothills and in the mountain parks west of the continental divide reviled the wolf. As elsewhere, most hunters felt that one less wolf meant 10 more deer.

Sinapu—a small but dedicated group of conservationists based in Boulder—want to right what they see as a historical wrong. To that end they are mapping roadless areas, ungulate concentrations and public lands to come up with a plan for reintroducing the wolf to the state.

Support for the idea is highest in the urbanized part of the state east of the continental divide. In rural areas west of the divide—where most wolves would likely live—there is no welcome mat out for wolves. Sinapu's Rob Edward, however, points out that a statewide survey, conducted in 1994 through the University of Northern Colorado for the U.S. Fish & Wildlife Service, "... showed that support for wolf recovery was amazingly strong, both along the Front Range and on the Western Slope. The Front Range residents support wolf restoration by a margin of 74%, and West Slope residents support wolf restoration by a margin of 65 percent—a level of support even higher than in Idaho or Wyoming."

If Coloradans wait long enough, some state wildlife managers suspect, the whole question will be moot. Wolves will come back on their own. Already, a growing population of reintroduced wolves in northwestern Wyoming is sending out dispersers into nearby areas. Wolves could also invade Colorado from the south if Mexican wolves recently released in Arizona and New Mexico reproduce and spread. Some state biologists think that the return of the wolf could prove to be good news.

In Colorado, wildlife managers face two thorny challenges. Elk populations have been growing for two decades and show no signs of slowing down. More elk are born each year than hunters can shoot. Elk herds are so large that they damage aspen forests in some parts of the state, overgraze some high mountain grasslands, and even displace rare native species such as the sage grouse.

At the same time, however, mule deer numbers continue to decline. Part of the problem, biologists be-

they can catch.

Wolves hunt small animals, too, such as beavers, ground squirrels and voles, but this occurs more often in summer than in winter. Pups at rendezvous

sites hunt and kill small mammals and birds, and pack members sometimes bring back beavers and other small animals.

Wolf feeding, protecting and marking a kill.

Does Colorado Need Wolves?

lieve, is that Colorado's most common and widespread predator—the coyote—is good at hunting deer.

John Seidel is a biologist with the Colorado Division of Wildlife. He assembles biological information and analyzes it to find out what's happening with the state's wild predator populations. The Division of Wildlife has no interest in reintroducing wolves, but Seidel suspects dispersing wolves from Wyoming could turn up in the state early in the 21st century.

"We've been working at the wolf question in relation to carnivore competition," he says. "We suspect that the coyote is such a generalist predator that it's been able to occupy niches that other predators like wolves used to. Even so, it probably preys more on deer than on elk. We think that coyotes would be really reduced in numbers and densities if wolves were here. The wolves would probably prey more on elk and less on deer, giving deer possibly a breather from predation since the coyote's numbers would be less dense. This is what they've been seeing in Yellowstone.

"Also the coyote is a direct competitor on the hares that are critical to the lynx. And coyotes have probably been able to invade the territory that the lynx previously occupied because of snowmobiles traveling in deep snow—country that those coyotes normally wouldn't have been able to get into."

Wolves rarely waste energy hunting snowshoe hares, but they kill coyotes whenever they get a chance. Seidel and other biologists suspect that more wolves will mean fewer coyotes. That in turn could mean more deer and hares. With more hares, the prospect of success for Colorado's lynx reintroduction program would increase dramatically. Wolves may also be more efficient than human hunters at controlling elk numbers.

"I really think we need to bring them back," says one Colorado biologist. "I think it'll be an influence on our deer mortality; real important for other carnivores, competitors. There's all these relationships all the way down. It would really influence some of our elk populations that we can't seem to touch with hunting."

If Sinapu has its way—and perhaps even if it doesn't—Colorado may soon find out.

By weight, ungulates amount to more than 90 percent of the diet of most wolves. Small prey makes an inefficient meal for so large a predator: it takes too much energy to catch such a small reward. Wolves, by design and preference, are big-game hunters.

Wolves in Cattle Country

Most modern ranchers have never seen a wolf and have no experience living with them. Nonetheless, all have heard stories about wolves wreaking havoc on horses, cattle and sheep during the late 1800s and early 1900s. Many worry about what might happen if wolves become common again; some wolves do eat livestock.

A late 1970s study in northern Alberta documented 16 cattle killed and 51 wounded by wolves in an isolated community pasture carved into the boreal forest. The losses happened over a six-year period during which wolf numbers increased from 15 to 40. North of Pincher Creek, in 1994 and early 1995, wolves killed more than a dozen calves and heifers and wounded 18 more.

Some wolves, however, do not eat livestock, despite ample opportunity.

Southwestern Alberta's Belly River wolf pack raised seven pups in 1994 at a den only a few hundred meters from a large cattle herd. The local ranchers suffered no cattle losses to wolves that year in spite of the high food demands created by such a large litter of pups. There were not even any suspicious deaths. Biologists speculated that the wolves simply did not recognize cows as potential prey. The wolves knew how to hunt white-tailed deer and elk effectively, and they managed to meet their needs with wild prey.

In Montana, Wyoming and Idaho, where the U.S. Endangered Species Act strictly protects wolves, animal damage control officers investigate all reports of wolf attacks on livestock. They look for evidence that wolves have actually made the kills, as opposed to scavenging on the remains of animals that died from other causes. If they confirm an attack, they trap and relocate the wolf to Glacier National Park. If it hunts domestic prey again, wildlife officers kill it. In Canada, stock-eating wolves get no second chances. Confirmed kills generally lead to a concentrated effort to eliminate the offenders, usually with poison.

Many wildlife officers dislike the job of killing wolves that eat cattle, but they know it makes ecological sense. Wolves, like domestic dogs, are intelligent animals that learn from success. A wolf that has successfully killed domestic stock will probably do it again and teach other pack members the same skill. Removing that wolf stops the livestock losses and leaves a healthy wolf population with experience of only wild prey.

A study in British Columbia recommends against predator control as a method of reducing wolf predation on livestock. It notes that not

Wolf Encounter

Late one February, I was skiing down the frozen channel of the upper Athabasca River in Jasper National Park. The landscape was frozen, the air still. When a tree cracked from the cold far back in the forest, it shocked the silence. The entire valley seemed devoid of life.

Something flickered in the trees a few hundred meters downstream. I stopped. Another flicker, then a wolf emerged onto the snowy flats, trotting steadily upstream toward me. I crouched behind some driftwood to watch. Three more wolves emerged.

Only a hundred meters away, the wolves encountered a patch of open water, turned, and crossed to the opposite side of the river. There, the lead wolf stopped and waited until the others had joined him.

They milled around together, sniffing one another's noses and wagging their tails. Then one of the larger wolves left the rest and continued up the frozen edge of the river. The largest wolf, a black, left the flats and disappeared into the forest at the base of a steep mountain directly across from me.

After a minute or so, the remaining two wolves headed into the forest too.

Upstream, I could see the first wolf sitting on its haunches, waiting. A long while later the big black came into sight, two hundred meters or so up the slope. He was shouldering his way through deep snow onto a narrow avalanche track, angling back downhill.

The two small wolves appeared next, spaced out along the slope below the black wolf. They too cut into the shrubby, open avalanche track, then vanished into the heavy forest on the opposite side.

Several minutes later, a wolf broke out of the trees downstream from the one that waited patiently on the flats. As they trotted to meet each other, tails wagging, the remaining two wolves emerged onto the flats. The pack regrouped, fell into single file and continued upstream out of sight. The valley was empty again except for the trails of four animals that had just executed an elegant, well-planned hunt through a small patch of moose habitat.

Will Wolves Wipe Out Their Prey?

Many hunters worry that wolves will eventually wipe out game populations.

John Gunson, Alberta's provincial carnivore specialist, says there is little basis for such worries. "Generally," he writes in the 1995 publication *Wolves in Alberta*, "when prey are healthy, in good habitat and without other major limiting factors, wolf predation alone should not cause a decline."

But wildlife populations today face more than wolf predation alone. A century of intense resource and land development has put many extra stresses on the prey wolves hunt.

Domestic cattle graze many wildlife ranges, even remote forested tracts of public land. If poorly managed, they can reduce forage and space for wild ungulates. Logging, rural residential development and other human uses have damaged critical ungulate wintering habitat. Roads and trails make it easy for human hunters to take a large share of available elk and deer. Recreational activities such as snowmobiling can make wolves more effective hunters too: they create hard-packed trails into areas that wolves might not otherwise visit because of deep, soft snow.

A wolf pack may kill two ungulates every week on average. Many kills, however, are animals already destined to die of disease, age and winter starvation.

Wolves never wipe out their prey—that is not how nature works. Nonetheless, wolf predation can reduce prey numbers and keep prey scarce, especially where human activities give wolves an advantage or where something else has already put stress on wildlife herds. After a bad winter, for example, ungulates recover more slowly with wolf predation than without.

Wildlife agencies in Alaska, the Yukon and British Columbia have responded to local declines of elk and moose by killing wolves. In most cases, prey populations rebounded. But killing wolves seldom increases prey numbers for long. Wolves usually compensate for high mortality with increased pup survival and the release of subordinate animals to breed. Where wildlife managers want to increase the numbers of deer, elk, moose or caribou, killing wolves provides only a temporary fix. A sustained increase in ungulate populations can only come from restoring habitat, closing roads and restricting snowmobile traffic.

One Alberta biologist points out that the number of big game hunters has dropped for the past decade. In areas with few wolves, deer and elk have increased. He says, "Our problem isn't that there's not enough game for hunters, it's that there are not enough hunters for our game herds. We probably need wolves just to help manage prey numbers in some areas."

Young wolf pups seldom venture far from the den.

all wolves kill livestock and that a pack that prefers wild prey protects livestock better than predator-control officers. A pack patrols its territory far more intensely and effectively. The study concludes that "the best line of defense against wolves that may kill livestock is an established pack that doesn't. That is, removal of such a pack may do more harm than good."

In western Canada, hunting regulations make it easy for virtually anyone to kill wolves. This often results in the exact opposite of good management. When hunters and ranchers randomly kill wolves, they break up wolf packs that prey only on wild game. The scattered survivors are less efficient at bringing down wary wild prey and more likely to kill naive domestic livestock.

Ironically, ranchers face wolf problems because they take good care of their land. Ranch country contains some of the best surviving wildlife habitat in western Canada. Wolves live there because ranchers have been good stewards, something wolf advocates sometimes forget.

Preventing Cattle Kills

Ranchers have reason to worry about wolves, but many fears and rumors that circulate today took root in the late 1800s, when ranchers managed sheep and cattle much differently.

In the 1870s and 1880s, settlers began to stock the West's empty wildlife ranges with domestic cattle. They regularly turned horses and cattle out onto the open range to fend for themselves during winter and the spring calving season. Wolves had little else to prey on: uncontrolled hunting had eradicated most of the big game. Untended domestic stock was easy prey, and when wolves scavenged on cattle that died of disease or exposure, they got blamed for those deaths too. Stories about frontier-era wolf kills became more gruesome with each retelling.

Most modern ranchers carefully tend their breeding herds during calving season. In winter, they pasture cattle herds close to civilization. Many haul away the carcasses of animals that die of natural causes so that wandering wolves or other predators will never get a taste of veal or mutton.

Even with the best of precautions, however, some wolves still learn to hunt domestic stock—especially when ranchers turn naive yearlings out to fend for themselves on remote private pastures and public forest reserves.

A dominant wolf scratches after scent-making.

Ranchers Matter

Consider your garden. You plant it in the spring, tend it carefully and keep your fingers crossed. One hail storm or bug infestation can wipe out all your work. You won't starve if that happens—there's always the grocery store, after all.

Now—imagine if instead of a garden, you had a cattle herd, and instead of a hobby, it was your main source of income. You worked day and night through February and March hauling bedding and tending to the births of dozens of baby calves. You've doctored them, fed them, watered them and moved them around to protect the health of the range that feeds them. Now it's late summer. Every night you go to bed knowing that your animals are out there, scattered beneath the stars. You can only hope they'll all be there in the morning. You've got some big loan payments that the bank isn't going to forget about. Cattle prices have dropped, so you don't have a lot of margin for losses. And your neighbor says he saw a couple of wolves a week ago. You've never seen a wolf, but you've heard horror stories about what they can do.
If nature takes too many of your livestock, you're going to go under. You might have to sell your ranch. Ranching is your whole life. Little wonder that you're fearful. Little wonder that you feel offended when

people who have never met you portray you as a redneck for worrying out loud about what wolves might do to your family's livelihood.

You don't have the time or inclination to go hunting for those wolves. But they're out there, and so are your cows and calves. What are you going to do? Who else cares about what might happen to your family ranch?

Too often, those who value wolves fail to respect the honest worries and legitimate concerns of the people who will have to live with them. For wolf recovery to work, it must work in ways that protect the interests of ranching families and other rural people who share—and care for—the West.

Defenders of Wildlife, fortunately, takes those concerns seriously. For many years this wildlife conservation group has not only promoted wolf recovery, but also raised money to pay ranchers for any animals killed by wolves in the western United States. Hank Fischer, long time Defenders field officer and a key figure in the successful campaign to reintroduce wolves to Yellowstone and Idaho, is adamant that wolves who develop a habit of attacking livestock should be relocated or killed.

Foxes

Ears laid back and tail curled under, one red fox communicates submission to another.

Fierce-eyed, small, swift and sly, foxes float wraith-like through the shadows lining the edges of the western night. Kit foxes nearly disappear when they stand still in the twilight desert. Gray foxes rarely stray far from the broken shade of dense shrubbery.

Startled, foxes straighten out like animated exclamation marks and seem to float suspended above the ground as they dart into cover.

Few humans know the world that foxes live in; at best, we get only glimpses. Foxes are creatures, for the most part, of the night. Most of the sounds that fill their world are too high pitched for our ears. Their pointed noses sift an unimaginable medley of scents from the air. What would it be like to live most of one's waking hours underground in snug earthen dens heavy with carbon dioxide and the smell of mould? Foxes know; we don't. Where fox and human worlds overlap is often along the roadside or close to the chicken coop. Small nocturnal predators such as foxes have evolved no behaviors to defend them against fast-moving automobiles. Their scavenging habits, in fact, often attract them to the decomposing bodies of previous roadkills. Being opportunistic and adaptable, foxes are no less ready to adjust to such new food supplies as domestic chickens, garbage dumps and bird feeders.

Increasingly, humans shape the world in which foxes live. We just are not particularly aware of it. Foxes are sensitive animals whose behavior seems to have more in common with housecats than with domestic dogs. Their eyes are large and catlike, as are their ears and whiskers. They watch movements intently, and stalk or even climb trees like cats. Unlike the larger coyotes and wolves, foxes never form packs. The large home ranges of male foxes and smaller, overlapping home ranges of females is a pattern more similar to how cougars or bobcats distribute themselves about the landscape than other wild dogs. But foxes, ultimately, are foxes: swift, shy and secretive creatures living out there at the edges of things.

The high-pitched yap of a dog fox as evening's half-light dims beneath the far edges of the meadow reminds us, briefly, that within our world there are other worlds that we can never truly know.

Red Fox

Some biologists still doubt that the red fox (*Vulpex fulva*) even existed in North America when the first European settlers stepped ashore to begin rearranging the landscape. Wherever else they may have dwelled, red foxes apparently did not inhabit the broad belt of deciduous forest stretching inland from the Atlantic seaboard and halfway across the continent. Early settlers imported red foxes from Europe in the mid 1700s for fox hunting and let them go in the southeastern United States.

Most biologists agree that native red foxes already lived in the boreal forests of northern Canada and many other parts of the continent. The native foxes and imports both found a growing abundance of ideal fox habitat as settlers opened up the eastern forests and created a mosaic of small farms, woodlots and wetlands.

Red foxes, like most wild canids, adapt quickly to new opportunities. Foxes colonized the prairies during the 20th-century when hunters encouraged by high fur prices depleted coyote populations. Coyotes aggressively pursue and kill foxes. Irrigation and windbreaks also helped make the prairie more friendly to foxes.

Red Fox snatching a meal.

Red foxes today are probably more widespread than ever before, thriving in the patchy habitats we have created across North America. Their range covers virtually all of Canada and Alaska, south through the Rocky Mountains and Atlantic watershed to parts of New Mexico, Texas and Florida.

Fox Life

Foxes like edges and contrasts. They avoid open prairie and dense forest, preferring places of ecological transition, where meadow, woodland and wetland meet and intermingle. Pioneer naturalist Ernest Thompson Seton described the red fox as a "creature of half-open country." Foxes commonly live along the edges of farmland, around wetlands and lakes, and in the riparian mosaics of forest, shrubbery and open

Red Fox Facts

Size: 0.8-1.1 meters / 2.5-3.5 feet
Weight: 3-7 kilograms / 6.5-15.5 pounds
Description: Slender, with a bushy tail, large pointed ears, slender muzzle; reddish-yellow with black lower legs and a white tip on the tail–sometimes black, or marked with a blackish cross on the back
Reproduction: First breeds at a year old
Gestation: 52 days
Litter size: 1-10 kits; average 5
Life span: 5 years
Food: Small animals, insects, carrion
Distribution: North America, primarily west of the Rockies and most of British Columbia

Saving For A Rainy Day

Foxes put away leftovers in case of future famine. Like dogs, they take food they do not need immediately and bury it carefully in out-of-the-way places. They may not return for several weeks to dig up the well-cured treasure and gulp it down. Foxes rely on caching, particularly in the winter, when they scavenge from the remains of large animals killed by other predators. Magpies, ravens, chickadees and other competitors all cache food too, so foxes waste little time hiding future meals before somebody else gets all the booty. Foxes take special pains to prevent other scavengers from spying on them; no animal that has to survive the northern winter is above pilfering from another.

Red Fox

meadows along streams.

Unlike wolves and coyotes, foxes are solitary creatures by preference. A male and female will collaborate on raising and feeding kits, but the rest of the time, foxes prefer life on their own.

Wolves, and sometimes coyotes, form packs to kill large animals more efficiently. When a wolf pack brings down a deer or moose, it has lots of meat to share. Foxes, by contrast, eat animals much smaller than themselves. They do not need help to make a kill, and the small size of their prey means they have no leftovers to share. Consequently, natural selection favors solitary foxes, not sociable ones.

The red fox belongs to the dog family, but its appearance and behavior have more in common with cats. Dr. David Henry's fascinating book, *Red Fox: The Catlike Canine*, explores the similarities in considerable depth.

Henry thinks convergent evolution accounts for the uncanny similarities between foxes and domestic cats. He points out that foxes and cats have similar hunting behaviors and that both have eyes with vertical, rather than round, pupils. Both arch their backs, hair erect, when threatened. They even play with their food the same way.

"The hypothesis," he says, "pivots on the fact that red foxes and small cats hunt similar prey: animals that try to avoid being captured by these two predators by using the same anti-predator devices." Small mammals and birds are alert and nervous, quick to retreat into burrows or high perches or to dodge into heavy cover. Both cats and foxes independently evolved similar physical characteristics and behaviors to overcome the defenses of this sort of prey.

Fox Hunting

Tally-hoing after foxes remains a valued, but increasingly controversial, part of English country life.

Hunting with hounds was originally the sport of kings and had nothing to do with foxes. During the Middle Ages, royalty chased deer or wild boar. When the English nobility took up hunting with hounds, after asserting right of ownership over forest estates previously controlled by the monarchy, deer and boar remained the preferred quarry. The nobility considered foxes sly, thieving vermin unworthy of serious consideration by civilized hunters.

Deer and boar numbers began to wane, however, as population growth in Britain whittled away at the forests. The gentleman-hunters turned to chasing hares. By the late 1600s with slimmer and slimmer pickings, hunters increasingly found themselves following hounds baying on the trail of foxes. Gradually, through the 1700s, the English aristocracy began to acknowledge that a fox's cleverness made it more than a worthy quarry. In 1793, the Prince of Wales took up fox hunting and finally made the red fox respectable—an honor the foxes, no doubt, would have gladly foregone.

Fox hunting encompasses a great body of tradition: hounds, horses, elaborate costumes and customs. From the fox's point of view, however, it simply entails getting chased, caught and killed by a bunch of noisy dogs.

As the British Empire expanded, the sons of English gentry took their taste for fox hunting to the colonies. They even took their foxes: North America's red foxes are probably a cross between foxes native to this continent and others shipped here for the amusement of expatriate Britons.

Sometimes, however, they had to make do with local quarry. In the early 1880s, a group of English aristocrats arrived in what is now southwestern Alberta and set up a ranch that covered much of the area west of present-day Okotoks, Alberta. They named the ranch the Quorn after a famous English fox-hunting club. Besides raising horses for English hunting clubs, the genteel ranchers and their visitors from overseas pursued the local coyotes on horseback.

The Quorn numbered among the many early ranches that failed. The all-play, no-work philosophy of its elite founders probably did not help.

Fox hunting never did catch on in western North America, partly for lack of foxes and partly because barbed wire and private property quickly rendered the landscape unfriendly to horsemen and hounds. Mostly, however, the practical-minded people who settled the West lacked the English nobility's interest in chasing small animals for sport.

Foxes as Hunters

Foxes specialize in small-game hunting, but no fox will turn up its nose at a meal laid on by other predators. The presence of a wolf pack is good news for foxes trying to make it through a tough northern winter. Wolves, unlike coyotes, seldom chase foxes. Their kills provide foxes with a rich, abundant source of protein.

Most of the time, however, foxes do their own hunting, catching small mammals, insects and birds. Their large ears and extremely acute hearing give them an uncanny, owl-like ability to locate and accurately pinpoint even the slightest rustle of a small mammal.

Once a fox locates a potential meal, its next move depends on what it has found. Mice, birds, rabbits and squirrels all require different hunting tactics.

A mouse or a vole generally scurries about beneath the grass, leaf litter or snow. The hunting fox delicately stalks the little animal, all the time listening and watching to locate its exact position. Then the fox bounds high in the air and comes down with all four feet and its pointed little snout ready to pin or grab the rodent before it can escape to its burrow.

Squirrels and birds dart upward when startled, so the fox crouches low and stalks as close as possible. It moves only when the intended victim will not notice. The belly-creeping posture and intent stare of the stalking fox resemble the herding behavior of blue heelers and border collies. Once the fox gets within range, its sneak turns into a crouching dash. At the last minute, it leaps at its startled target.

Foxes stalk rabbits, hares and ground squirrels in the same catlike manner. These prey cannot climb trees or fly away, however, so the final dash can turn into a hell-bent-for-leather chase that only ends when the intended victim suddenly becomes a meal, escapes into a burrow or dense cover, or out-distances its pursuer.

Fox Families

Male foxes use a larger home range than females, so the range of a single male can overlap

A hopeful fox is reluctant to forsake its squirrel.

Fox Food

Foxes take advantage of just about any readily available food source. They eat roadkill, forage in garbage dumps, raid poorly designed chicken coops and follow wolf packs to scavenge for carcasses. In summer, foxes eat insects and rodents. They rely more heavily on carrion once snow blankets the landscape.

Studies from across North America have found that foxes concentrate on the following general groups of prey, listed from most important to least:

Mice and voles	Carrion
Cottontail rabbits	Birds
Snowshoe hares	Insects
Red squirrels	Plants

Adult red foxes need between 2-3 kilograms / 4-6 pounds of food each week. Kits need close to two kilograms / four pounds, meaning that foxes hunt most when they have a den full of young. This heavy hunting season for foxes coincides with the season when food is most abundant. It's no accident that predators raise their offspring at the same time as insects swarm, birds nest, and mice, ground squirrels and other small mammals produce their young.

Foxes cache food to keep it safe from other scavenging animals.

with those of several females, all of whom he may end up breeding. Females go into heat between late December and early February, somewhat earlier than wolves and coyotes. Seven weeks later, the vixens give birth to two to seven kits in underground dens. They generally take over the den of a woodchuck, badger or ground squirrel and enlarge it for their own use.

Occasionally, two females give birth in the same den, a phenomenon only rarely seen in coyotes and never in wolves.

The kits, blind and covered with fine fur at birth, open their eyes after they are a week old and begin to walk two weeks later. The adult foxes move the kits from one den to another as the kits grow, no doubt partly because fleas and other parasites thrive in the crowded environment of a fox den. At about 10 weeks of age, the kits begin to explore around the den on their own, and within another week or two, they wander widely.

Male kits depart to seek their own fortunes by late fall, but female kits may remain with their mothers through the winter and help care for the next year's litter. Foxes can breed when they are less than a year old, but they rarely live past the age of six.

Gray Fox Facts

Size: 0.8 to 1.1 meters / 2.5 to 3.5 feet
Weight: 3-5 kilograms / 6.5-12 pounds
Description: Salt-and-pepper grey with reddish undercoat and black-tipped ears; bushy grey tail has a black line along the top and a black tip; rust-colored along the edge of the belly and throat and on the backs of the ears and legs
Reproduction: First breeds at a year old
Gestation: 52 days
Litter size: 1-10 kits; average 4
Life span: 5 years
Food: Insects, fruit, small mammals and birds, carrion.
Distribution: Deciduous eastern parts of the United States, the southern Rockies north to Colorado, Utah and Oregon and the Pacific Coast

Falling Hard

Victor Calahane, in his Mammals of North America, describes an incident in New York state where two male gray foxes were found dead at the base of a 90-foot-high cliff. Tracks in the snow above indicated that they had evidently been fighting over a female when they tumbled off the edge; a third pair of tracks led away from the area.

Foxes can vanish in a wink, thanks to their ability to use small spaces for cover.

How Do Foxes Die?

Starvation is probably the biggest threat to small-bodied animals with high energy demands. Many young foxes die during their first winter simply because they cannot find enough food. Hunting and trapping can result in heavy mortality of young foxes too. Fur farms, which now raise foxes in captivity, have helped to reduce the demand for wild furs.

Roads pose a major threat to foxes. In many agricultural areas, roadsides are important habitat for mice, voles and other small animals. Foxes, hunting at dawn and dusk, often get run over.

Foxes can die of sarcoptic mange, a condition caused by small mites that burrow into hair follicles and cause the fur to fall out. Mange-infested foxes die of exposure when cold weather hits.

Other diseases and parasites take their toll too: foxes are particularly vulnerable to rabies, distemper and a wide range of internal parasites.

Gray Fox

Of all the foxes, the gray fox, (*Urocyon cinereoargenteus*) spends the least time in open country. Gray foxes are woodland creatures which forage for berries, nuts, insects and small rodents beneath the dappled shade of oaks, hawthorns and other deciduous trees. Not all forests will do—gray foxes prefer second growth and riparian woodlands to older, more mature forest, and they also seem to prefer hillsides and canyons to more level terrain. Graceful and cat-like, a startled gray fox is as apt to scamper up into the branches of a tree as to vanish into the undergrowth. They are far and away the most arboreal of all the dog family.

Unlike their open-country relatives, the kit and Swift foxes, who spend most of their time in burrows, gray foxes rarely take shelter underground. Even in April, when females give birth to their young, they are more likely to den in a hollow tree, under a rock outcrop or beneath a brush pile than in a borrowed burrow.

Gray foxes rarely wander far. The average home range is barely 1.6 square kilometers (one square mile)—expanding when drought or other factors make food scarce and shrinking when food is abundant. They are not aggressively territorial and their home ranges often overlap, especially among related animals. Like red foxes, grays take advantage of whatever food is most readily available. Most places where gray foxes are found, cottontail rabbits are also common. Cottontails place high on the list of most commonly eaten foods in most

91

studies of the gray fox. In summer and early fall, gray foxes feed on ripening fruit, sometimes climbing into trees to pick them.

Roads are as deadly to gray foxes as they are to most other predators. Young foxes, in particular, die on roads as they disperse into new habitat. Rabies and distemper also kill many gray foxes and, in some areas, gray foxes are important sources of rabies in domestic dogs and cats. Diseases spread through fox populations most virulently during the late winter mating season and again in the fall, when young foxes disperse into new habitat.

Gray Fox Food

A Texas study found that gray foxes ate mostly cottontails, cotton rats, pocket gophers and pocket mice in winter. They also consumed insects and small birds. In spring, small mammals and insects became even more important. As summer progressed, gray foxes ate increasing amounts of vegetable foods, especially persimmons and acorns, as well as many insects. The biologists got their information by examining the stomach contents of 42 dead foxes. They found chicken remains in only one stomach and game bird remains in only two, and concluded that gray foxes rarely come into conflict with human interests.

Other researchers have found that gray foxes prey heavily on cottontail rabbits, especially in winter. In summer, biologists have found gray foxes eating huckleberries, wild grapes, apples, hawthorns, elderberries, mesquite beans and even juniper berries.

Rabies

In the late 1800s, rabies forced the Quorn, one of England's leading fox-hunting clubs, to destroy all its hounds—a little poetic justice for foxes. Foxes are usually among the first animals that a rabies outbreak affects, though not in this case. Thousands of dogs and several hundred humans died, but no one reported infected foxes.

Rabies can infect any warm-blooded animal, but it occurs far more often in some species than others. In North America, the most important carriers of the disease include red foxes, skunks, bats and raccoons. Further north, arctic foxes carry a form of rabies endemic to them.

Rabies is spread by viruses so small that 40 laid end to end, would barely equal the length of one red blood corpuscle. Rabies spreads through saliva, often from an infected animal that goes mad and attacks other animals. The viruses take over nerve cells near the infection site and chemically trick them into producing more viruses. Gradually, the viruses travel through the nervous system to the brain. After infecting the brain cells, the viruses spread back out through the nerves to the rest of the body, including the saliva glands.

Rabies leads to a progressive nervous disorder that results in either a state of frenzied madness, during which infected animals may attack and bite dozens of other animals, or a state of passive depression that makes a wild animal such as a fox appear strangely tame. Either way, people can become infected from contact with rabid animals: in the one case from being bitten, in the other from handling apparently friendly or sad animals. The disease can take more than two weeks to develop in humans, manifesting itself as hydrophobia (fear of water) and other forms of madness. Left untreated, rabies is always fatal.

The last major rabies outbreak appears to have started among arctic foxes around 1950 and then spread south. By the summer of 1952, farmers in northeastern Alberta were encountering crazed red foxes and a small number of rabid wolves. Within a year, public concern about the spread of the disease had mobilized governments across Canada to launch the most intense and well-coordinated anti-predator campaign in North America's history. Guns, traps and poisons eradicated millions of foxes, coyotes and wolves.

Rabies persists across Canada in skunks and foxes, but governments no longer resort to scorched-earth poison campaigns to control it. Veterinarians have developed a vaccine that, laced into drop-baits, can immunize wildlife against rabies. Public fear of rabies has declined with the development of effective treatment.

Prevention remains the best defense. Never approach a fox, skunk or other wild animal that seems sick, unusually friendly, or aggressive. If bitten or even if you just come in contact with an animal's saliva, call wildlife authorities immediately and then go to the nearest emergency services. It is essential to get anti-rabies treatments as soon after infection as possible.

Red foxes have pointed noses and larger ears.

Red foxes have a coughing bark; they never howl.

Kit Fox

So closely related to the Swift fox that some taxonomists consider it the same species, the kit fox (*Vulpes macrotis*) has a narrower face and longer ears. Where Swift foxes are prairie animals, kit foxes live only in the deserts of southwestern North America—from Colorado and Texas to California. One subspecies, the San Joaquin kit fox, is endangered because of habitat loss to farming, industry and urban development. Since much of its surviving habitat serves as training and weapons testing grounds for the U.S. Army, however, the San Joaquin subspecies is one of the most intensively studied of all North American foxes. Endangered species legislation requires the military to prove that its activities don't threaten the little fox. It does this by paying for research and monitoring studies that have provided valuable insights into the life of an animal that could scarcely be harder to

Kit Fox Facts

Size: .6-.8 meters / 2-2.5 ft
Weight: 2-3 kilograms / 5-7 pounds
Description: Tan or yellowish brown with very large ears, black margin on the back edge of its ears, and black tip on its bushy tail
Reproduction: First breeds at 2 years old
Gestation: 52 days
Litter size: 2-6 pups
Life span: 4 years
Food: Small rodents, kangaroo rats, ground squirrels, rabbits, insects, birds
Distribution: Desert locales of North America, from Mexico and Texas north to Colorado and Utah and west to central California

Home Is Where You Find It

Gray foxes rarely den underground like other foxes. Instead, they shelter under rock overhangs, brush piles and fallen trees. Their adaptable nature has produced surprises for biologists studying them—gray foxes have been found denning in places as diverse as a hollow oak limb 7.5 meters / 25 feet off the ground, a wood pile, a den dug into growing sorghum, and a discarded 10-gallon milk can.

study —spending most of its life underground and going about its above-ground life after dark.

Kit foxes live in some of the driest and hottest environments in the west. Kit foxes have hairy pads on their feet which help them to travel on soft sand and protects them against heat. It might seem logical that a desert fox would have thin fur, but the kit fox actually has a fairly dense pelage, probably as insulation against both high and low temperature extremes. Their large ears are important both as radiators, helping their bodies dispose of extra heat without wasting precious water in the process, and as magnifying devices for the high pitched, low intensity sounds of the small rodents that are their main prey.

Desert life imposes one cardinal rule on every living thing: conserve water. Small animals like the kit fox need not only to use water efficiently, but also to protect against overheating.

Kit foxes get most of their water from their prey, since other sources of water are rare in desert habitats. Scientists have found that kit foxes kill more prey than they need for food; the extra meals have more to do with meeting their needs for water. This is not a very efficient way of getting water, but the little foxes reduce their need by using their underground dens to avoid daytime heat and wind. The small body size of kit foxes may help too, by reducing their need for moisture.

The larger coyote occupies the same desert habitats as the kit fox. It, too, gets some of its water needs from the prey it eats. However, coyotes are less able to avoid heat and their larger bodies demand more water. Most coyotes rely on drinking water at least part of the time, so they are more common near streams, rain pools and stock tanks. Because of their large bodies, coyotes are less efficient than kit foxes when it comes to dissipating body heat, but they appear to be better able to store heat in their body tissues without suffering ill effects.

Kit foxes can tolerate a greater range of temperatures and higher temperatures in general, without showing any stress, than can coyotes. Biologists studying kit foxes in Arizona found that kit foxes have the ability to dissipate heat from their bodies efficiently, rather than relying on sweating, panting or other methods that waste body moisture. Because of their small size, however, kit foxes can quickly overheat when the temperature climbs above 35 degrees Celcius / 95 degrees Fahrenheit.

In the desert environment, with its dramatic shifts in temperature from midday to dawn, there is one way to solve that problem: dig a den and stay below ground where temperatures never get so extreme. Kangaroo rats, lizards and many other animals use the same strategy. Kit foxes create elaborate complexes of dens in some places, with numerous entrance holes and bedding chambers. Since they get these dens by taking over burrows previously dug by ground squirrels, badgers or other animals, they are quick to exploit artificial dens that result from human activities. Kit foxes readily set up camp in culverts, well casings or even abandoned outhouses.

Tree Foxes

British colonists in the southern U.S., eager to continue their tradition of pursuing foxes with horses and hounds, found the gray fox frustrating. Instead of running across country while the hunters tally-hoed behind, most gray foxes simply climbed the nearest tree. The homesick fox hunters ended up importing English red foxes to make up for the failings of the arboreal locals.

With their almost cat-like front legs—they twist more flexibly than any other wild dog—gray foxes can even climb straight, branchless trees when they must. They clasp the tree with their fore legs and hitch themselves along with their rear legs—much like a cat. Their descent—sliding down backwards or running down inclined branches—is no less cat-like. Young gray foxes can climb within a few weeks of birth. Ernest Thompson Seton once saw a gray fox resting in a red-tailed hawk nest. Although some early naturalists told fanciful tales of gray foxes chasing squirrels through the tree tops, the little foxes climb trees most frequently to escape predators or to feed on fruit.

Licking his lips, a red fox takes a break from hunting.

Kit Fox Country

Deserts offer a lot of poor places for small predators to live, and only a few habitats where prey is abundant, the ground good for burrowing, and human activity light. Desert shrub habitats and shortgrass flats are home to most kit foxes. In Utah, one study found that eight out of 10 kit fox dens were in open shadscale flats. Elsewhere, foxes occupy ground squirrel or prairie dog colonies in dry pastureland. In California's San Joaquin valley, kit foxes use oak woodlands, orchards, pastures, desert scrub

Kit Versus Swift

They both have big ears and small bodies and live most of their lives underground. So why do biologists consider Swift foxes to be different from kit foxes?

Well—they do and they don't. Taxonomy—the science that classifies living things according to their relationships—doesn't always provide clear answers. Taxonomists sometimes get different results from different methods. They can measure and describe different physical features and look for measurable differences between what they suspect to be separate species. Early taxonomists relied on this alone. Based on subtle differences among museum species they not only considered the Swift fox and kit fox separate species but believed that there were two subspecies of Swift fox and eight of kit fox.

More recently, advances in cellular biology have made it possible for taxonomists to look inside the cells of animals for genetic differences. The newer genetic techniques suggest that Swift and kit foxes are so similar as to be almost indistinguishable. Where kit and Swift foxes live close to one another—for example, along the Pecos River in southeastern New Mexico and adjacent Texas—they commonly hybridize. The hybrid offspring, however, fare poorly compared to purebred offspring of either species—evidence that there are important differences between the two.

One more method of distinguishing species, however, may be the most meaningful—comparing how they live and behave in the real world. Ecologically, the prairie-dwelling Swift fox and desert-dwelling kit fox are sufficiently different from one another that most biologists continue to treat them as different species.

A newborn Swift fox is scarcely larger than a mouse.

and even irrigated farmland.

Otherwise desirable kit fox country loses a lot of its value to the little foxes as soon as someone builds a road. The nocturnal habits of the little foxes make them vulnerable to road-kill. Since kit foxes readily fall prey to coyotes, agricultural development of their desert valleys can be bad news because not only does it eliminate the open country they prefer, but it increases the number of coyotes that can find a living there.

Swift Fox Facts

Size: 0.6-0.8 meters / 2-2.5 feet
Weight: 2-3 kilograms / 5-7 pounds
Description: Buff yellow with large ears, a black spot on either side of its nose, and a black tip on its tail
Reproduction: First breeds at 2 years old
Gestation: 52 days
Litter size: 4-5 kits
Life span: 4 years
Food: Insects, rabbits, small rodents, birds
Distribution: Dry prairies, primarily east of the Rockies from northern Texas and eastern New Mexico north to southeastern Alberta and southwestern Saskatchewan

Kit Fox Life

Female kit foxes move into their brood dens in fall or early winter. Shortly after they establish themselves, their mates join them. In late January or early February the pair breed. Unlike wolves or coyotes, kit foxes are usually monogamous: one male mates with one female. In a few rare cases, however, biologists have found two females denning together, both apparently bred by the same male.

Late in the winter, mother foxes give birth to tiny red and brown pups, each about the size of a potato. The mother nurses the pups while her mate takes care of hunting for both parents. After about a month the pups venture out of the den on their own for the first time; usually by this time their mother is ready to move them to another nearby den with less puppy odor and fewer fleas. Over the next few months the family may move several times.

By June, young kit foxes have lost their puppy coloration and look like small versions of their parents. The family remains together for several months—in fact some female kit foxes remain with their mother for more than a year, helping her raise next year's litter.

How many young kit foxes reach maturity depends on weather and prey abundance. Both

extreme drought and unusually heavy rainfall can reduce the amount of prey. Undernourished young kit foxes die of starvation or disease. If they make it through their first year, kit foxes can live from seven to 10 years.

Kit foxes eat whatever is available, and that varies from one region to another. In Utah jackrabbits, cottontails and small rodents play a significant role in kit fox diets. California's endangered San Joaquin kit foxes eat kangaroo rats, ground squirrels, cottontail rabbits, birds and, at some seasons, grass. Deer mice, pocket mice and other night-dwelling rodents are most active at the same time as kit foxes, making them particularly vulnerable to sharp-eared little predators.

Swift Fox

David Thompson, a young Englishman, explored western North America between 1786 and 1812, meticulously mapping the landscape and recording his observations of native people, land and wildlife in an extensive set of journals. In 1787, Thompson journeyed into the heart of Blackfoot country near the modern site of Calgary, where he watched natives hunt eagles. A hunter would lie in a shallow hollow at the top of a hill, cover himself with branches and grass, and set a piece of meat on his chest. When an eagle landed on the meat, he would grab the bird by its feet and kill it quickly.

"The greatest plague to the Eagle catcher," Thompson later wrote, *"are the gray Foxes of the plains, they are almost as tame as dogs and while the Indian is lying patiently looking at the sky, watching the Eagle, one or two of these Foxes suddenly jump on his breast and seize the piece*

of meat, a battle ensues in which his covering of willows and grass is destroyed. As the Foxes will be sure to return, the Indian is obliged to shift his place to some other knoll several miles off and there try his chance."

Thompson's "gray foxes" were Swift foxes (*Vulpes velox*), once abundant throughout the grassland regions to east of the Rocky Mountains.

Trappers killed Swift foxes for their pelts. The Hudson's Bay Company shipped more than 117,000 pelts between 1853 and 1877, though traders never valued the fur highly. Most foxes died accidentally when wolfers and later, ranchers and early settlers, set out poison baits for coyotes, wolves, prairie dogs and ground squirrels.

Highly vulnerable to poisons, Swift foxes soon disappeared. By 1928, they no longer survived in Saskatchewan. Alberta's last Swift fox died about a decade later. The last confirmed record of a wild Swift fox in Canada was in 1938. In 1978, Canada's Committee on the Status of Endangered Wildlife In Canada (COSEWIC) declared the Swift fox extinct in Canada.

The Swift fox is little larger than a jackrabbit, dusty-colored and slender, with large, pointed ears and distinctive dark markings on either side of its sharp little muzzle. Swift foxes frequently kill their preferred prey—jackrabbits and cottontails—by stalking them, catlike, and then dashing out with surprising speed. Swift foxes also hunt mice, ground squirrels and ground-nesting birds.

Miles and Beryl Smeeton, a retired British couple who lived on a ranch near Cochrane,

Life Down Under

Prairie summers can be blazing hot. Prairie winters can be bitterly cold. And there are things up there that like to eat small foxes.

Little wonder that—from the time it is born in its mother's whelping den a meter / three feet or more below the earth's surface until the day it dies—a Swift fox spends most of its life underground. Pioneer naturalist Ernest Thompson Seton considered Swift foxes to be the most subterranean of North America's fox species.

Swift foxes appropriate abandoned rodent or badger burrows. Through the winter female foxes re-

main in large brood dens with their mates. In May or June the female moves her offspring to a smaller nearby den and continues to change dens regularly through the summer. Swift foxes may use as many as 13 dens over the course of a year, moving out when fleas and other vermin build up to uncomfortable levels, or when they begin to run out of local prey. Their restless ways result in an ongoing surplus of unused dens which other animals like rattlesnakes and burrowing owls often take over for their own use.

Alberta, imported two pairs of Colorado Swift foxes in the early 1970s to raise in captivity. Dr. Stephen Herrero of the University of Calgary encouraged them to begin a captive-breeding program in 1973 with the goal of releasing Swift foxes back into the wild. Herrero's students identified places where extensive tracts of wild mixed-grass prairie still survived, along with the jackrabbits, voles, ground squirrels and other animals that Swift foxes depend on for food. In 1983, the Smeetons and the researchers set the first captive-raised foxes free.

Coyotes, golden eagles and bobcats quickly killed most of them. Other foxes starved or went missing as they tried to adapt to life in the real world. For the next decade, many organizations continued to work on the reintroduction program, including the University of Calgary, the Calgary Zoo and the Canadian Wildlife Service. They released wild Swift foxes caught in the U.S. when it became clear that captive-bred foxes were too naive to avoid coyotes.

Because of the reintroduction program, 200 or so Swift foxes now live in southwestern Saskatchewan, southeastern Alberta and adjacent parts of Montana. Other Swift foxes may soon recolonize these areas naturally, since remnant populations in Colorado, Wyoming, the Dakotas and Montana appear to be spreading north. "The reintroduction experiment—because, really, that's what it is—has reached the logical point to walk away from it," says Herrero. "Nature will now tell us whether there is still an ecological niche for the Swift fox in the southern Canadian prairies.

Arctic Fox

Life in the far north is demanding for warm-blooded terrestrial animals; winters are long and merciless, and summers are brief and cool. Arctic foxes (*Alopex lagopus*) have short ears, snouts and legs compared to the more southern species of foxes. These adaptations expose less surface area to the cold and enable the little foxes to save body heat. Luxuriantly thick winter coats and furred soles help too.

The arctic fox, as a result, inhabits the coldest regions of the northern hemisphere. The small white or dirty-gray foxes (there are two common color phases) range along the arctic coasts of Canada, Greenland, Europe and Asia.

When they are not hunting, arctic foxes spend much of their time curled up in tight little balls, with the least-furred parts of their bodies—feet, face and underparts—tucked away out of the wind. Foxes have to expose these

A Dog's Life

Swift foxes need more than protection from poisons and roadkill if they are to recover their former abundance. According to the Predator Project, a Montana-based group that promotes the protection and recovery of native predators, Swift foxes and other predators can only survive in healthy ecosystems which include native prey animals. Among the most important is the black-tailed prairie dog. But while the persecution of Swift foxes may have ended, prairie dogs still have few friends.

Aggressively trapped and poisoned for more than a century, prairie dogs now survive on less than 5 percent of their original prairie range. Even there, they receive little protection; some western towns even stage annual prairie dog shooting festivals to attract tourists.

The Predator Project thinks these chunky rodents deserve more respect. "The fact is that prairie dogs are the keystone species for the grasslands of the Great Plains region," says a campaign flier, "because they are critical in maintaining the biological integrity of that region. Forty species of mammals, 10 species of amphibians, over 90 species of birds, 15 species of reptiles, 29 species of insects and over 80 species of plants have been found on Black-tailed Prairie Dog colonies. Some of these species, in one way or another, need the prairie dog and its colonies to survive."

Swift foxes, for example. The original range of the Swift fox and the prairie dog overlap closely -- and that's no coincidence. Not only do Swift foxes eat prairie dogs when they get the chance, but the superior burrowing abilities of prairie dogs provide the little foxes with prefabricated dens. Wildlife conservation groups like the Predator Project point out that it is not just Swift foxes or black-footed ferrets that are in trouble -- it's the whole prairie world. Trying to protect just one or two endangered species while choosing to ignore the rest of their ecosystem simply can't work in a world where all things are connected.

Foxes change dens frequently as pups grow larger.

parts when they hunt, and the loss of heat drains energy. But a successful hunt more than repays this loss with food energy.

Arctic foxes prey mostly on lemmings, large mouselike creatures that sometimes become extremely abundant in the low-growing, scrubby vegetation of arctic islands and coastlands. Lemming populations plummet every four or five years, forcing the foxes to put more energy into hunting waterfowl and other birds during the short arctic summer.

Foxes hunt lemmings mostly during the snow-free season. Once winter arrives, arctic foxes become scavengers, shadowing wolves, humans and polar bears and feeding on the remains of their kills. They often follow bears far out onto the pack ice.

Arctic foxes are opportunists. Like most other carnivores, they are adapted to the north's boom-and-bust ecosystem. Arctic foxes commonly steal dog food and scrounge for garbage around northern settlements and remote camps. Often, the foxes become quite tame.

Arctic foxes die from a number of causes. Some get trapped for their fine fur. Others make the odd meal for bears, wolves, eagles and other predators. But starvation kills the most foxes, especially young ones. Northern wildlife populations swing through dramatic and predictable cycles of abundance and scarcity. When prey populations diminish, foxes starve to death or, in their weakened state, become more vulnerable to diseases such as rabies.

Like other foxes, arctic foxes spend most of their time alone or in family groups. They mate in late winter and give birth in June to a large litter of kits from as few as two or three to as many as 25, but averaging 10. Well-fed kits born during a year of abundant lemmings and other prey, breed the following winter. Chronically undernourished kits may take two years to reach sexual maturity.

Both parents care for the kits. Late in the summer, the parents abandon the kits, a sink-or-swim survival strategy that results in high mortality as the young foxes disperse in search of food.

Arctic foxes travel great distances, especially in winter when food is scarce and patchily distributed. Some radio-collared wild arctic foxes have ranged nearly a 1,000 kilometers / 620 miles from their point of capture.

Arctic Fox Facts

Size: 0.8 meters / 2.5 feet
Weight: 1.5-3.5 kilograms / 3-8 pounds
Description: In winter, white or bluish gray; in summer, dirty gray with cream underparts; short, rounded ears and blunter muzzle than other foxes; well-furred feet; no white tip on tail
Reproduction: First breeds at a year old
Gestation: 52 days
Litter size: 1-20 kits; average 10
Life span: 5 years
Food: Carrion, lemmings, voles, birds
Distribution: Arctic regions of North America, Greenland, Europe and Asia

Wild Cats

Wild Cats

A large bobcat places each foot deliberately, making little sound.

N ot long ago, as the mountains know time, remarkable wild cats roamed western North America. Prides of North American lions hunted bison and stag-moose along the Rocky Mountain front ranges. Sabretooth cats fed on mammoths and horses.

The last of the giant Pleistocene cats died out only a few thousand years ago, along with many of their prey species. The North America we know today is a tamer place than it was during the period that biologist Valerius Geist describes as the predator hell of the Pleistocene.

Tamer it may be, but remarkable wild cats nonetheless range today's landscape too. The cats surviving today are specialists who have evolved remarkable relationships with their preferred prey species. Cougars prey mostly on deer and other hoofed creatures. Their tawny coloring and size makes them look almost deer-

like themselves. Lynx have large ears and eyes, facial whiskers, powerful hind legs and over-sized feet, very much like their preferred prey: the snowshoe hare. Bobcats differ from lynx as their favorite prey, the cottontail rabbit, differs from snowshoe hare: they have smaller feet and ears, longer tails, and an aversion to deep snow.

On other continents wildcats form pack-like prides, such as lions, or run down their prey in high-speed chases, as the cheetah does. Modern North America's wild cats, however, are all cut from a similar cloth. They are mostly solitary, and all hunt by lying in wait or stalking to

Well equipped for detecting prey, the cougar's elongated face enables its powerful jaws to grip and crush a deer's neck.

within close range, then launching a short, surprise attack from cover. Because of their furtive hunting style, wild cats put their prey under different kinds of pressures than coursing predators like wolves or coyotes. Cats kill the unwary and unlucky; dogs often kill the young, weak, slow or sick. In both cases, predators select for the survival of only the very best.

Cats rely on extremely acute vision and hearing to help them locate and isolate their prey, unlike members of the dog family whose elongated noses reflect the importance of scent in their hunting. A cat's disconcerting, round-eyed stare makes most humans uncomfortable. Perhaps we are reacting to the same sensation prey animals feel when these wild hunters lock-on on their ocular radar systems and begin the slow, infinitely patient stalks which will lead to their next meals. Few predators are as efficient hunters as wild cats such as the cougar, lynx, bobcat and the subtropical cats ranging into the very southern edge of the western U.S. These are not sabretooth cats or giant American lions. Even so, they are no less remarkable and awe-inspiring.

The Desert Cats

In the cottonwood bosques and mesquite tangles that line the rivers of southwestern New Mexico and southeastern Arizona, a near mythical cat still leaves pug-shaped tracks along sandy washes and cattle trails. Half again as large as the mountain lion, stockier and more muscular, the jaguar ranges back and forth across the Mexico-U.S.A. border where once it was believed extinct.

Until the 20th-century, jaguars ranged widely across the southern U.S.—from California's Palm Springs across southern Arizona and New Mexico into Texas and Louisiana. The heavyset predators were most at home along river bottoms and in low elevation shrublands where they could hunt javelinas and deer, but they ranged well into the southern mountains along canyons and wooded slopes. Domestic sheep and cattle were temptations too hard for some jaguars to resist, so early ranchers in both the U.S. and Mexico spared no effort to rid their ranges of the spotted cats.

By 1973, biologists documented the killings of more than 60 jaguars in Arizona between 1900 and 1973 when the United States government passed the Endangered Species Act. Most believed the jaguar to be extinct in the U.S. by that time, but in 1986 a trapper killed an adult jaguar in Arizona's Dos Cabezas Mountains. When the U.S. Fish and Wildlife Service proposed to list jaguars as endangered in the United States—a legal status that would automatically mandate total protection from trappers and agricultural agencies, as well as development of a recovery plan—controversy erupted.

Some people felt that listing the jaguar would achieve nothing because the species was already extinct. If it wasn't, others argued, it should still be considered a Mexican animal that only wanders across the border by accident. Some ranchers felt that legal protection for the jaguar would only mean restrictions on their ability to raise, and protect, cattle. Hunting groups wondered if this might be part of a hidden campaign to eliminate hounds and other forms of hunting. State wildlife agencies feared loss of control over wildlife management on state lands.

In 1987, however, another jaguar appeared in Arizona. A year later, after seeing suspicious looking tracks for several days, a rancher set hounds on the trail and soon treed an adult jaguar in Pima County's Altar valley. More jaguar sightings followed in Coronado National Monument and the Buenos Aires National Wildlife Refuge. In 1996 a jaguar was photographed in New Mexico.

It had become undeniably clear that jaguars still roam the sky island mountains and desert rivers of the southwestern United States. In 1997 the spotted cats finally received full protection under the endangered species act. Listing of the jaguar protects it from deliberate killing, restricts the use of traps and predator poisons within its known range, and limits the ability of landowners and land management agencies to clear brush or forest from places where jaguars live.

Jaguars, however, are not the only exotic cat to range into the southwestern United States' Sonoran and Chihuahuan Desert regions. Another spotted cat—the ocelot, which is slightly larger than the bobcat—haunts southern Arizona's mesquite and catsclaw tangles. Jaguarundis—even smaller cats, about twice the size of a common house cat -- also occupy dense thorny thickets at low elevations. Unlike the spotted jaguars and ocelots, jaguarundis are either slate-gray or reddish-brown.

Jaguars, ocelots and jaguarundis may also live along the lower Rio Grande Valley in Texas. A fourth subtropical cat—the Margay—lives there too. All four species are listed as endangered species and—if the fast changing Southwest succeeds in protecting and restoring its much abused river valley habitats—all may someday cease to be exotic rumors and become, instead, a familiar part of how Arizonans, New Mexicans and Texans know themselves and the places they call home.

Cougars

A cougar eases silently along a fallen log, watching for prey.

That first encounter with a cougar changes the whole landscape. The hills and forests never look quite the same once you have gazed, however briefly, into those pale yellow eyes and have seen the long muscles rippling lean beneath the tawny hide. Before, it was scenery.

Now, it is the place where North America's giant cats prowl. They really are out there.

The first European explorers encountered cougars soon after arriving in North America.

Cougar Facts

Size: 1.5-2.7 meters / 5-8 feet
Weight: 35-90 kilograms / 75-200 pounds
Description: Slender, lionlike, with a small head; tawny-brown except for white underparts and facial markings
Reproduction: First breed at 2-3 years old
Gestation: 90 days
Litter size: 1-6 kittens; average 3
Life span: 10 years
Food: Deer, other animals
Distribution: Mountainous areas from northern British Columbia south to Argentina

Until barely a century ago, the cougar was one of the most widely distributed large predators in the western hemisphere, ranging from what is now southern Canada to the very tip of South America. The trackless forests that rose from the shores of the New World looked ominous enough to people used to the towns, roads and farmlands of Europe. The sight of a lionlike beast—nearly half again as long as a man—lurking in the forest shadows, must have haunted superstitious minds.

The people who already lived in North America knew the cougar well. Most indigenous peoples revered it as an animal of great power and spiritual potency. Tribes occupying the eastern deciduous forests called it names that translate as "cat of God," or "greatest of wild hunters." Farther west, the desert peoples of the southern Rocky Mountains called the cougar the "father of game." For a hunter to see and be seen by a cougar was an honor that might bestow extraordinary good fortune.

Most indigenous peoples lived by hunting, gathering and small-scale crop farming, but the Incas raised livestock. They did not revere the great cats. According to the accounts of early Spanish missionaries, the Incas organized elaborate cougar hunts to protect their domestic herds of vicunas and guanaco. By contrast, when Jesuit missionaries arrived in California with sheep, goats and cattle, they found that the native people would not permit them to kill cougars. The people had a long tradition of appropriating cougar kills, which they found by watching for circling condors and vultures. They refused to kill an animal whose superior hunting prowess helped feed them.

For settlers who cleared the forests, plowed fields and pastured domestic stock the cougar became a target of fear and loathing. Newcomers who settled different parts of the continent gave the cougar different names: catamount ("cat of the mountain"), panther, puma, mountain lion and cougar. But no matter what they chose to call it, they killed it.

The cougar is now extinct throughout much of its former range. A few may linger in the border region between the Canadian provinces of New Brunswick and Quebec and the American states of Maine and Vermont. A very few survive in southern Florida, but their critically low numbers have probably doomed them. Healthy populations of cougars now survive only in the mountains, foothills and rain forests of western North America—from British Columbia and western Alberta south to Texas and Mexico.

Cougar Country

Scenic settings and mountain lions seem to go together. Although cougars live in heavily forested valley bottoms too, they seem to have a stronger affinity for the open woodlands of canyons, ridge tops and foothills. Their tastes in habitat probably have a lot to do with the distribution of mule deer, bighorn sheep and other favored prey.

Rock outcrops serve cougars in a number of ways. On sunny winter days and summer mornings the big cats often seek out south-facing rock outcrops to bask in the sun—not unlike a house cat on a sunny windowsill. Female cougars often den in sheltered niches beneath rock outcroppings. Since cougars like to attack from cover, rocky terrain can also give them an advantage in hunting.

Cougars are rarely found far from cover—they are creatures of wooded country. They also avoid deep snow because their long, low-slung bodies force them to waste energy they can't spare when the snow gets deep.

In the northern Rockies, cougar habitat is patchy and corresponds mostly with small pockets of mule deer and sheep winter range at low elevations. Farther south, cougars range throughout the ponderosa pine, Douglas fir and pinyon-juniper country where mule deer and other prey are abundant and winters are mild.

Cougar Society

Cougars do not mate for life. Once the deed is done, the male moves on and leaves the female to raise and feed her offspring by herself. She's probably just as glad to

Cougar mothers hide their kittens while they hunt.

see him go. Mating can be a marathon affair that takes an entire day and repeated copulation. Biologists suspect that the female needs many couplings to induce her to ovulate. They think this may serve a useful biological purpose by ensuring that only fit males succeed in passing on their genes. An unfit male would lack the stamina or would prove unable to fight off other suitors during such an extended bout of mating.

Female cougars have another good reason to prefer single-parent families: given the chance, males kill kittens.

Except for mating season, cougars are solitary creatures that generally avoid each other. Females with kittens sometimes associate briefly with female kittens from the previous year. Temporary groupings of as many as six cougars have been reported from places such as Waterton Lakes National Park.

Males have large home ranges and do not tolerate the presence of other males. In the Alberta foothills, some males occupy ranges larger than 364 km^2 (140 square miles). A few males just wander, too young or too old to establish or defend a territory. Female home ranges occupy less than half the area of male home ranges and commonly overlap with those of neighboring females. A single male's range may cover the territory of several females, all of which he may breed.

Sunbelt Roadkill

The Florida panther, *Felis concolor coryei* is one of North America's most endangered predators. A handful of panthers survive in the fragmented remains of Florida's once-mighty Sea of Grass—the Everglades. Sugar plantations, expressways and development have reduced the Everglades to a patchwork of habitats too small and fragmented to ensure a future for the panther. The big cats have started to exhibit deformities that point to inbreeding, a worrying indication of how few remain. They continue to die on the high-speed highways that slice through their remaining wild habitat.

Ouch!

Researchers found porcupine quills in more than a third of the cougars they examined in southern Alberta. Young cougars accounted for most of these. Mature cougars are more adept at killing porcupines, batting them in the face with a lightning-fast paw and biting them before they can regain their defensive position.

Cougar kittens are spotted, unlike their mothers.

Sly Beasts That Kill In The Night

Historians describe the Earl of Southesk as the first tourist in the Canadian Rockies. In 1860, the wealthy young Englishman traveled through what is now part of Jasper National Park.

Southesk's explorations took him through trackless wilderness, but he did not let that stop him from enjoying civilized amenities. He bathed each night in a rubber bathtub filled with water heated over the campfire. He also studied the works of William Shakespeare and other writers. Southesk's horses packed a complete hardbound library.

Southesk killed most of the animals he saw—more than a dozen bighorn sheep in one day, for example—but much to his chagrin, he never got the chance to kill a grizzly or a cougar.

"Neither in the mountains nor elsewhere did I even catch a glimpse of a puma, or observe its tracks, or any other sign of its existence," he wrote.

That, however, did not stop him from becoming an instant expert, based on campfire tales.

"In the Rocky Mountains, though probably not north of the Bow River and its headwaters, there exists a savage and treacherous wild beast," he wrote, *"more dangerous in some respects than even the grisly [sic] himself."*

He continues:

Marking out a small party of hunters or travellers, it will follow them secretly for days, and watch their camp at night, till at last it discovers one of their number resting a little separate from his companions. Then, when all is dark and silent, the insidious puma glides in, and the sleeper knows but a short awakening when its fangs are buried in his throat.

These details I gathered from my men, and I see no reason to doubt their truth.

Cougars Out East?

If eastern cougars survive, they are so rare that successful mating is unlikely.

Early settlers clearing farms in the forests of eastern North America occasionally glimpsed and sometimes killed a uniquely attractive variety of cougar, more reddish-brown and smaller than the western subspecies.

Two centuries later, the eastern cougar teeters on the brink of extinction.

Eastern cougars once roamed throughout the range of the white-tailed deer (their preferred prey) as far north as the deciduous forests of southern New Brunswick, Nova Scotia, Quebec and Ontario and as far south as the Mississippi delta and eastern Texas.

In 1938, a hunter killed a cougar near the U.S.-Canada border between Maine and New Brunswick. This was the last record of a cougar in eastern Canada until recently. For many years, biologists believed that habitat loss and overhunting had eradicated Canada's eastern cougars. From time to time, tantalizing reports surfaced of sightings or tracks, but none could be confirmed.

In May 1990, however, a New Brunswick man spotted what appeared to be a cougar outside his brother's woodworking shop, southeast of Fredericton, New Brunswick. He got it on videotape. The tape quality was poor and the animal was filmed at a distance, but the image appeared sufficiently like a cougar to excite a new round of debate about the possibility that a few eastern cougars might still survive in the northern edge of their former range.

Then, in 1992, a hunter killed a cougar near St. Lambert, Quebec. A few months later, biologists, investigating a report of cougar tracks north of Fredericton, found a dropping that had cougar hairs in it.

Biologists could not confirm whether the Quebec cougar, or the cougar that dropped scat in New Brunswick, belonged to the eastern subspecies. But they know that the eastern subspecies, if it survives at all, must hover close to extinction. Conservation biologists estimate a population needs several hundred cougars to remain viable over the long run. The few cougar reports do not support that possibility.

In 1939, whooping cranes numbered only 15 individuals. Today, they number more than 150. The tenuous, but impressive, recovery of the whooping crane offers hope for other endangered species such as the eastern cougar.

Eastern North America certainly needs cougars, one of its most dramatic and effective predators. White-tailed deer have become so numerous that they threaten the ecological health of many protected areas and small fragments of native forest, from Ontario and the Canadian Maritimes south to Alabama and Georgia.

Cougar Families

Unlike other native predators, cougars can come into heat and breed at almost any time of year, though most mating seems to take place in May and June. The female finds a cave, a hollow beneath deadfall or some other sheltered spot and, about three months after mating, gives birth to between one and five blind, spotted kittens.

The mother has to provide for both herself and her offspring. After the first few days, she may be away from the den for as much as a third of the time, sometimes for several days in a row. Separation brings risk to the kittens: hunters or other dangers may kill the mother, male cougars or other predators may kill the unprotected kittens. But kittens are not necessarily safe even with their mother around. Toni Ruth found evidence that a grizzly bear had tracked a mother cougar to her den and killed a kitten in Montana's Flathead Valley. Further north, a female cougar (which another British Columbia researcher, Brian Spreadbury, was monitoring) lost both her kittens in an attack by a male cougar. She attempted to protect them and suffered serious injuries to her legs, chest and head.

Once the kittens can travel, they accompany

Cougar Food

Elk

Mule deer

Moose

Diet of cougars near Sheep River, Alberta:

Mule deer	26%
Moose	15%
Elk	12%
Porcupine	10%
Unclassified deer (mule or white-tailed)	9%
Unclassified cervid (moose or elk)	8%
Beaver	6%

Other: white-tailed deer, bighorn sheep, cougar, squirrel and grouse

Source: Pall, Jalkotsky and Ross 1988, *The Cougar in Alberta*

Diet of cougars near Elk River, British Columbia:

Elk	66%
Mule deer	13%
White-tailed deer	4%
Bighorn sheep	4%
Cougar (2 of 3 killed were eaten)	6%

Other: coyote, porcupine, snowshoe hare, weasel (not eaten)

Source: Spreadbury 1989, *Cougar ecology and related management implications and strategies in S.E. B.C.*

The white muzzle and black moustache mark are characteristic of most cougars.

the female and begin to take part in hunting. Kittens usually remain with their mothers for more than a year. When they disperse, males may wander more than 100 km (62 miles) before carving out a new home range of their own. Female kittens often establish a home range that overlaps with their mother's. Many kittens die when they venture off on their own because of their inexperience at catching prey and also because their travels take them into unfamiliar territory where they meet hunters or other cougars.

Cougars as Hunters

The cougar is superbly designed for preying on deer and other animals of similar size; no other predator in North America matches it. Wolves hunt large prey too, but they must rely heavily on teamwork. Cougars hunt alone. Where they share territory with other large predators, cougars kill more prey partly because wolves and bears steal cougar kills when they can.

A cougar's technique involves stealth and surprise. Popular myth has cougars lying in wait above a trail, stretched out on an overhanging tree limb. Cougars do spend a considerable

amount of time bedded on the limbs of large coniferous trees, but they rest there for comfort, not for ease of hunting. Cougars do most of their hunting on the move. They travel furtively from one spot to the next and return to places where they have found deer, elk or other prey before.

Cougars move from one patch of cover to another, spending as little time as possible in the open. Radio-tracking studies in B.C. have shown that cougars use logged areas, but only at night. Open terrain does not suit cougars' hunting style, which requires stalking cover. In Waterton Lakes National Park, where cougars occasionally hunt in the townsite, their tracks show that they rely on houses, bushy young spruce trees and even parked cars for cover, rarely venturing into large open areas such as the town campground.

Once a cougar has scented or sighted a potential meal, it crouches and becomes perfectly still, fixing its eyes on its prey. The cougar may then stalk carefully into range, or remain hidden and wait for the animal to wander closer. As its prey draws near, the cougar becomes increasingly tense, lashing the tip of its tail and

shifting its powerful hind legs. Finally, when the prey gets within range, the cougar suddenly charges and launches itself at the animal's neck or shoulders. Cougars like to attack downhill to take advantage of gravity for speed and impact.

An attacking cougar grips its prey with its long forelegs, raking the sides and flanks with its claws and biting at the neck. A cougar's claws, usually retracted into its paws (they almost never show up in cougar tracks) function mainly to keep the big cat attached to its prey. Most victims die when the cougar's powerful jaws crush their throats or break their spines.

Most prey probably escape before the cougar can attack, given the necessity of a close approach. Researchers have found that cougar kills turn up regularly at specific places where the right combination of terrain, vegetation and wildlife-movement patterns improves the odds of success. Other places simply do not provide the ingredients for a successful ambush or stalk.

Once a cougar makes a kill, it usually drags the carcass under a tree or bush or into some other sheltered location and feeds on it. Then it carefully rakes leaves or grass over the carcass to completely cover it and finds a quiet spot to lie down and digest before returning to finish off the remains.

In the western U.S., 14 of a total of 16 cougar studies over the past half-century have identified deer as cougars' main prey. Hares and rodents are important too. Some research suggests that more kittens survive when these small prey are abundant because they are easy prey for mother cougars.

Martin Jalkotsky and Ian Ross studied

Hunting equipment: powerful jaws and forearms.

Have Cougar, Will Call

Hunting guides who do "will call" hunts don't advertise it. It's unethical and—in most places—illegal. But Kevin Hansen, in his book *Cougar: The American Lion*, quotes one law enforcement specialist as saying that at least 30 percent of guides in Arizona do will call hunts for cougars and black bears. Guides contract in advance with clients who want a trophy without the trouble of hunting. The guide and his dogs trail and tree cougars until they find a big one. The guide then calls the hunter, sometimes even from a cellular phone, and holds the cougar in the tree long enough for the hunter to fly or drive out and shoot it.

Tiger, Tiger . . .

"On the twenty-second of April [1808] in hunting we were not successful, but killed an animal of the tiger species. He was three feet in height on the fore leg, from the nose to the insertion of the tail seven feet and a half, the tail two feet 10 inches, very strongly legged with sharp claws. The back and upper part of the tail were of a fawn colour, the belly and under part of the tail and its tip white. The flesh was white and good, in quantity equal to the antelope; the liver was rich, and the two men that ate it for several hours had a violent headache which passed away. The Indians say that the habit of this animal is to lie in cover and spring on the back of the deer, to which he fastens himself by his claws, and directly cuts the back sinew of the neck. The deer then becomes an easy prey."

-David Thompson, 1808
Near Kootenay Falls in
what is now Montana

Cougars have muscular bodies and grace.

sive wolves and bears.

In the early 1990s, the north fork of the Flathead River in western Montana and southeastern British Columbia became the focus of intense research on large predators and their prey. Biologists had already identified the valley as the core area for the densest population of grizzly bears in the Rocky Mountains and as a refuge for the wolves which began to repopulate Montana's Rockies in the late 1980s. They also discovered that it harbored a healthy population of cougars.

By 1995, the Flathead's elk and deer numbers were dropping rapidly from the combined predation of wolves, cougars, coyotes and, in some areas, grizzlies. Something had to happen to predator populations as the prey base dwindled. The cougars showed the first signs of stress.

Although cougars killed the most large animals in the valley, they could not defend their kills from wolves and bears, some of which started following the cougars around. Cougars frequently kill coyotes, but not wolves. One Yellowstone study turned up more than 13 cougar-killed coyotes and Flathead researchers recently documented four more. The Flathead Valley has also provided examples of wolves killing cougars—at least four in the mid-1990s.

Even in areas where cougars face little competition from other predators, they have another enemy: deep snow and cold. When cougars became numerous in Jasper National Park in the 1930s, park wardens brought in a professional cougar hunter. The wardens noted many of the cats he killed had frozen ears or parts of their tails missing. The cold north has few cougars, and when bad winters hit the Rockies, cougar numbers can drop suddenly.

Researchers in Alberta's Sheep River Valley, southwest of Calgary, found that cougars may have more to fear from one another than from starvation, wolves or other dangers. They docu-

cougars for almost a decade in the foothills and front ranges of the Rocky Mountains southwest of Calgary, Alberta. They found that male cougars, which are up to twice the size of females, can even bring down adult moose.

How Do Cougars Die?

If the cougar has an Achilles heel, it is its timidity in dealing with other large carnivores. Cougars readily surrender their kills to aggres-

Say Cheese

A lot of houndsmen and hunters I've talked to have spent so much time out there that they've just totally changed. They've switched to going in and treeing cougars and sharing the experience through photographing. I've met more hunters that way than the other way. It's a real neat process of evolution where hunters have learned so much about cougars through their hunting that they don't want to kill them any more.

-Toni Ruth,
Cougar Researcher

Playing The Odds

According to the Sierra Club, bees have killed 300 people for every one killed by cougars in the 20th-century. For every fatal cougar attack, more than 750 people have died in vehicle collisions with deer and more than 1,200 from lightning strikes.

mented five natural cougar deaths: one young cat that died accidentally while trying to kill a deer, another that died of an infection and three killed by male cougars. Male cougars often try to kill young cougars and other males, a behavior they share with other carnivores. The behavior helps keep cougar densities within the carrying capacity of their habitats: cougars spread out across the landscape partly to avoid each other. Males get an added benefit from killing kittens: when a female loses her young she soon goes into heat, increasing the odds that the male will populate the wilds with his own offspring.

Human hunting kills many cougars in areas where it is allowed. Hunting accounted for eight of 16 deaths documented in one Alberta study. In the western U.S., hunting ranks as the largest single cause of cougar deaths.

Cougar populations can compensate for consistently high mortality up to a point: the availability of vacant home ranges and abundant prey enables female cougars to mate at a younger age and produce more kittens that survive to maturity.

Cougars Get Mugged Too

Toni Ruth, known to many as the "Lion Lady" after nearly a decade of studying cougars from Florida and Texas to the Canadian border, began studying the Flathead River Valley's cougars in 1993. She is trying to find out how cougars coexist with wolves; so far, it looks like the cougars come out the losers. Wolves have killed at least four cougars and, as prey populations decline, both wolves and bears have increasingly turned to robbing cougars of their kills.

"Grizzlies are scavenging cougar kills, wolves are scavenging kills. Most of the cougar kills we find are hit by one or both of those. Some kills they're being chased from. With others, the wolves will come through and scavenge the pieces left by cougars.

This last summer, the berry crop was not very good. I know that bears make significant use of carrion in the spring, but it seemed this year that they were using it throughout the spring, summer and fall, and staying in the valley bottoms quite a bit more than last year.

That kind of pressure has got to have an impact on cougars' reproductive status. With my radio-collared sample, there were 10 or 12 females who potentially should have had kittens during the summer but we never did see denning behavior.

I finally found one female that did have a litter of kittens. I went back into the den to mark them about two days later and there was fresh track sign but we couldn't really figure out where the kittens were. We started searching a little farther from the den, and right away we hit very fresh grizzly bear tracks. We started backtracking those and found out that he had followed her in from some kills she'd made not too far from the den site and he'd killed one of the kittens. All we found was its matted hair.

Toni Ruth

She did make it out of there with one kitten that we ended up marking later. But going back in to track her and see if the kitten was with her, we found a kill of hers that a bear was on. He'd tracked her into it and the minute he got done on that kill he immediately went back to her tracks and followed her.

The last three radio-collared cougars that we've found dead died of starvation. We had five carcasses examined earlier, and several of those had starved.

Looking at the combined impact of all these predators on ungulate populations, we're finding out that cougars are the number-one predators on white-tailed deer. Wolves are a close second. Cougars are also number-one on elk.

Maybe that's so, but now I'm asking what are predation rates for cougars and how are they different in this population, with wolves, compared to others? I would say that they would have to kill quite a bit more often just to get enough food. They may be the most significant predators in that system in terms of the number of animals they're killing, but they're not getting the benefits of all those kills."

Cougars and Agriculture

Considering how many cows, horses and other domestic animals live in cougar habitat, surprisingly few fall prey to the big cats. Domestic animals have weak defenses against predators, after all, and cougars have been known to kill animals as large as moose.

Cougars do kill domestic sheep, horses and, less frequently, cattle. Young cougars dispersing into new terrain, with poor hunting abilities, sometimes hunt domestic dogs or even raid chicken coops but such incidents are rare, except in parts of the American southwest. Utah and Nevada—where ranchers often allow sheep to graze wilderness tracts of public land—account for the vast majority of documented cougar attacks on domestic livestock. Ranchers in that area have reported several cases of surplus killing by cougars, especially female cougars with growing kittens learning to hunt.

Elsewhere in the American West, cattle and sheep rarely exceed even three percent of the cougar diet. Cougars that kill livestock usually prey on young calves and sheep, so most ranchers simply keep young calves well protected or buy guard dogs to protect their sheep herds. In Alberta, ranchers and farmers worry about wolves but are often unaware of the robust cougar population. Losses of livestock to the big cats are rare and episodic. Wildlife officers recorded only 61 cougar attacks on livestock between 1974 and 1986. Some of those attacks, however, cost farmers dearly. One cougar killed 14 goats in one night. Another killed 420 chickens.

A California study analyzed the carcasses of 19 cougars known to have attacked domestic livestock. Most were either transient males (that is, males too young or too old to defend a territory successfully) or old animals no longer able to catch wild prey.

Many governments used to pay bounty for cougars, just like for coyotes and wolves. Bounties, however, failed to eradicate cougars or reduce livestock losses. Montana's state cougar management plan acknowledges this. "In recognition of its ecological importance, and the futility of most government-sponsored

Cougar Encounter

I was working in the San Andres Mountains in New Mexico, helping snare cougars. I'd been working real hard to catch this one female that we didn't have a collar on. One day, I found a carcass. I didn't know which cougar had killed it, so I went ahead and set snares around it. The next morning, I'd caught the female. She'd been tagged as a kitten and had stayed in the area. We put a radio collar on her.

The next day I went back down the canyon to check on her. She wasn't around and I couldn't pick up her radio signal, but as I headed down the canyon I started picking up the signal of one of the radio-collared males. The female's kill was near a spring below a little ledge. There were a bunch of cottonwood trees and willows at the edge of the spring, and her kill was in there.

As I came closer to that ledge, the male's signal grew stronger and I still had no signal from the female. I came up fairly quietly. I was on rock, and as I approached I heard this scraping noise. It sounded like somebody raking leaves. When I got to the ledge, that's exactly what he was doing.

He'd come upon the kill and I guess she had already left, or maybe he d chased her off it, but he'd

eaten and was caching the kill.

So I stood on the ledge and his rear end was toward me and he was just very busy with pulling up leaves and covering the thing. I'd been very silent and the wind was in my favor. There wasn't much of a breeze but I do remember that I stood there for a little while and it's not like he turned around and saw me, it was like he stopped suddenly. I don't know if he had smelled me finally or what, but he stopped. Then he just turned and looked over his shoulder at me. We only looked at each other for two seconds and that was it. He just took off.

I'm sure he didn't hear me because he was very busy raking the leaves. It was more like he just felt my presence and suddenly realized somebody was watching him. That's still one of my favorite encounters with a cougar in the wild.

I have a peeve about paintings and taxidermists' mounts that show mountain lions snarling. I have rarely ever, ever seen that facial expression in the wild. They're a very timid, docile animal even when they're pressed.

-Toni Ruth,
Cougar Researcher

An exhausting business: cougars mate repeatedly over several hours.

predator-control programs, most states had declared the cougar a game animal by 1972."

"Game animals" have more protection than "pest" species. People cannot kill game animals indiscriminately; they need hunting licences and have to observe hunting seasons and bag limits.

In the U.S., and to a limited degree in B.C. and Alberta, wildlife officers continue to snare or hunt down cougars that kill livestock. Such losses are so rare, however, that some ranchers do not even realize they live in cougar country. In Yellowstone National Park, biologists thought that no cougars survived until they investigated the feasibility of reintroducing them to the park. To their surprise, they discovered that the park and surrounding areas already had cougars. The big cats had gone undetected because of their secretive behavior and because nobody had lost any domestic animals to them.

Hunting Cougars

The only consistently reliable way to hunt mountain lions is with hounds, but most hunters cannot afford to raise, train and care for hounds. Cougar hunters usually contract with outfitters who keep cougar hounds.

During the snowy season, cougar hunters drive back roads in good cougar habitat and watch for telltale round footprints. When a

Cougar AIDS

Feline immunodeficiency virus, or FIV, infects more than a third of the cougars living on Vancouver Island, based on blood analyses from a study in the early 1990s. Florida panthers have a similar rate of infection, which has led researchers to speculate that FIV has existed in cougar populations for a long time.

Like the notorious HIV that appeared in humans in the early 1980s, FIV weakens the immune systems of infected cats, making them vulnerable to a wide range of infections. The virus is spread in body fluids: blood, saliva and mucus, which cougars sometimes exchange during territorial fights, grooming and mating.

Biologists believe that FIV does not threaten wild cougar populations: it appears widespread and not particularly virulent. Like many other endemic diseases and parasites, FIV simply forces cougars to adapt through natural selection.

hunter finds fresh tracks, he releases the hounds. The hounds bay excitedly as they chase the scent trail of their quarry. The cougar, as the dogs close in, usually climbs a tree and drapes itself over a limb safely out of reach of the excited pursuers. It seems to relax, even to the point of appearing to fall asleep.

The hunter, once he decides the cat is large enough and not a nursing mother, shoots it in the tree. He hopes that it will fall out on its own. If it gets hung up, he has to climb the tree and work it loose. This can prove strenuous and, if the cat is not dead, downright hazardous.

Nobody really understands why cougars (more than capable of quickly dispatching most dogs) tree so readily when pursued by hounds. It may be a defensive behavior they have evolved against wolves. It may also help cougars conserve energy; they don't possess the stamina for prolonged chases. Their slow-stalk, sudden-dash type of hunting requires little lung capacity.

Climbing a tree works well against wolves and dogs, but not against people with guns.

Kerry Murphy monitored a heavily hunted cougar population in western Montana in the early 1980s and found that hunters almost always got cats when they released their hounds on tracks. He estimated that hunters killed half the males and a quarter of the female cougars in his study area in one hunting season. Hunters had the highest success rate in areas with good winter vehicle access.

Hunters usually kill about twice as many males as females because regulations require them to spare females with kittens. This should theoretically improve the survival rate of kittens by reducing the number of adult males that might kill them. But studies in Montana have shown that fewer kittens actually survive in hunted populations because hunters orphan kittens by inadvertently shooting mother cougars.

Most western states and provinces allow cougar hunting but have regulations that prevent houndsmen from taking too many

A Part Of The Circle

I've got a big tom cougar on my place right now. One of the trappers came to our door one day and said that he wanted to go up and kill it. And I knew that my kids would never let that happen, but I said, Well, why would you want to kill it? And he said that they'll kill all the kittens.

I said, "Gee I didn't know that."

And he said, "Well, we just get it if he's a certain age of a tom that we think is going to do that, because he's protecting his breeding rights"

And I paused, because here my love for nature right away had said no, and yet I realized that I didn't really know much about cougars. Here I thought that this guy just wanted to kill a cougar and yet because he was in the business of being a guide, what he was really saying was that he needs to do this so he can manage things. He's trying to be a part of it. So even though I took that request to the kids and they said no, so I'm not going to let him shoot the cougar, my main response to him was: Educate me.

Because that's part of the problem: we're not letting people know that man is a real part of that circle and has to be to make things work. We've always been there.

Some kids from Medicine Hat were staying at

Keith Everts

the McRaes and they were walking down the road (this was on New Year's Day) and the cougar ran in front of them. Man, it was like those kids had got the best Christmas present ever. "Do you know," the one young guy says to me, "that you've got a cougar on this place, and do you know that I've never seen a cougar before!" And he was just babbling along, he was so excited. I never did get to say anything. It was priceless. And those kids are going to relate this place to wildness, you know, and hopefully it'll stay that way.

-Keith Everts, rancher,
Beavermines, Alberta.

Hunters usually select large male cougars, leaving females and young cats alone.

cougars. They set quotas conservatively and close the hunting season as soon as hunters register a predetermined number of kills.

Impacts of Cougars on Game

Any predator as effective as the cougar will have an impact on the populations of its preferred prey, but cougars rarely become so abundant that they are able to reduce game populations. Cougars prefer to avoid one another, so they never become as common as other animals that can tolerate more crowding. Their home ranges shrink when deer become abundant, which means the same landscape holds more cougars. Low deer populations, however, force cougars to expand their home ranges. The result: fewer cougars.

Ungulates rarely increase or decline because of predation. Severe winters, habitat loss and low food supplies have far more impact on deer, elk and moose populations. Predation by animals such as cougars, however, shaves off population highs and extends the time it takes for populations to recover from lows.

There Goes The Neighborhood

Cougars do just fine if they don't have to share. But they have a harder time once other predators move into the neighborhood.

Western Alberta probably has more cougars today than at any other time in the 20th-century. The region has lots of big-cat food—abundant mule and white-tailed deer, and increasing numbers of bighorn sheep and elk. It also has few other large predators. Grizzly bears are scarce, liberal hunting regulations have nearly eradicated wolves and the number of human hunters has dropped steadily for almost a decade.

Just across the Continental Divide in the Flathead Valley of British Columbia and northern Montana, however, cougar populations began to decline in 1995. The Flathead's cougars compete for food with wolves and grizzlies, and their prey populations have plummeted. Cougars could face the same pressure in Alberta if a severe winter reduces ungulate populations or in the unlikely event that the Alberta government brings in more reasonable hunting regulations for wolves and other predators.

Farther south, cougars are abundant in Colorado and New Mexico—for now. Wolves are likely to arrive there within the next few years.

Cougars that concentrate their hunting in a small area can temporarily reduce the local deer population because the deer move away. Overall, however, the prey population remains healthy. When deer and elk populations crash dramatically, as they did in the Flathead River valley in the 1990s, the combined hunting pressure of many predator species including humans is usually responsible.

Staying Alive in Cougar Country

Lightning kills more people every year than cougars have killed over the past century. Bees, statistically, are more dangerous than cougars.

Cougar populations have reached all-time highs in many parts of western North America, yet the number of serious attacks on people in any given year can be counted on one hand.

Between 1890 and 1990, records document only 53 cougar attacks on humans in Canada and the United States. To date, fewer than 20 people have died from cougar attacks.

Even so, the frequency of cougar attacks has increased in recent years as both cougar and human populations have grown. Vancouver Island, California and the Front Range of Colorado, as well as the edges of cities such as Vancouver, British Columbia, have had the highest number of cougar attacks. In Boulder, Colorado and other growing western cities with urban deer populations, cougars have begun to hunt in yards and alleys from time to time, increasing the frequency of their encounters with human beings.

Cougars rely on very specific search images to identify likely prey. Fortunately for us, an upright, two-legged ape looks quite different from a four-legged deer. Thousands of unsuspecting people walk into the intense gaze of a cougar every year and right out again, blissfully unaware that they have been examined and dismissed. Cougars seem to attack people when:

- People behave in a way that makes them look like potential prey.
- A sudden movement triggers an instantaneous chase reflex in a cougar.
- The cougar is starving and desperate.

Small children or people who spend a lot of time crouched, kneeling or sitting in one spot can look like prey to a cougar because of their size and behavior. Of 58 cougar attacks documented before 1991, 37 involved victims less

than 16 years old. This group included nine of the total 10 fatal maulings.

People who walk dogs in cougar country may find themselves in a tug-of-war; cougars attack dogs more readily than they do humans. Joggers or cyclists moving rapidly along narrow trails can trigger spontaneous chase behavior.

Most cougars attack from behind or from the side, but inexperienced young cats may approach a person from the front. If a cougar confronts you, make your profile as large as possible: raise your arms, stretch open your jacket or open an umbrella. Then shout loudly and aggressively. Cougars rarely press an attack against an alert or aggressive target.

If, in spite of everthing, a cougar actualy attacks, never play dead or turn to run. Fight back aggressively. Use a stick or camera as a weapon, shout angrily and do whatever you can to bluff the cat into deciding the risks of continuing the attack outweight the benefits.

"No Hunting, Children At Play"

When urban people go rural, their new lifestyle often produces ideal cougar habitat...and the potential for trouble.

Cougar attacks have increased in recent years partly because more people have developed a taste for country living. Rural subdivisions continue to proliferate in the foothills west of Calgary, the Colorado Front Range, the interior valleys of British Columbia and the islands and rainforests of the Pacific Northwest.

Montana's cougar management plan describes how the modern penchant for building homes in wildlife habitat may create cougar problems: "Reasons for the increase in incidents have included habituation of cougars due to increases in both cougars and human housing in cougar habitat, increased deer populations developing in human subdivisions, and increased use of recreational lands by urbanized humans."

Cougar need to live in cougar habitat. People do not. The long-term interests of cougars, their prey and people may all depend on the voluntary restraint of the only animal with free choice in the matter: us.

Unlike humans, cougars have little choice about where to raise their families.

Cougar Hunting Lingo

Bawl-mouth A hound noted for its deep, loud baying while on the scent of a cat.

Cold-nosed A hound able to follow a cold cougar track having little scent left in it.

Freshening A cougar trail that suddenly grows warmer as the hounds follow it.

Jumping a cat When a cougar suddenly realizes it's being trailed and begins to flee.

Jumping tree When a treed cougar jumps to the ground and flees again.

Locator bark The distinctive baying of a hound that has spotted the cougar it's following.

Pop-up A cougar that climbs a tree immediately instead of fleeing.

Running wide When hounds run beside rather than on the track, be cause it's so fresh that they can smell the body odor of the cougar in the air.

Trash-free dog A hound that refuses to be distracted by the scent of deer or other animals.

Treeing a cat When a cougar finally stops running and climbs a tree.

Tree-and-see Like catch-and-release fishing the cougar is treed but only shot with a camera.

Bobcats

Sleek and small, bobcats frequent dry, broken country.

Each of North America's wildcats has a hunting specialty. Cougars have evolved into ideal deer-hunters, lynx specialize in snowshoe hares, and the little bobcat is perfectly suited for catching cottontail rabbits. Bobcats hunt other prey too: whatever is locally abundant.

This makes them less vulnerable to downswings in prey numbers than their northern relative, the lynx.

Bobcat Facts

Size: 0.6-1 meters / 2-3 feet
Weight: 7-15 kilograms / 15-31 pounds
Description: Brown with dark spots or streaks, small face, short tail–barred and tipped with black
Reproduction: First breeds second year of life
Gestation: 62 days
Litter size: 1-8 kittens; average 3
Life span: 10 years
Food: Small animals
Distribution: North America, primarily south of Canada

Based on fossil evidence, most biologists believe that the bobcat evolved fairly recently from a species of lynx that once ranged across most of the northern hemisphere. The glaciers that advanced across Europe, Asia and North America during the ice age isolated primitive lynx into several different populations. In North America, the ice forced the species south into what is now the United States and Mexico. These eventually evolved into the modern bobcat.

As the ice retreated and advanced again several times, the primitive lynx again managed to colonize North America across the Bering land bridge that, until 10,000 years ago or so, connected Alaska to Siberia. The Bering Sea flooded the land bridge as the glaciers melted, isolating the more recent immigrants. These evolved into the Canada lynx.

Today, the two very similar-looking small

wildcats each occupy different parts of the continent. Lynx prefer the dense northern forests and only extend into the U.S. in the east, where coniferous forests bulge south around the Great Lakes and in the west at high elevations in the mountains. They are creatures of deep-snow country.

Bobcats prefer less snowy terrain. They range from the southernmost part of Canada across most of the U.S. into Central America. This vast area contains several races of cottontail rabbit (their preferred prey) and, depending on which museum taxonomist you want to believe, from one to 14 varieties of bobcat.

Northern Bobcats

Neither bobcats nor cottontails can survive where winter brings deep snow. Compared to lynx and snowshoe hares, bobcats and cottontails have smaller feet and legs in proportion to their bodies, so they bog down and quickly exhaust their energy in snowy terrain. Bobcats' small bodies and poor ability to regulate their body temperatures also make it hard for them to cope with extreme cold.

In western Canada, bobcats are rare and very locally distributed; western Canada lies at the northern edge of their range. Bobcats live along prairie river valleys and coulee systems as far north as Regina and Drumheller. Farther west, small numbers of bobcats live in the foothills of southern Alberta, where frequent chinook winds keep winter snows shallow, and in the dry valley bottoms that separate British Columbia's southern mountain ranges even though cottontails do not inhabit these areas. Few bobcats live in the protected landscapes of western Canada's national parks, except for the southern corner of Kootenay National Park and the Frenchman's River valley of Grasslands National Park.

Bobcat Country

Bobcats like broken rocky terrain and dense shrubby cover. Put those two habitats close together in an area that gets little deep snow and the combination is great potential habitat. Kick around in the bushes if you find the droppings or runways of cottontail rabbits; it is almost certainly bobcat country.

In southern Alberta and Saskatchewan, the best bobcat habitat lies along the sides and bot-

Big eyes and ears enable bobcats to locate prey.

Pronghorn Prey

Bobcats account for almost 10 percent of predation on newborn pronghorns in southeastern Alberta. Researcher Morley Barrett found that most fawns fell prey to bobcats at about a week old. Barrett speculated that this corresponded with the most vulnerable period for the fawns. For the first several days of a pronghorn's life, it lies flat on the ground during its mother's absences, a behavior that makes it hard for predators to detect it. By the end of its second week, a baby pronghorn can walk and run strongly, and can accompany its mother during her daily travels. Between those two stages of development, however, fawns often raise their heads or stand, but remain too weak to outrun predators. During this season, some bobcats forsake the shrubby coulees and river bottoms they usually prefer and hunt baby pronghorns on the sagebrush flats—a risky business since their dangerous enemy, the coyote, hunts fawns too.

Bobcats have longer tails, and only a partial black tip, compared to lynx.

Bobcats Versus Lynx

Most biologists agree that bobcats are more aggressive than lynx. They base this on what happened when bobcats colonized Cape Breton Island. Before a causeway linked the island to the rest of Nova Scotia, only lynx lived on Cape Breton Island. After the causeway, bobcats started to turn up. Within a few years, the bobcats had taken over the valley bottoms and the lynx had retreated to higher elevations.

"Bobcats are considered to be a little bit more of an aggressive animal than the lynx," says bobcat researcher Clayton Apps. But he considers the conventional interpretation of what happened on Cape Breton Island too simplistic. He points out that the two cats simply fell into the pattern seen anywhere the two species live in close proximity, such as western Canada.

In their dealings with humans, however, bobcats have repeatedly shown themselves fiercer than the much larger lynx or cougar. Cougar researcher Toni Ruth says cougars keep their composure when cornered, but bobcats become little spitfires.

Cat specialists speculate that the bobcat evolved a fiery disposition to compete with and defend itself against a wide range of larger predators. The lynx, by contrast, evolved in northern forests where it encountered few other predators.

"With a little 10-pound bobcat," says Apps, "you would never hope of handling it unless it was totally immobilized, but trappers tell me they can hold down a lynx by the neck. It's because of this difference in personalities people think that bobcats will drive out the lynx from an area."

Still, bobcats may not always chase out lynx. In western Canada, it appears that they sometimes mate with them. Trappers in southern B.C. occasionally register lynx-cats—something between bobcats and lynx. Modern DNA analysis may help biologists determine whether crossbreeding happens in the wild. So far, it has only happened for sure in captivity.

"I suspect that it's occurring in southeastern B.C.," says Apps, "where fairly stable populations of both species overlap, separated by elevation. Some of the trappers say this lynx-cat is a hybrid between the two. I've seen a picture of one and it looks like a bobcat except for those big paws. I've plotted on a map the locations where trappers have registered lynx-cats, and almost every time they come from areas such as Luxor Pass or the St. Mary's River which are in the margins between good bobcat habitat and good lynx habitat."

For the most part, lynx and bobcat live apart simply by virtue of their differences. In the western mountains, lynx occupy the high elevations and latitudes where their large feet enable them to cope with deep snow. Bobcats stick to patches of low-elevation habitat where the snow remains shallow.

A bobcat family investigates a promising sound.

toms of prairie river valleys and the large coulees draining into them. Trees and shrubs grow here, making ribbons of green through the dry prairie grasslands. Cottonwood forests and tangles of willow and silverberry border the water. Higher on the slopes, near-impenetrable tangles of wild rose, buckbrush and saskatoon provide ideal shelter for rabbits, grouse and other animals that bobcats hunt.

Cottontails thrive along parts of the Milk and South Saskatchewan watersheds, but they are rare in the Alberta foothills and southern B.C. Bobcats dwell there, however, since these areas rarely receive deep snow for any significant length of time and other prey animals make up for the lack of rabbits. The Similkameen, Okanagan, Kettle, Kootenay and Columbia valleys all lie in the rain shadows of large mountain ranges, and their mild climates make for rainy winters more than snowy ones. East of the Rockies, Chinook winds howl down off the Front Ranges to sweep the snow from the Porcupine Hills and southern foothills and pile it up on sheltered slopes where, melting in the spring, it waters the dense shrubbery tangles favored by bobcats.

The upper Columbia Valley near Invermere and Cranbrook contains most of the best sur-

viving bobcat habitat in British Columbia. Bobcats in this area need mature stands of Douglas fir forest, especially on the rocky slopes that line the east side of the Rocky Mountain Trench.

"Coyotes play a pretty important role in defining suitable bobcat habitat," says bobcat researcher Clayton Apps. "Bobcats avoid open areas that would be good habitat otherwise, because they're so vulnerable to coyote predation. They spend a lot of time in rocky areas where there's lots of escape cover."

Living On The Outside

There are no areas of core bobcat range in western Canada that are afforded any type of protection. It's a unique situation compared to what we're used to thinking about with carnivores. Most people consider national parks as core population sources for carnivores, and provincial lands as being the mortality sinks. With bobcats, it's very much the opposite. In fact, for Kootenay National Park to hang onto the bobcat population it currently has completely depends on how the land outside the parks is managed.

Clayton Apps,
Bobcat Researcher

Apps says environmental conditions, not available prey, control bobcat distribution. Diverse, uneven-aged Douglas fir stands are critical habitat, he says. The brushy young saplings are important for stalking purposes, while the big mature trees are important because of how their canopies intercept snowfall. Clumps of Douglas fir growing together with lots of branch

Bobcat Food

Cottontail Rabbit

Bobcats eat whatever they can catch, but across most of their range they specialize in hunting rabbits. When cottontail rabbits are scarce, or in areas that have no cottontails, bobcats hunt squirrels, birds, mice and voles, packrats, snowshoe hares and other small animals. Large male bobcats hunt deer, pronghorn and bighorn sheep, especially young fawns and, in winter, small adults.

In the 1980s, researchers in Idaho's Frank Church/River-of-No-Return Wilderness examined bobcat droppings to find out what bobcats ate. They recorded the percentage of scats that contained remains from these prey:

Prey	Summer Scats	Winter Scats
Vole	40%	65%
Cottontail rabbit	36	2
Ground squirrel	32	0
Mule deer	0	27
Bighorn sheep	0	16
Unknown rodent	12	10
Birds	12	4
Wood rat	8	7
Deer mouse	4	4
Red squirrel	4	2

Other: Pocket gopher, unknown ungulate, chipmunk, shrew

interconnection intercept so much snow that the ground beneath them is often virtually snow-free all winter. Also, interconnected branches are excellent red squirrel habitat.

Southern B.C. has only patches of this kind of high-quality bobcat habitat. The area's bobcats consequently have the largest home ranges ever documented for the species—they have to travel widely in search of livable habitat. Western Canada's bobcats use more energy and face more hazards than bobcats that live farther south. They also find fewer prey animals within their preferred size range.

Farther south, where the climate is more friendly to bobcats and their prey, bobcats occupy a greater range of habitats from oak-brush thickets and pinyon-juniper stands up into the ponderosa pine and aspen forests of the Rockies. Even here, however, bobcats prefer broken, rocky terrain—canyons, foothills and desert washes.

Bobcat Families

Bobcats mate in late winter or early spring. Several males may court a female, but they rarely fight even after the female chooses a mate. The pair may travel together for a while and hunt as a unit, teaming up to flush rabbits to one another. They stay together only long enough to breed. The female gives birth, on her own, to a litter of one to five kittens about two months after mating.

The female bobcat generally dens in or near a rocky area. Rocky areas offer shelters inaccessible to coyotes and wolves, which hunt bobcats. Small caves and shelters in rocky slopes protect bobcats from extreme weather too.

The kittens are born blind with spotted fur. Within less than a month, they start to explore around the den and to supplement their mother's milk with meat she brings back for them. If the hunting is poor, most will sicken or starve before they leave the den. If the hunting is good, the female usually weans them at two months of age and they begin accompanying their mother on her hunting forays.

Kittens remain with their mother for less than a year before venturing off on their own. Bobcats reach their full adult size at about one-and-a-half years old.

Yearling female bobcats can become pregnant and give birth, but usually a female does

not have her first litter of kittens until her second year of life.

Bobcats as Hunters

Some hunting beds of bobcats resemble UFO landing sites: trampled circles of vegetation in the tangled shrubbery of prairie coulees.

Where cottontails are abundant, bobcats often hunt them by lying very still in the middle of cover and watching for the telltale movements of a passing rabbit. The bobcat changes position to face different directions and eventually makes a circle of flattened grass or snow. In winter, the prints of the bobcat's front paws sometimes mark the edge of the circle.

Bobcats, like other cats, use their acute senses of vision and hearing to locate prey, then carefully stalk to within a short distance before dashing suddenly out of hiding and grabbing at their quarry with extended claws. One researcher watched a bobcat take 13 minutes to creep only one meter / three feet as it carefully stalked a small rodent. Sensitive whiskers on the face and feet help the bobcat stalk silently, detecting twigs or leaves which might rustle under its weight.

The hunting strategy of a bobcat depends on the abundance and type of potential prey. Where rabbits or other small mammals are abundant, a bobcat may spend most of its time waiting beside trails, watching from a hunting bed or crouched on a vantage point where it can look down over a large area. Where food is scarce, bobcats travel to search for prey.

Female bobcats hunt smaller prey than males. They kill mostly squirrel-sized animals

and rabbits. Male bobcats, up to half again as large as females, can kill animals as big as deer. In some areas, bobcats hunt deer in winter, even though deer make dangerous prey for such a small predator. But one deer delivers as much food value as 50 or more hares, so the risk makes sense for cats facing the high-energy demands of a hard northern winter.

When hunting deer, bobcats try to maneuver into position for an attack from above, probably so that they can take advantage of gravity to give them extra speed and impact. Usually, bobcats attack bedded deer, landing on their backs and biting the deer rapidly in the throat, at the base of the jaw or at the front of the chest. The rapid biting helps the little cat sever enough blood vessels or crush the wind-

Bobcats In The Fur Trade

Trappers have killed more bobcats in the last twenty years than any other cat species in the world, according to a recent review by the Cat Specialists Group of the IUCN (International Union for the Conservation of Nature). In the 1960s trappers received less than $20 for each bobcat pelt, but after an international treaty banned trade in endangered cat skins in the mid 1970s the price of bobcat pelts climbed as high as $600. Most of the demand for bobcat hides came from Europe where fur-loving consumers could no longer buy clothing made from ocelot, margay and other exotic cat skins.

Inevitably, trappers saw the chance for windfall profits. In the 1960s ,U.S. trappers killed only about 10,000 bobcats each year. By the 1980s, however, they were trapping more than 90,000 a year. Like previous fur trading booms and busts, the bottom fell out of the market once supply exceeded demand. "At present, trade in bobcat pelts is declining . . ." says the 1995 IUCN report. "In addition, the European Community has announced that, after 1995, all imports of furs from countries allowing the use of leghold traps will be prohibited."

Trapping has probably never seriously threatened bobcat numbers where the little cats occupy high quality habitat. In some parts of the northern Rockies and Canada, however, intense trapping pressure can have long-lasting impacts on bobcat numbers.

No Lap Cat

Naturalist Victor Calahane described a California rancher's attempt to raise an orphaned bobcat kitten. Until it was about half a year old, the kitten was friendly and tractable, but it soon developed a nasty habit of climbing up a door frame and pouncing on people as they entered the house. When scolded, it would hide under a bed spitting, snarling and grimacing. The rancher finally gave up the struggle to befriend the little wildcat and turned it loose. "I have kept several bobcats," wrote Calahane, "and never found them friendly. Some were coldly aloof, and others plainly disagreeable."

Its dappled spots camouflage a bobcat in a birch tree.

Hunting Bobcats

More and more hunters have become interested in chasing cougars and bobcats with hounds. Cougar populations seem able to handle the pressure, but that may not be true of bobcat populations. Bobcats in British Columbia live under extreme environmental stress: patchy habitat, demanding winters and poor-quality prey.

Clayton Apps does not oppose hunting in general, but when it comes to bobcats at the northern fringe of their range he says, "I don't think it's quite appropriate considering how sensitive and vulnerable they are. Hound hunting is a growing sport in the area, and there's access everywhere that bobcats occur. You've got roads almost everywhere."

Bobcats are so rare, compared to cougars, that hounds generally tree more than 15 cougars for every bobcat. Unfortunately, that makes the bobcat a valuable novelty for some hunters.

In many cases, houndsmen do not kill the bobcats they tree; like catch-and-release fishers they tree-and-see.

Even being treed, though, causes stress, says Apps. *"For a lot of these animals that are so stressed to begin with, chasing and treeing them may be all it takes to push them over the edge. It doesn't look like they're under a lot of stress when they're in the tree. They look calm and relaxed but nobody's ever done any research on what their heart rate actually is and how much internal stress there is. The point is that while they're up there, they should be hunting and they're not."*

pipe before the struggling deer can throw its attacker off or injure it by crushing it against a tree or rock.

Threats to Bobcats

Bobcats live virtually invisible lives, attracting little attention from hunters, fur trappers or farmers. On rare occasions, especially during hard winters, bobcats may learn to prey on chickens or other domestic animals, but these individuals are soon trapped and killed.

Starvation and cold winters with deep snow threaten bobcats the most. Starvation is the biggest threat facing any predator. When cottontail or snowshoe-hare populations die off, as they do periodically, many bobcats die. Few other animals are sufficiently abundant, espe-

Bobcats On The Fringe

Clayton Apps feels at home in the forest, summer or winter. He doesn't like offices and he doesn't enjoy meetings. But he spends a lot of time in both, because he's concerned about the future survival of animals such as the bobcat and lynx in western Alberta and southern B.C.

Apps and his fellow researcher, Trevor Kinley, spent several years radio-collaring bobcats in British Columbia's Kootenay River valley north of Cranbrook and following them around to learn more about bobcat ecology.

"A lot of people assumed that everything under 1,300 meters elevation [4,300 feet] was bobcat habitat," says Apps. "I found out that this is just not the case here in the northern edge of their North American range.

"The bobcat should be managed as a species of concern, because there is no de facto refuge in southern B.C. for bobcats. The most suitable bobcat habitat coincides exactly with the areas that are most heavily impacted by humans."

Apps monitored the activities of 22 individual bobcats, but most of his work concentrated on six males and seven females that ranged along the edges of the Rocky Mountain Trench, a semiarid valley of open ponderosa pine forests with thickets of aspen, pine and Douglas fir, and very few streams or lakes.

"It's disturbing," he says, "to hear people describe bobcats as habitat generalists. In this area, they have very specific habitat needs that make them particularly vulnerable to human land-use decisions."

Few rabbits inhabit the Rocky Mountain Trench. In the absence of their favorite prey, bobcats have had to develop other specialties. The males Apps followed killed several deer. The females and young, which are considerably smaller than males, relied heavily on red squirrels.

Clayton Apps

Compared to a rabbit, a deer makes dangerous prey. Apps found one bobcat killed by their sharp hooves. And compared to a rabbit, a squirrel is little more than an *hors d'oeuvre*. It takes twice to four times as many squirrels to provide the same amount of food as a rabbit, and squirrels, alert and dodgy, are harder to catch.

During hard, snowy winters, squirrels spend a lot of time under the snow or curled up in a sort of semi-torpor. Apps found that hard winters resulted in high death rates among female bobcats and kittens. By contrast, male bobcats made it through those same winters in good shape, possibly because deep snow and cold make it easier to capture deer. Large males, since they have larger bodies that lose less heat and don't have young to feed, don't require as much energy as females with kittens.

When a population has found a way to survive in marginal habitat, as the bobcats of southern B.C.'s Rocky Mountain Trench have done, they are particularly vulnerable to habitat loss. Bobcats in this region rely on steep rocky slopes that face the sun and mature, uneven-aged Douglas fir forest with diverse understories.

Camouflage coloration helps bobcats evade detection by both prey and predators.

cially in winter, to meet the energy requirements of these cats.

Deep snow makes bobcats waste a lot of energy simply getting around. Severe cold adds to the energy deficit. Since Canada offers only marginal bobcat habitat and nowhere near the abundance of rabbit-sized prey found farther south, a bad winter can tip the balance for bobcats and result in very high mortality. Small pockets of high-quality bobcat habitat become critically important to our northern populations during severe winters.

If human land-use decisions remove some of these pockets, even though the rest of the landscape may remain relatively untouched, whole populations of bobcats can disappear. Dams on prairie rivers, for example, interrupt the natural cycle of spring flooding that sustains river-bottom cottonwood forests. Dams have eliminated, in some areas, more than half the cottonwood and willow stands which bobcats use in the prairie regions and low elevation inter-montane valleys Throughout the Rocky Mountain West vital bobcat habitat faces threats from rural subdivisions, golf courses and agriculture.

Go South, Young Bobcat

Location matters in bobcat country.

Northern bobcats are larger than their southern relatives. They breed only once a year, usually in spring, and their chances of survival are relatively slim.

Southern bobcats, on the other hand, may breed any time of the year. Their average size is smaller but they enjoy a more abundant food supply than their cold-country cousins. Where a northern bobcat might need to travel a long way to find a neighbor—bobcat densities in the north can be less than one cat every 25 square kilometers / 15 square miles—southern bobcats have no difficulty finding someone to squabble with. In the chaparral country of coastal California, biologist have found as many as 38 bobcats per 25 square kilometers / 15 square miles.

Longer growing seasons, more continuous habitat and a diverse and abundant supply of prey makes life easier for bobcats living in Texas, New Mexico, Colorado and other southern ranges. Farther north winters are snowier, habitat patchier, and prey less easy to find.

Canada Lynx

Lynx communicate by scent, often rubbing their faces against vegetation.

The lynx looks as if it is all legs and feet, the feline equivalent of those jacked-up muscle trucks whose huge tires make the vehicle body look puny. Big tires on a four-wheel-drive truck spread the vehicle's weight over a large area, enabling it to travel over swampy terrain and muskeg where normal vehicles would bog down. Lynx, by the same token, rely on oversized feet and long legs to enable them to travel over deep snow where other animals sink. Lynx live in deep-snow country. They range throughout the forested, snowy parts of North America.

Until ten thousand years ago, the Bering land bridge occasionally connected North America and Asia between Alaska and Siberia. As the glaciers of the last big ice age melted, the Pacific Ocean grew deeper and covered the land bridge, isolating North American lynx from those of Asia and Europe. European lynx are up to twice as large as their North American relatives and their faces are more brown. The long isolation of the two populations from one another has resulted in genetic drift, a process which concentrates different genetic characteristics in different populations. Four varieties of lynx now exist: the European lynx, which ranges throughout northern Europe and Asia; the endangered Spanish lynx of the Iberian Peninsula; the Canada lynx; and the bobcat. Some taxonomists consider each a separate species, but most believe the four

Lynx Facts

Size: 0.65-1 meters / 2-3 feet
Weight: 7-14 kilograms / 15-30 pounds
Description: Gray, short-tailed cat with large feet, long hind legs, tufted ears and a black-tipped tail
Reproduction: First breeds in second year of life
Gestation: 65 days
Litter size: 4-12 kittens; average 4
Life span: 10 years
Food: Snowshoe hare, other small animals
Distribution: Northern forests of Canada and Alaska, south at higher elevations in the mountains to Utah and Colorado

strains are closely related.

The name "lynx" comes from the Greek root *leuk,* which means "white" and may refer to the gray color of the animal. French fur traders adopted a Cree word for the same animal, *peshewa,* and named this gray shadow of the northern woods *le pichu.*

Lynx range across Canada wherever snowshoe hares live—mostly in the boreal forest. Few survive in the western mountains, where they were probably never as common and heavy trapping through the 1800s and early 1900s made them even more uncommon. Even today, with more enlightened trapping regulations and fewer trappers, lynx remain relatively rare in the southern fringe of the northern coniferous forests and in the aspen parkland: agriculture and other development have severely fragmented their habitat. In the northern U.S., they are scarce and patchily distributed, and may soon be listed as a threatened species.

Lots of hares can make for lots of lynx. During the cyclic peak of hares in 1991, the Mackenzie Bison Sanctuary recorded the highest density of lynx in western Canada: more than 300 per 1,000 km^2 (390 per 500 square miles). The following year, lynx numbers dropped by nine-tenths and young lynx from the area began turning up hundreds of kilometers away.

Most of the lynx that disperse are kittens or yearlings. Few survive; they are poor hunters, food is scarce and their wanderings take them into marginal habitat and unfamiliar terrain. Trappers find that during the first year after hare numbers crash, young lynx account for almost nine out of 10 of the lynx they trap. Researchers in one Yukon study lost all their study animals to trappers when the lynx left the study area during a decline in hare numbers.

These long-range dispersals only lead to a range expansion for lynx if some of the wanderers find good habitat with no trappers and with adequate numbers of hares or other small mammals. The aspen parkland of central Alberta, Saskatchewan and Manitoba contains some areas like this, but only a few patches of high-quality habitat exist in the Rocky Mountains.

Lynx Country

Lynx walk on snowshoes, just like their primary quarry, the aptly named snowshoe hare. Both predator and prey have feet that seem out of proportion to the rest of their bodies.

A lynx's tracks are nearly the same size as a cougar's even though a lynx weighs only a about a fifth as much as the larger cat. Bobcats weigh about the same as lynx, yet lynx feet mea-

Lynx or Bobcat?

Bobcat

Lynx

If it looks like a giant house cat with a short tail, it is probably a bobcat. If it looks like someone accidentally put size-large legs on a size-medium body, the odds are you are looking at a lynx.

Lynx are gray and have a prominent black tip on the end of their tails. Their hind ends seem higher than their front ends because of the long, powerful hind legs. Their paws are conspicuously large.

Bobcats are usually reddish-brown. Their tails, un-

like the tails of lynx, do not look like they have been dipped in ink. A bobcat tail has several narrow black rings and a black patch near the end which does not extend all the way around as on a lynx. A bobcat's legs seem to be the right length for its body. From the side, it resembles a common house cat—no jacked-up rear end here. Bobcat rear ends differ from lynx rear ends in one other way: a bobcat's tail is markedly longer than the stubby tail of a lynx.

The Lynx And The Hare

Snowshoe hare

The lynx lives on rabbits, follows the rabbits, thinks rabbits, tastes like rabbits, increases with them, and on their failure dies of starvation in the unrabbited woods.
- *Lives of Game Animals*,
Ernest Thompson Seton,
1926

The remarkable relationship between lynx and snowshoe hares can help lynx recolonize former territory. Lynx depend heavily on snowshoe hares for food. Every 10 years, the snowshoe hare population peaks and then crashes. In a peak year, it seems like hares are everywhere: the next year, they seem to have vanished utterly.

Abundant hares means well-fed lynx. Well-fed lynx breed prolifically and most of the kittens survive to maturity.

When the snowshoe hare population crashes, it forces hungry lynx to wander far afield. Hungry young lynx have dispersed more than 1,000 km (621 miles). Some turn up as far south as the Dakotas.

sure twice the size of bobcat feet. Lynx pad over landscapes of soft, deep snow where bobcats and cougars would sink, flounder and starve.

Forest fires help shape the boreal forests of Canada and Alaska. Without frequent fires, many species of northern animals would not exist. Snowshoe hares depend on the young forests that sprout soon after fires. Young pines and spruce have rich inner bark and grow much more densely than in older forests. Dense young thickets offer hares protection from cold and wind as well as from hawks and owls.

As forests mature, they become less and less desirable for hares and, consequently, for lynx.

Logging removes mature forests and replaces them with younger stands too. Unlike fire, however, logging rarely creates lynx habitat. Forest companies scarify the soils of many clearcuts, which encourages grass to grow more than shrubs. They also spray herbicides to hold back willow, poplar and other shrubs. Even when young stands of trees become well-established on logged areas, many forest companies return to thin them. "Just as it starts to get good," says lynx biologist Dr. John Weaver, "we go back in and thin it out and reduce its value to hares."

Muskeg covers much of the north. Most trees have difficulty living in these waterlogged lowlands, which have filled up gradually with sphagnum moss and sedges during the 10,000 years since the last great glaciers melted back. Dense growths of black spruce, a specialized tree which can grow in wet, acidic soils, often cover the driest parts of muskegs. Unlike the young forests which sprout after fire, these black spruce stands provide reliable, if less-productive, habitat year after year for snowshoe hares and the cat hunting them. They are core habitat for the few hares surviving after population crashes.

Both hares and lynx are scarce and patchily distributed in southern British Columbia and the mountain states of the western U.S. In the Rocky Mountains and other mountain ranges of the west, muskeg is rare and fires less frequent than in the north. Hares rely on coniferous forests at high elevations, and willow thickets and dense spruce forest along river floodplains. Although mountainous terrain produces a wide variety of habitats from grassland and pine forest to alpine tundra, snowshoe hares cannot survive in most of them.

Lynx Families

As the days lengthen toward the spring equinox and the sun begins to crystallize the aging snow, normally solitary lynx begin to look for mates. Finding a mate proves easy or difficult, depending, as with so much else in the existence of a lynx, on the abundance of snowshoe hares.

When hares are abundant, lynx have relatively small home ranges and the range of a male may overlap with those of several females. But in times of scarcity, fewer lynx range over bigger areas, making it harder for them to find one another.

Even when a male lynx finds a female during hungry times, they may not mate and, if they do, they may not produce kittens. Several research studies have found that, when food is abundant, more than 25 percent of all 10-month-old female lynx mate and produce kittens. But when hares are scarce, virtually none do. Adult females, hungry and undernourished, have smaller litters if they give birth at all and fewer of their kittens survive.

As a prelude to mating, the male lynx displays a form of behavior also seen in some deer: tasting or smelling the female's urine and then posing for a minute or two with its face contorted. As courtship progresses, the male chases and bumps against the female, bites and holds her by the nape of her neck, and eventually mounts her. They couple one to five or more times. The characteristic odors given off by the female in heat sometimes attract other males, which often fight one another fiercely.

Lynx do not form long-lasting attachments. Male and female resume their solitary lives shortly after mating and, about nine weeks later, the female gives birth to her kittens in a den beneath the upturned roots of a windblown tree, or inside a hollow log or under an overhanging bank. Researchers in the northwestern U.S. believe that female lynx may need old-growth forest both for denning and to hide their kittens while they hunt.

Kittens are blind and look faintly mottled at birth. If their mother can find enough food close to the birth den, three to five of them may grow to maturity. But when food is scarce, most kittens die early; mother lynx feed themselves first. Kittens usually remain with their mother for about 10 months and rely on her for food. When they strike out on their own, yearling lynx have little experience hunting. During hare-abundant years, yearlings usually get enough chances that dumb luck keeps them alive until they perfect their hunting skills. When food is scarce, inexperience often leads to starvation.

Yearling lynx, however, have one advantage over their parents. Their smaller bodies put no more pressure on snow than the hares they hunt. Large adult lynx may put twice the pressure and must use more energy to travel and hunt in winter.

Lynx as Hunters

Biologists have found evidence that lynx sometimes attack deer, caribou and even mountain goats. Like the much larger cougar, they stalk close, then suddenly charge from cover and pounce on the back of the startled animal, biting at its neck. Lynx risk death hunting such big prey. Park wardens in Yoho National Park in the the Canadian Rockies once pulled the bodies of a lynx and a mountain goat out of the debris of a large avalanche. The lynx had died of puncture wounds from the goat's horns and the goat had died in a snow slide triggered, perhaps, by the battle.

Even though big game seldom forms an important part of the lynx's diet, lynx occasionally become significant ungulate predators. In Newfoundland, for example, one researcher found that lynx had become so efficient at hunting caribou calves that they limited the growth of one herd.

Lynx have two primary techniques for hunting snowshoe hares, their preferred prey: they stalk them, often along the trampled hare trails that run through the deep winter snow of black spruce muskegs, willow thickets and young conifer forests, or they lie in wait beside the trails. Lynx watch and listen for the slightest trace of movement, testing the subtle breezes of the forest understory for the scent of their prey.

Once it spots a hare, the lynx crouches low, fixing its quarry in its slit-eyed gaze. It may stalk closer, or simply remain still and wait for the hare to move nearer. Then it leaps forward in a sudden, sprinting attack and reaches with its large forepaws to hook the fleeing hare with extended claws. If the hare is too slow or inattentive, the attack ends with the lynx pinning the hare and biting through its neck, severing its spine or crushing its windpipe.

Normally solitary except in mating season, lynx have more docile natures than bobcats.

Threats to Lynx

Lynx have luxurious, long-haired fur that makes attractive coats and trim. Since Europeans first invaded the North American interior, fur trappers have had a lot of interest in lynx.

But trappers who want lynx face a problem.

Lynx populations fluctuate dramatically every 10 years or so. When lynx are common, lynx saturates the fur market and prices stay low. When lynx are scarce, prices soar but trappers have little luck catching any. It is worth their while to try though. In the 1980s, during a cyclic low in

Boom and Bust

Explorer James Hector got his first taste of lynx meat during the winter of 1858-59 and reported that it was fatty but quite delicious, especially when mixed with the meat of bighorn sheep. Hector had lots of opportunity to enjoy the taste. His host, Walter Moberley, killed 88 lynx that winter in the vicinity of his wilderness trading post beside the Athabasca River in what is now Jasper National Park.

Ten years earlier, artist Paul Kane had encountered similarly large numbers of lynx near Fort Pitt. Eighteen years later, American zoologist J. Alden Loring followed Hector's trail into the Athabasca River country. He, too, found abundant lynx.

The reports of these early adventurers mirrored a pattern that the Hudson's Bay Company, which held a fur trade monopoly over much of the north, had already noted in its records of furs purchased from year to year. Lynx populations oscillate, gradually building to very high numbers every nine or 10 years and then crashing to very low levels.

During the last half century, the lynx population

has peaked in 1953, 1963, 1972, 1981 and 1991. We can expect the next peak around the year 2000, but the population may not top out as high as last time. Each of the last three population peaks for lynx has been lower than the one before, a trend that worries conservation biologists. It may indicate a long-term decline in the overall health of the lynx population.

Simple predator-prey systems such as the boreal forest's lynx-hare system show pronounced cycles of abundance and scarcity more often than complex systems. In the boreal forest, lynx have little else to hunt when snowshoe hares die back, and snowshoe hares have few other predators than lynx. Lynx cycles follow hare cycles, which fluctuate mostly with food supply. Lynx numbers in the Mackenzie Game Sanctuary crashed 90 percent in one year, following a decline in hare densities from seven to nine per hectare in 1990 (3 to 3.5 per acre) to less than one per hectare (0.4 per acre) in 1991.

Lynx are gray and less spotted than bobcats.

Lynx have pronounced black ear tufts.

lynx numbers, some northern trappers got more than $1,000 for each lynx pelt.

Supply and demand makes trapping pressure greatest when lynx numbers are lowest—when lynx populations can least afford the added mortality.

"The heavy trapping pressure that resulted from the high fur prices of the late 1970s and early 1980s," says Dr. John Weaver of the University of Montana, "even though state wildlife agencies made useful regulation changes and lowered quotas, appear to have taken lynx down to extremely low levels in most of the northwestern U.S., to the point where they are having trouble recovering."

Partly because of this economic imbalance, the number and distribution of lynx all across North America declined through the first half of the twentieth century. During the last few decades, most provinces, territories and states have classified the lynx as a fur-bearing animal and some wildlife agencies regulate the trapping kill through quotas that they adjust as the population swings. Even so, recent research in the Mackenzie Bison Sanctuary and other northern areas has clearly demonstrated that lynx need safe havens from trapping when their population bottoms out.

Many trappers recognize the importance of protecting breeding stock during low ebbs in the lynx cycle and voluntarily abstain from trapping in parts of their territories. Over the past century, governments have established some sanctuaries, places such as the Mackenzie Bison Sanctuary, where they either do not permit trapping or strictly regulate it. Fur farmers have begun raising lynx in captivity, further reducing trapping pressure on wild lynx populations.

Habitat loss poses a more subtle, but severe, problem for wild lynx. Young lynx disperse widely during peak lynx years, taking advantage of an opportunity to repopulate suitable habitat. But fire control, peat moss mining and the draining of wetlands for agriculture have reduced the available habitat.

Lynx Food

Between 1961 and 1963, when the lynx population swelled across Canada, C.G. Van Zyll de Jong, a graduate student at the University of Alberta, had the rare opportunity to examine the stomach contents of dozens of lynx. Based on his autopsies, he determined the relative importance of different prey species to lynx. Van Zyll de Jong went on to become one of Canada's leading taxonomists. Lynx eat far more hares than any other prey species, especially in winter. They eat other small mammals too, most often in summer. In winter, ground squirrels hibernate and voles live beneath the snow. But even in summer, hares top the list. Their larger size means they contribute more to the total volume of lynx food than other species.

Prey Item	Percentage of lynxes' stomachs	
	Winter-killed	Summer-killed
Snowshoe hare	79%	52%
Meadow vole	10	22
Red-backed vole	—	9
Red squirrel	2	9
Ground squirrels	—	8
Beaver	2	—
Deer	6	—
Grouse	10	4
Other birds	13	17

Oversized paws and hind legs adapt lynx for travel in deep-snow country.

The Year Lynx Invaded Calgary

I spent much of my tenth year of life searching for wildcats in the coulees and river bottoms around Calgary. The newspapers were full of stories about the great lynx invasion of 1963 and I was determined to catch sight of one.

The first lynx arrived in Calgary late in the winter. Wildlife officers caught it that spring. By late November, they had netted or live-snared more than 50 wildcats.

They returned some of the wandering lynx to the wild, killed others and shipped several to zoos.

Lynx invaded many prairie cities that year. They turned up in Minneapolis, St. Paul, Winnipeg and Edmonton. Most of the cats were only a year or two old. Males outnumbered females two to one. Most reports described them as fearless.

Wildlife biologists never clearly established the cause of the mass southward dispersal. It probably resulted from an abundant population of lynx coping with a cyclic crash in snowshoe hares. But one researcher noted that northern Alberta still had lots of hares when lynx first started to arrive in the southern prairies.

Whatever the cause, the 1963 population eruption was one of the most dramatic in recent decades. I saw three different lynx that year and have spotted only two of the ghostlike creatures in all the years since.

In the long run, global warming presents an even greater threat to this northern predator. The earth's temperature will rise over the next century, primarily because of excess carbon dioxide in the atmosphere from people burning fossil fuels such as gasoline and coal. Scientists project that forest fires will increase as the earth warms—good news for lynx. But if winter snow cover decreases, the hunting success of lynx may also drop and the smaller bobcat, which some biologists believe outcompetes its larger relative, will extend its range north into areas that were previously the exclusive domain of lynx.

Are Lynx Endangered?

The U.S. government has listed lynx in the Rocky Mountain states as a threatened species. In fact, the lynx has been extirpated in the southern parts of its range, and Colorado biologists have recently reintroduced them in the southern San Juan Mountains. The problem they faced, not surprisingly, involved snowshoe hares.

The mountains of the northwestern United States and southern Canada contain tracts of spruce and pine forest, just as northern Canada does. The mountains also have a lot of countryside where snow accumulates deeply in winter, again like the north. But the resemblance between northern forests and Rocky Mountains ends there.

The Rockies and other mountain ranges to the west contain large areas where little snow accumulates in winter. Because the snow remains shallow here, predators such as cougars, coyotes and bobcats thrive; mountains have more kinds of predators than northern forests. Mountains also have many more kinds of prey since the variety of slope, drainage and elevation in the mountains create many types of habitat.

Snowshoe hares concentrate in only the small part of the landscape (10 per cent or less) that has high-quality habitat, just as they do in Canada's northern forests during periods of low population. Unlike in the north, however, when young hares disperse into other habitats they find themselves in very unfamiliar vegetation and surrounded by several kinds of predators only too ready to eat them. As a result, hare populations in the mountains rarely grow or expand like they do in the northern forests.

Lynx, like the snowshoe hares they hunt, also concentrate in the small patches of high-quality hare habitat. This keeps lynx populations in the mountainous west in a perpetual low ebb. Kitten survival is poor, population densities are low and mortality is high. Ecologically, these lynx populations cut it close, even under ideal conditions.

Add logging, roads, trapping, dams and a host of other land-use changes and the future begins to look grim for the already vulnerable lynx. Thirteen U.S. environmental groups sued the U.S. Fish and Wildlife Service early in 1996

The Cat That Looks Like A Rabbit

Snowshoe hare: big ears, whiskers and feet.

Lynx: big ears, whiskers and feet.

"You are what you eat," seems to be a particularly apt adage in describing the bizarre degree to which lynx have evolved adaptations that resemble those of their main food source, the snowshoe hare. Both lynx and hare have large, splayed feet that function like snowshoes. In fact, when compared for weight and paw size, lynx tread with little more pressure than the much smaller hares and sink about the same depth in snow. Lynx and snowshoe hares both have very long hind legs that help them to bound—in the one case to pursue and in the other to escape. Both have enlarged ears and rely heavily on sensitive hearing to detect one another. Both have exceptional night vision and sensitive facial whiskers.

Snowshoe hares, however, can breed far more prolifically than lynx, which only makes ecological sense . And snowshoe hares turn dark brown in summer, when they need to blend into forest shadows, and white in winter, when they need to disappear against the snow. Lynx, by contrast, turn only slightly more brown in summer and a shade grayer in winter.

Lynx are threatened by habitat loss in the U.S. Rocky Mountains.

for failing to list the lynx as an endangered species in the American northwest. Conservation groups had first petitioned in 1991 to have the lynx protected under the Endangered Species Act, but the Fish and Wildlife Service repeatedly deferred a decision, pleading the need for more information and money.

Dr. John Weaver, a specialist in the conservation of carnivores, feels that lynx are not endangered in the Great Lake states where, though rare, they only occur as dispersers from northern populations. He says, however: "It's my strong opinion that the number of resident lynx in the northern Rockies and Pacific Northwest has declined since the late 1970s and that lynx should receive some degree of listing in this area."

Mitch Friedman, executive director of the Northwest Ecosytem Alliance, warned in 1996: "If this species is not listed and policies are not changed, I think we're going to see the extirpation of the lynx in Washington and Montana

No More Secrets

Biologist John Weaver has found a new way to count lynx without ever laying eyes on one. He takes advantage of their cattish compulsion to rub their faces on objects like branches or stones.

The idea, according to Dr. Weaver, came to him one day while walking with his captive lynx, Chirp. Watching her rubbing her cheeks on things, he came up with the idea of designing a rubbing post that would snag facial hair from lynx that paused to rub. If the sample contained enough hair follicles, lab technicians should be able to come up with a unique DNA "fingerprint" for each lynx. DNA analysis has become increasingly accurate and inexpensive in recent years, making it useful for criminal investigators and biologists alike.

Dr. Weaver rigged up a simple hair trap by studding a piece of carpet with sharp tacks. He sprayed cat odor on the hair trap and evaluated the response of captive lynx and bobcats. They loved it. Scientists in a New York lab used the resulting hair samples to develop a DNA technique for telling one cat from another.

When the lynx researcher took his low-tech hair snagger out into the woods of northern Montana, it worked. In the first season he gathered 28 hair samples from twenty scent stations. "All results to date," reports Dr. Weaver, "indicate that this . . . will provide a new technique for gaining crucial information on these elusive cats."

and Idaho."

With the 1999 listing of the lynx, federal agencies must ensure that logging, road building, winter snowmobile traffic and other uses of forested habitats do not increase the danger of extinction for this rare cat. Fortunately, since most lynx habitat is at high elevations, most lynx habitat is federal public land. Every surviving acre of mountainous habitat is critical if Americans hope to see Friedman's dire prediction proven wrong.

Lynx Returns Home To Colorado

Lynx were probably never common in the Colorado Rockies; their habitat—high elevation conifer forest with good snowshoe hare populations—is not abundant in the Centennial State. Trappers had little difficulty mining the few good pockets of lynx habitat. Surviving lynx from other areas—faced with intervening patches of unfriendly terrain—could not easily find their way to the emptied forests. Trappers turned in only 14 lynx in the half-century leading up to 1935—and none at all during the following three decades. The Division of Wildlife closed the trapping season for lynx in 1971.

Even so, a trapper illegally killed the state's last known lynx in 1973 at the Vail ski resort. Belatedly, Colorado declared the lynx endangered in 1976.

From the late 1960s on, lynx habitat became even rarer. Real estate developers chopped it up for ski hills and mountain resorts. Some of Colorado's last and best lynx habitat became the site of a controversial ski resort expansion at Vail in the late 1990s. Despite strong opposition by Division of Wildlife biologists to the destruction of high quality lynx habitat—and in spite of a $6 million fire which extremists set to protest the deal—U.S. Forest Service officials permitted the expansion.

After 20 years of futile searches for lynx, state biologists concluded in 1998, "If any lynx remain in Colorado, their numbers are so small they do not represent a viable population . . . It is quite possible that lynx have been extirpated from Colorado." The Colorado Wildlife Commission decided, in November 1998, to return lynx to the state. The commissioners reasoned that only by releasing radio-collared lynx and closely monitoring them could biologists ever know whether viable lynx habitat survives in the state. Colorado voters, after all, had improved the odds of lynx recovery when they passed a 1996 ballot initiative restricting poisons and leghold traps. With those threats removed, the future recovery of lynx became a possibility.

The first four lynx arrived in Colorado from British Columbia within weeks of the commission's decision. Released in early 1999, into the San Juan National Forest's Weminuche Wilderness, three of the animals soon died of starvation. Biologists recaptured the fourth to prevent her suffering the same fate.

Based on the initial failure, biologists in charge of the reintroduction program changed their approach. As more lynx arrived from Yukon, Alaska and B.C., biologists kept them in captivity longer to fatten them on pen-reared rabbits until spring. They reasoned that this would not only start the lynx out in better condition, but promise them better hunting as ground squirrels emerge from hibernation in March and April.

Critics of the re-introduction campaign included some ranchers who feared that a new predator in the woods may result in more dead sheep, directly due to lynx, or because of increased coyote predation if hare numbers decline. Some wildlife groups worried that the imported lynx might live short, miserable lives before dying of starvation or falling prey to other predators.

John Seidel, Colorado's predatory animal specialist in charge of the reintroduction, thinks the effort may well succeed. He feels that lynx food—hares, beaver, porcupines, and squirrels—is abundant and that the big-footed cats' taste for deep snow will keep them separated from coyotes, bobcats, cougars, and importantly, domestic livestock.

In a 1999 statement, Seidel said, "There is a chance that the U.S. Fish and Wildlife Service will list the lynx as a threatened or endangered species later this year. If they do, then there are more than a dozen other states that will be considering reintroduction efforts as part of their recovery strategies. We're learning a great deal from this reintroduction, information that will make it easier for us and other states."

Afterword

Willows can live without deer. Deer can live without cougars. Cougars, however, can't live without deer, willows, wild spaces and human tolerance. A cougar or wolf is persuasive proof that entire ecosystems, including the people who use them, are still healthy.

Wild hunters live at the top of the food pyramid. They range widely across the landscape. If a landscape still has predators, then it must certainly still have all the animals they eat, all the plants those animals eat, and all the habitats and connections that all those plants and animals require. Some ecologists call predators "umbrella species" because ecologically, they represent so much more than just themselves.

Humans have often taken pride in their ability to master nature—eradicating predators is only one of many ways we prove that ability. Where large predators survive and thrive in our shared western landscape, it proves that we can master something more challenging: our own fears and prejudices. When we choose to make room for predators we demonstrate our ability to accept the right of all species to exist simply because they, like us, are among the astonishing products of Creation.

Unlike other animals, we humans can rearrange or destroy whole ecosystems. We've been doing that, one way or another, for decades. But we also have other unique and important attributes that make us different from other animals: we can reason, imagine the future and make moral choices.

What if we imagined a future in which we allow wolves, cougars, bobcats, foxes and other wild hunters to reclaim much of North America, to return to places from which our historical choices displaced them? What if we made the kinds of choices that led to such a future?

We know that we can eradicate predators if we really want to. But the fact that we choose not to is a hopeful sign that we may be capable yet of becoming full citizens of North America's ecosystems, able to live here with humility, wisdom and restraint—not arrogance, fear and self-centredness.

We can learn to belong to the natural world, rather than to expropriate it. We can rediscover ourselves as "Creation made conscious" in the words of theologian Thomas Berry, rather than as rulers of Creation free to destroy anything we don't understand. All we need is to use the intelligence, reason, imagination and moral judgment that make humans unique among animals. And one measure of our success will be the fate of predators and other animals we sometimes find it hard to live with.

At the turn of the century—a shocking time for earth's living ecosystems—hope is something we all need. The return of wild hunters to the landscapes we now occupy may be one of the most compelling signs of hope for a future in which we finally become full citizens of the living West.

Reference

Conservation Organizations

Organizations Buying or Protecting Critical Habitat

The Nature Conservancy of Canada
794A Broadview Avenue
Toronto, Ontario M4K 2P7
Canada

Vital Ground Foundation
(focus on grizzly bear habitat)
Box 447
Heber Valley, Utah 84032-0447
USA

The Nature Conservancy (U.S.)
1815 - North Lynn Street
Arlington, Virginia 22209
USA

The Predator Project
Box 6733
Bozeman, Montana 59771
USA

National Organizations Promoting Wilderness or Habitat Conservation

Canadian Parks and Wilderness Society
1019 - 4th Ave. SW
Calgary, Alberta T2P 0K8
Canada

World Wildlife Fund Canada
90 Eglinton Avenue East, Suite 504
Toronto, Ontario M4P 2Z7
Canada

Canadian Nature Federation
Suite 520, 1 Nicholas Street
Ottawa, Ontario K1N 7B7
Canada

Canadian Wildlife Federation
2740 Queensview Drive
Ottawa, Ontario K2B 1A2
Canada

National Parks and Conservation Association
1776 Massachusetts Avenue, N.W.
Washington, D.C. 22036
USA

National Audubon Society
700 Broadway
New York, New York 10003
USA

The Wildlands Project
1955 W. Grant Road #148-W
Tucson, Arizona 85745
USA

Sierra Club of Canada
412-1 Nicholas St.
Ottawa, Ontario K1N 7B7
Canada

Sierra Club
85 Second St., Second Floor
San Francisco, California 94105-3441
USA

Regional Organizations Promoting Wilderness or Habitat Conservation

Alberta Wilderness Association
Box 6398, Station D
Calgary, Alberta T2N 1Y9
Canada

Sierra Club of Western Canada
314 - 620 View Street
Victoria, British Columbia V8W 1J6
Canada

The Valhalla Wilderness Society
Box 329
New Denver, British Columbia V0G 1S0
Canada
vws@web.apc.org

Western Canada Wilderness Association
20 - Water Street
Vancouver, British Columbia V6B 1A4
Canada

Alliance for the Wild Rockies
PO Box 8731
Missoula, Montana 59807

Southern Rockies Ecosystem Project
Box 1182
Nederland, Colorado 80466
USA

Yellowstone to Yukon Conservation Initiative
710 - 9th Street, Studio B
Canmore, Alberta T1W 2V7
Canada

Organizations Promoting the Protection or Welfare of Wildlife

Defenders of Wildlife
1534 - Mansfield Avenue
Missoula, Montana 59801
USA

Northwest Wildlife Preservation Society
Box 43129, Station D
Vancouver, British Columbia V6J 4N3
Canada

The Humane Society of Canada
347 Bay Street, Suite 806
Toronto, Ontario M5H 2R7
Canada

The Mountain Lion Foundation
Box 1896
Sacramento, California 95812
USA

Organizations Raising Funds to Compensate Ranchers for Losses to Predators

Defenders of Wildlife
(Wolf; northern U.S. Rockies)
1534-Mansfield Avenue
Missoula, Montana 59801
USA

Glacier Institute
Box 1457
Kalispell, Montana 59903
USA

The Jasper Institute
Parks and People, Jasper
Box 100
Jasper, Alberta T0E 1E0
Canada

McCrory Wildlife Services
Box 146
New Denver, British Columbia V0G 1S0
Canada

Waterton Natural History Association
Box 145
Waterton Park, Alberta T0K 2M0
Canada

Wolf Awareness International
G-2 Farms, RR #3
Ailsa Craig, Ontario N0M 1A0
Canada

The Yellowstone Institute
Field Courses and Nature Study Vacations
Box 117
Yellowstone National Park, Wyoming 82190
USA

Calendar of Programs

Twice a year, the bi-weekly Colorado-based *High Country News*—"A paper for people who care about the West"—publishes special issues listing conservation education and outdoor programs available across the Rocky Mountain West. More information: www.hcn.org/

Government Addresses

Alberta Minister of Environmental Protection
Legislature Building,
Edmonton, Alberta T5K 2B6
Canada

British Columbia Minister of Environment
Parliament Buildings
Victoria, British Columbia V8V 1X5
Canada

Saskatchewan Minister of Environment and
Resource Management
Government of Saskatchewan
3211 - Albert Street
Regina, Saskatchewan S4S 5W6
Canada

Manitoba Minister of Natural Resources
Legislative Building
Winnipeg, Manitoba R3C 0V8
Canada

Yukon Minister of Renewable Resources
Government of Yukon Territory
Box 2703
Whitehorse, Yukon Y1A 2C6
Canada

Prime Minister of Canada
Ottawa, Ontario K1A 0H3
Canada

Alaska Department of Fish and Game
Box 25526
Juneau, Alaska 99802-5526
USA

Arizona Game & Fish Department
2221 W. Greenway Rd.
Phoenix, Arizona 85023-4399
USA

Colorado Division of Wildlife
6060 Broadway
Denver, Colorado 80216
USA

Idaho Department of Fish and Game
Box 25
Boise, Idaho 83707
USA

Montana Fish, Wildlife and Parks
1420-E. 6th Avenue
Helena, Montana 59620
USA

Nevada Division of Wildlife
1100 Valley View Road
Reno, Nevada 89512
USA

New Mexico Department of Game and Fish
PO Box 25112
Santa Fe, New Mexico 87504
USA

Oregon Department of Fish and Wildlife
Box 59
Portland, Oregon 97207
USA

Wyoming Game & Fish Dept.
5400 Bishop Blvd.
Cheyenne, Wyoming 82006
USA

Utah Division of Wildlife
1596 W. North Temple
Salt Lake City, Utah 84116
USA

Zippy way to say it

Want to let your elected representatives know your views about predator conservation and management, but you don't know how to find them? Just visit www.voxpop.org/zipper/ on the World Wide Web. This website prompts you to enter your zip code and then tells you the email and surface mail address of your congress person or senator.

Internet Sites

National and Provincial Parks

U.S. National Parks:
http://www.gorp.com/gorp/resource/US_National_Park/main.htm

British Columbia:
http://www.env.gov.bc.ca/

Canadian National Parks:
http://www.worldweb.com/ParksCanada_Banff/parks.html

Yukon:
http://parallel.ca/yukon/YUKON-03.HTM

Eco-tourism

http://www.gorp.com/gorp/activity/wildlife.htm

Government Agencies

U.S. Fish and Wildlife Service:
www.fws.gov/index.html/

U.S.D.A. Animal Damage Control:
aphisweb.aphis.usda.gov

U.S. Forest Service:
www.fs.fed.us/
Canadian Wildlife Service
www.ec.gc.ca/cws-scf/

Predator Control

http://151.121.3.135/adc/adchome.html

Predator Research

Wolves:
http://www.nncc.scs.unr.edu/wolves/desertm.html

Canada:
http://www.rr.ualberta.ca/~lmorgant/

General:
http://www.york.biosis.org/zrdocs/zoolinfo/wildlife.htm

Selected Readings

Dekker, D. 1985. *Wild Hunters.* Edmonton, Alberta: Canadian Wolf Defenders. ISBN 0-919091-16-4.

Fischer, H. 1995. *Wolf Wars.* Helena and Billings, Montana: Falcon Press Publishing. ISBN 1-56044-352-9.

Gadd, B. 1995. *Handbook of the Canadian Rockies.* Jasper, Alberta: Corax Press. ISBN 0-9692631-1-2.

Hansen, K. 1993. *Cougar: The American Lion.* Portland, Oregon: Northland Publishing. ISBN 0-87358-544-5.

Henry, J.D. 1986. *Red Fox: The Catlike Canine.* Washington D.C.: Smithsonian Institution Press. ISBN 0-87474-520-9.

Hummel, M. and S. Pettigrew. 1991. *Wild Hunters: Predators in Peril.* Toronto: Key Porter Books. ISBN 1-55013-362-4.

Leopold, A. 1949. *A Sand County Almanac.* Toronto: Random House of Canada. ISBN 0-345-34505-3.

Scotter, G.W. and T.J. Ulrich. 1995. *Mammals of the Canadian Rockies.* Saskatoon, Saskatchewan: Fifth House Publishers. ISBN 1-896618-55-X.

Index

About the Author

Kevin Van Tighem's western roots run deep; his family has lived in Alberta since 1883. Graduating with a BSc in plant ecology from the University of Calgary, Van Tighem has studied wildlife in various western national parks and protected areas. He has written more than 200 articles, stories and essays on conservation and wildlife.

His work has garnered many awards, including the Western Magazine Award, the Outdoor Writers of Canada Award and the Journey Award for Fiction. Van Tighem has served on the executive committe of the Alberta Naturalists, and has organized two major conferences to promote conservation of rivers and river valleys.

Currently, Van Tighem works as a biologist in Waterton Lakes National Park, where he lives with his wife, Gail, and their three children.

Author's Note

While many of the photographic images presented in this book are of wild animals living free, some difficult-to-find species or behaviors were photographed under controlled conditions.

Photography Credits

In the following list, photographers are indicated by page number. When there are two or more photographs on a page, the top or left image is indicated as "a" and the bottom or right photograph is referenced as "b," etc.

Lu Carbyn: 97

Rolf Kopfle: 12, 38

Jim Osterberg: Front Cover, Back Cover, Frontice, 8-9, 36-37, 39, 45, 48-49, 52, 62-63, 68, 91, 102-103, 104, 108, 116-117, 122

Terry Parker: 46, 47, 54, 70, 79, 128, 140

Dennis Schmidt: 10-11,15, 17, 18a, 18b, 19, 23, 24a, 24b, 25a, 26, 28, 29, 30, 32, 34, 35, 42, 43, 44, 50, 55, 59, 60, 65, 74a, 74b, 74c, 76a, 77, 81, 84, 85, 90, 101, 106, 107, 110, 111a, 112, 114a, 114b, 114c, 119, 123, 127, 129, 130a, 131, 132, 137, 139, 141, 142b, 143, 145, 146a, 146b, 147, 149a, 149b, 150, 152

Esther Schmidt: Back Cover inset, 13, 16, 21, 25b, 40, 41, 51, 56, 67, 71, 72-73, 76b, 80, 82, 83, 86, 87, 88-89, 93a, 93b, 94, 96, 99, 105, 109, 111b, 113, 115, 118, 125, 130b, 133, 134-135, 142a, 148

Courtesy of Kevin Van Tighem: 57, 69, 120, 124, 138, 160

Quilts of Valor

A 50 STATE SALUTE

QUILTS *of* VALOR®
FOUNDATION

CONTRIBUTING AUTHORS:
Ann Parsons Holte

Renelda Peldunas-Harter

Ann Rehbein

Sue Reich

★

Foreword by
Marianne Fons

4880 Lower Valley Road · Atglen, PA 19310

Type set in Desire/Times New Roman/NewsGoth
ISBN: 978-0-7643-5630-8

Printed in the United States of America

Published by Schiffer Publishing, Ltd.
4880 Lower Valley Road
Atglen, PA 19310
Phone: (610) 593-1777; Fax: (610) 593-2002
E-mail: Info@schifferbooks.com
Web: www.schifferbooks.com

For our complete selection of fine books on this and related subjects, please visit our website at www.schifferbooks.com. You may also write for a free catalog.

Schiffer Publishing's titles are available at special discounts for bulk purchases for sales promotions or premiums. Special editions, including personalized covers, corporate imprints, and excerpts, can be created in large quantities for special needs. For more information, contact the publisher.

We are always looking for people to write books on new and related subjects. If you have an idea for a book, please contact us at proposals@schifferbooks.com.

Other Schiffer Books by the Authors:

Making the Lancaster Diamond Sampler:
A 19th Century Quilt Design by Fanny's Friend,
Ann Parsons Holte, ISBN 978-0-7643-4549-4

From Ensign's Bars to Colonel's Stars:
Making Quilts to Honor Those Who Serve,
Renelda Peldunas-Harter, ISBN 978-0-7643-4719-1

World War I Quilts, Sue Reich, ISBN 978-0-7643-4754-2

Other Schiffer Books on Related Subjects:

World War II Quilts, 2nd Edition, Sue Reich,
ISBN 978-0-7643-5334-5

Civil War Quilts, Pam Weeks & Don Beld,
ISBN 978-0-7643-3936-3

The Last Veterans of World War II: Portraits and Memories, Richard Bell, ISBN 978-0-7643-5362-8

Dedicated to

The men and women of the Armed Services who selflessly serve our nation.

The thousands of Quilts of Valor volunteers who honor our nation's service members.

Catherine Roberts, founder of the Quilts of Valor Foundation.

"It Started with One Quilt."

CONTENTS

Foreword

National service, at one time a common household activity, thrives—day in, day out—in the lives of thousands of quilters all across America. Alone at their sewing machines, or in groups that meet in quilt shops, libraries, bank community rooms, and church fellowship halls, these unpaid volunteers cut out and stitch patchwork blocks by the thousands. They join the blocks into rows, and the rows into completed quilt tops. The tops become quilts thanks to volunteer machine quilters nationwide. The quilts these women (and some men) make, Quilts of Valor, may be awarded privately in recipients' homes, or in more-public places, with family, friends, and a larger community looking on. Regardless, a Quilt of Valor says unequivocally to the awardee, "Thank you for your service, your sacrifice, and your valor. Thank you for putting your life on hold to protect and defend me."

Like Quilts of Valor Foundation founder Catherine Roberts, I came of age in the 1960s—during an unpopular war. My college classes were often interrupted by campus protests. In those days, no one spoke of national service. In the conflict's aftermath, an insensitive public often blamed the veterans themselves.

Until I awarded my first Quilt of Valor, I had never given a quilt to a stranger; when I did, I found my own heart healed, and have repeated the act frequently. Catherine Roberts's gift to me has been a clear path for rediscovering my own personal patriotism, in the company of people who know what I know—that nothing expresses love like a quilt. Now that our Quilts of Valor Foundation's mission has broadened to include not just combat veterans but all service members touched by war, we have set ourselves an impossible task—one we bravely embrace with our time, our skills, and our hearts.

National service can be as complicated as giving your life for your country, or as simple as making a quilt and giving it away. I hope this book will inspire you to join our ranks!

Marianne Fons awarded Shannon Shepard with a Quilt of Valor in May 2014,
at the commemoration of the awarding of the 100,000th Quilt of Valor. The commemoration took place
in the USO Warrior and Family Center located at Naval Support Activity Bethesda,
home of Walter Reed National Military Center, in Bethesda, Maryland.

ACKNOWLEDGMENTS

To all of the QOVF state coordinators for providing a quilt
from each of our great states.

To Jeff Thorne, QOVF Marketing and Public Relations Director, and
Doris Long—your combined photography captured the soul of QOVF.

To Carolyn Goins and Barbara Garrett for their assistance
in photographing the quilts.

To Schiffer Publishing, Ltd., for welcoming Quilts of Valor Foundation
into the Schiffer publishing family.

To Saundra Chambers, QOVF Under Our Wings Coordinator, for her
contribution to the Under the Wings patterns, and to Phyllis Schoenholz
for her assistance.

Quilt of Valor award ceremony in Colorado Springs, Colorado, June 2017.

Quiltmaking in Times of War

"Needle in Hand to Vanquish Those Foes"[1]

Quilts of Valor Foundation is carrying on the age-old tradition of comforting service members with quilts. During the Revolutionary War, charged with the responsibility of providing for our troops, the women of the colonies sent their household quilts directly to the battle front. In 1890, from the pulpit of the First Congregational Church, Goshen, Connecticut, the Reverend A. C. Thompson recounted his grandmother replenishing supplies for local soldiers during the harsh warring winter of 1777–1778. Responding to a call for more provisions, Ruth Benton Thompson quickly gathered up "all the blankets, quilts & bedspreads in the house."[2] She was remembered to have said, "We can make ourselves comfortable with wearing apparel till we make a new supply of bedding."[3] The sufferings of Revolutionary War soldiers at Valley Forge and throughout the war are well documented. Consequently, few quilts from this era have survived to the twenty-first century. After the war,

General Washington recognized Ruth's state of Connecticut as a great supplier of necessities to the Revolutionary War militia, dubbing it "the Provisions State."

The War of 1812 (1812–15) and the Mexican War (1846–48) were our country's next big military conflicts. The War of 1812 was fought primarily in coastal communities of the Atlantic, the Gulf, and the Canadian frontier. Commerce and trade by sea were greatly affected by the blockades of goods, including textiles destined for the new nation. The Mexican War was fought primarily in the American South. Precious few quilts survive from the early nineteenth century. Period quilts tended to be simply pieced, appliquéd, or framed with center medallions made with imported textiles. Quilts with a direct connection to these two wars have yet to be discovered. The same cannot be said for quiltmaking during the Civil War (1861–65).

"Mending the Old Flag" illustrated in *Farm Ballads* by Will Carleton, page 157 (New York: Harper & Brothers, 1873).

'Twas made for brave boys,

who went from the West;

And swiftly the fair fingers flew,

While each stitch,

as it went to its place in the quilt,

Was a smothered "God bless you, boys," too.[4]

Two days after Fort Sumter was fired upon, President Abraham Lincoln called up 75,000 volunteer soldiers from the North. This began the "War between States," known as the Civil War. As in Revolutionary War times, towns and villages on both sides were charged with providing their soldiers with supplies. Local ladies' aid societies and sewing circles, most with church affiliations, leapt into action sewing uniforms, shelters, and bedding. The provisions they produced were sent directly to their local soldiers on the battlefront or to the Sanitary Commission for further distribution.

TOP Detail of the Mary Silliman Chapter DAR Founders' Quilt.
This quilt was embroidered by the members of the Mary Silliman Chapter from Bridgeport, Connecticut.
The squares of cream-colored satin were inscribed, displaying their lineage to their Revolutionary War soldier relative.
In the collection of the Daughters of the American Revolution Museum.

BOTTOM Wholecloth, ca. pre-1800, made by Ruth Benton Thompson (1742–1813), Goshen, Connecticut. Glazed wool.
Owned by the Henry Whitfield State Museum, Guilford, Connecticut.

Civil War quilt, ca. 1890, made by Sarah Bright Anderson Lea,
wife of Benjamin Franklin Lea of the Fineview section of Allegheny City. Benjamin served in the
Union Army between 1863 and 1865 as a guard and later as a cook at Camp Reynolds in Pittsburgh.
He was active in the Grand Army of the Republic through the 1890s.

Sarah incorporated many significant wartime images into her quilt: an encampment,
regimental patches, the *Monitor* and *Merrimack*, the Patriot Shield, eagles, Lady Liberty, presidents,
war heroes, and much more. *Courtesy of Mark May Photography, Bridgeville, Pennsylvania,
and the Sewickley Valley Historical Society, Sewickley, Pennsylvania.*

The *Springfield Republican* (published in Springfield, Massachusetts) printed this article, "A Word for the Sanitary Commission," by P. Thorne. It accurately presented the effort on the home front to supply local soldiers fighting in the War between States.

Soldiers' aid societies were inaugurated, and the women of the Union wheeled into the ranks, needle in hand, to vanquish those foes more fatal to our soldiers than rebel hosts; diseases, want and suffering. Shirts, socks, wrappers, bed-quilts, lint, bandages, wines, jellies, pickles, have been rained down upon these foes in quantities, rivaling those of iron powder, and lead fired into the much-enduring confederacy. More healing, more sanitary than the stores themselves, is the home air they bring to the soldier. Sick and away from home—what expression more dreary to those who know its meaning? To the soldier, sick and wounded, but only one of many, surrounded by sense of discomfort and wretchedness, suffering most of all from all worst sickness, home-sickness, come these gifts, saying, "Your sufferings are not forgotten. There are those still who care for you. We come to you from homes of the North, the work of those who appreciate what you have done and borne for them, and would gladly comfort you."[5]

Today, those historic Civil War quilts are referred to as Sanitary Commission quilts. They were packed in barrels along with apples, pickles, bandages, sewing kits, and other supplies and sent to hospitals and forward positions on battlefronts. Benevolent organizations could be found both in the North and the South. "It is estimated that more than 20,000 soldiers' aid societies were formed in the entire country, with two-thirds of them in the North."[6]

Children also participated in quiltmaking during the war. A young lady from Manchester, Connecticut, was most diligent in her efforts to provide comforts for soldiers. Her quilts were also referred to as Album quilts.

Grace L. Bissell commenced in October to go among the little girls and boys soliciting blocks for soldiers' bedquilts, with the name of the child contributing each inscribed thereon. On the 17th of Nov. she came to our rooms with her first one, and presented it as her birthday offering to the soldiers (only nine years old). Accompanying the quilt was a letter to the soldier which she requests him to write her, not alone that she may know who is made comfortable thereby, but also that she "may remember him in her little prayer that God would shield him in the hour of battle. And if he had a little girl she would pray for her too, as she had no Papa at home to care for her now." In little more than two months she has collected the six quilts which the ladies of the League have quilted and forwarded to the Commission. She has traveled many miles in leaving patterns, collecting blocks for each quilt, and yet her patriotic little heart and willing hands and feet tire not, and she is as earnest and enthusiastic in the work as at the commencement.[7]

Civil War newspapers from across the South record thousands of quilts sent to relief and hospital associations. In October 1862, the *Savannah Republican*, published in Georgia, printed the following articles, titled "Covering for the Soldiers—a Lady's Suggestion":

This sampler quilt was made to raise monies for the Sanitary Commission during the Civil War.
Dated July 1864, Tarrytown, New York. Cotton. *In the collection of the Tarrytown Historical Society.*

We take great pleasure in giving publicity to the following proposition from a patriotic, whole-souled woman of Georgia. Let those to whom it is more especially addressed respond to the call.

Waresboro, Ga. Oct. 8, 1862.

Mr. Editor: You who have appealed so eloquently in behalf of our noble defenders, will not refuse us sufficient space to put in a petition for them.

Our tailors, and contractors for clothing for the Army, must have many small scraps—remnants of cloth which are useless to them—which might be made into comforts for our soldiers in Virginia. A little labor might accomplish much good; if only a few were benefited, it will be a pleasing reflection that we have "done what we could." A single quilt, comfort or blanket, from each woman in the Confederacy would furnish our Army and hospitals.[8]

It was estimated more than 250,000 quilts were sent from the North to the battlefronts of the Civil War. Ohio quilt historian Virginia Gunn wrote in her paper "Quilts for Union Soldiers in the Civil War":

Most of the quilts made for soldiers did not survive the war or hard use in the years which followed. Many became lost or destroyed in the heat of battle. Refugees and destitute families quickly picked up quilts laid aside by marching soldiers trying to lighten their loads . . . when field hospitals moved, they often left behind piles of quilts and comforts caked with blood and dirt.[9]

The Spanish-American War was primarily fought in the Caribbean and the Philippines. It lasted just three months, three weeks, and two days. Most quilts memorializing the war tend to have a patriotic flair. The *Press and Horticulturist* from Riverside, California, reported on June 18, 1898, "The present war has created a tremendous enthusiasm for the stars and stripes, and

ABOVE 1864 Sanitary Commission quilt, Ladies of Vernon, Connecticut. This Civil War–era quilt was sent through the US Sanitary Commission to Captain Robert Fisk of the 132nd New York Infantry, stationed in North Carolina.
After the war, Captain Fisk married Elizabeth Chester, the sister of Fannie, one of the makers of the quilt. Robert and Elizabeth spent most of their years in Montana, working in the newspaper business and raising a family. In 1919, the Fisks retired to Berkeley, California. Their granddaughter, Elizabeth White Dittmar, donated the Sanitary Commission quilt to the Lincoln Memorial Shrine of Redlands, California, in 1982.
Courtesy of the Lincoln Memorial Shrine, Redlands, California.

RIGHT This Sanitary Commission stamp found on the back of this quilt is the most reliable indicator that it was made to be sent to our soldiers on the battlefield. It is important to note that not all comfort quilts for soldiers received a stamp.

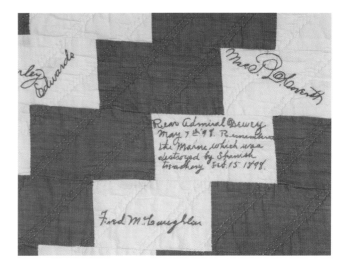

the display of flags in all parts of the country is an inspiring lesson in patriotism." The war was remembered in quilt-making with a Redwork penny square, "The Maine." This slogan, "Remember the Maine," will forever commemorate the sacrifice of our military who fought in Cuba, Puerto Rico, and the Philippines.

On April 6, 1917, America declared war on Germany. The first war of the twentieth century became known as "the Great War." During the next nineteen months, all quiltmaking was dedicated to the war effort and raising monies for the Red Cross. The popular styles of quiltmaking in the 1910s included crazy quilts, Redwork quilts, wool quilts, tobacco flannel and cigar silk quilts, and quilts made with thousands of pieces; however, quilts made in the patriotic colors of red, white, and blue were the most popular. The *Modern*

Priscilla Magazine's Red Cross quilt pattern, published in December 1917, became the iconic quilt of World War I. Exact copies and variations of this fundraising quilt have been well documented across the nation. Constructed with Turkey red fabric and muslin, and embroidered with colorfast Turkey red threads, quilts of this design have remained in good condition these past one hundred years.

TOP LEFT Detail of a silk and velvet Log Cabin quilt, ca. 1898.
The Spanish-American War was fought over a period of a few months. Consequently, very few quilts exist from this time period. Many feature the American flag and the Cuban flag.

TOP RIGHT Detail of a Redwork penny square, ca. 1898.

BOTTOM RIGHT Detail of a Redwork fundraising quilt dated Feb. 15, 1898.
Signatures on this quilt are from Michigan.

Newspapers printed during the war recorded hundreds of quilts made to raise monies for the Red Cross. The *Evansville Courier and Press*, Evansville, Indiana, reported on July 14, 1918:

A Red Cross quilt, containing 1,057 names, has been completed here. The quilt contains a large Red Cross in the center, with the names of 100 soldier boys from this city grouped around it. The names of 957 citizens of this vicinity form the border of the quilt. The quilt will be sold at auction and the proceeds, together with the sum charged each person for the placing of their name on the quilt, will be given to the Red Cross.[10]

This is a newspaper description of the iconic World War I Fund-Raising quilt. Subscriptions were sought as people paid money to have their names signed or embroidered on the quilt. It was then raffled as a double fundraising quilt. Everyone was encouraged to "Do Your Bit."

The Blue Star Service Flag was an important home front symbol originating during World War I. In 1917, US Army Captain Robert Queisser of Cleveland, Ohio, designed the flag in honor of his two sons serving in the war. On September 24, 1917, the following was read into the Congressional Record:

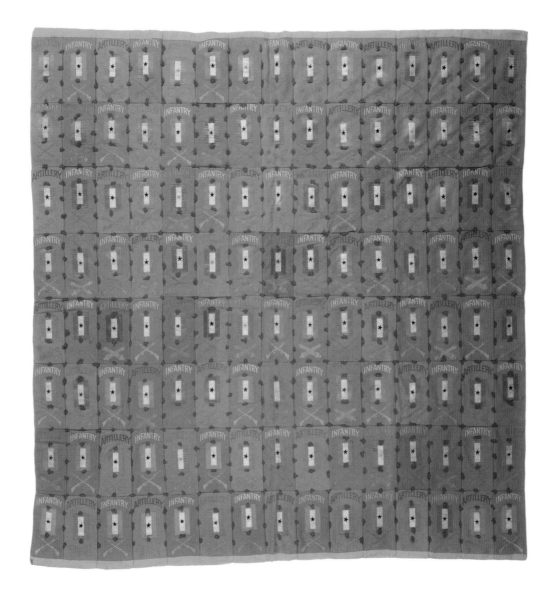

World War I Service Flag quilt, ca. 1918. Wool. The embroideries of Blue Star Service flags, artillery, infantry, and their symbols were accomplished on industrial-strength embroidery machines of the era. This is one of the few examples known of these World War I service flag embroidery quilts: two are housed at the World War I Museum in Kansas City, Missouri, and one is in the Des Plaines History Center, Des Plaines, Illinois.

The mayor of Cleveland, the Chamber of Commerce and the Governor of Ohio have adopted the service flag. The world should know of those who give so much for liberty. The dearest thing in all the world to a father and mother—their children.

The Service Flag or Banner symbol, still in practice today, was designed with a blue star centered on a white ground and was made like a quilt. Displayed in the front window of homes, it represents a loved one deployed. It is a show of family pride in their loved one serving in the military and it serves as a reminder to all that preserving America's freedom demands much.

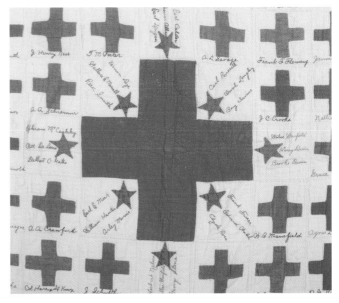

TOP RIGHT Detail of a 1917 *Modern Priscilla Magazine*–designed Red Cross fundraising quilt from Washington County, Ohio. The blue stars blocks indicate soldiers of World War I.

BOTTOM RIGHT Detail of an embroidered quilt block featuring Uncle Sam, a World War I doughboy, and sailor.

World War I, Red Cross quilt, East St. Louis, Illinois. Dated 1919. Cotton.
This quilt was made for fundraising to welcome home the 124th Field Artillery. The names of soldiers
are featured with red stars, and the gold stars indicate soldiers killed in action.

At the 11th hour on the 11th day of the 11th month of 1918, World War I ended. America's nineteen-month involvement ended abruptly, hastened due to the Spanish flu. This pandemic plague killed 50 to 100 million people worldwide.

World War I was supposed to be "the Last Great War." The unresolved issues of World War I would sow the seeds of the second major war of the twentieth century, World War II.

From World War I until their passing, veterans who served in that war were held in the highest esteem. To this day, organizations such as the American Legion and the VFW (Veterans of Foreign Wars) hand out paper poppies over Memorial Day and Veterans Day. When veterans returned home from the war, they recounted the beauty of the poppy fields in bloom among the ruins of war. Quilt designers quickly took note and published kits and patterns for Poppy quilts. Women's auxiliaries of the American Legion and the VFW made Poppy quilts for raffle to raise monies specifically to honor and benefit the veterans of World War I.

Americans were deployed in support of our European allies in World War II from the late 1930s onward. After the bombing of Pearl Harbor on December 7, 1941, President Franklin Roosevelt signed the declaration of war. Once again, American men and women were drafted into the service of their country. For the next three years and eight months, our military fought a war on two fronts: in Europe and in the South Pacific.

On the home front, benevolent efforts to support our troops and raise monies for the Red Cross immediately sprang up in cities, towns, and villages. Quiltmakers responded by making patriotic red, white, and blue quilts, fundraising quilts, Victory quilts, and quilts to honor our service men and women.

LEFT This silk pillow cover showcases the Blue Star Service flag. The flag was designed in 1917 by Army captain Robert Queisser in honor of his two sons serving in World War I. The blue star indicates that a member of your family is deployed into war. It serves as a symbol of hope that he/she be returned home safely. After the war, President Wilson designated the Blue Star Mothers as an official national organization.

RIGHT Cigar Silk quilt, ca. 1918. Silk.
The center of this small piece features the flags of the Allied nations of World War I.

Quilt companies and patternmakers designed quilts specifically to pay tribute to our troops and rally support on the home front. Military-inspired quilt patterns were printed in newspapers and magazines and on the inside of quilt-batting wrappers. Despite the limited availability of fabric, women dipped deeply into their scrap bags and made thousands of quilts with a patriotic flair for soldiers. They also made more-utilitarian quilts, which were sent to Bundles for Britain and the Red Cross for distribution to the refugees in Europe.

Unique to World War II is a group of quilts called Roll Call or Honor Roll quilts. Made by women's auxiliaries, these quilts were displayed in local libraries, churches, and town halls. The quilts were embroidered with the names of soldiers and sailors from their communities serving in the war. Quiltmakers often included ranks, branches of the military, and deployment status. Today, these unusual quilts provide a textile-based battlefront record of men and women from the big cities to the plains across America in World War II.

Except for the Midwest and the South, interest in quiltmaking generally waned from after World War II until the nation's Bicentennial in 1976. The Korean War and the Vietnam War fall into this time period. To date, no Korean War–related quilts have been discovered. It is also rare to find a quilt related to the Vietnam War. The Vietnam quilt featured here was most likely made in the early twenty-first century as a memorial remembrance. The intricate machine

TOP LEFT Detail of a Redwork quilt from World War I.

BOTTOM LEFT Post–World War I postcard featuring a float with the white crosses and poppy fields of World War I.

TOP RIGHT Red, white, and blue Poppy quilt, ca. 1940. Cotton. After the poppy was designated as the flower of World War I, quiltmakers made Poppy quilts to honor the service of veteran from "the Great War." This quilt was most likely made from a published quilt pattern.

TOP LEFT Detail of a silk, flocked Victory quilt block.
It features the eagle with its wings in the shape of a V, the Morse code for V, and "Remember Pearl Harbor."

TOP RIGHT "Sea Wings to Glory" quilt, ca. 1944. Silk.
Designed and published by Mountain Mist, Cincinnati, Ohio, in 1943 to honor the US Navy Aviation.

BOTTOM LEFT "Wings over All" quilt, ca. 1944. Cotton.
Designed and published by Mountain Mist, Cincinnati, Ohio, in 1943 to honor US Army Aviation.

BOTTOM RIGHT Detail of an Honor Roll / Roll Call quilt from Seminole, Oklahoma. Dated 1945.
Made by the Women's Society of Christian Service, this quilt is embroidered with the names of men
who served in World War I and World War II from the Seminole Creek Nation.

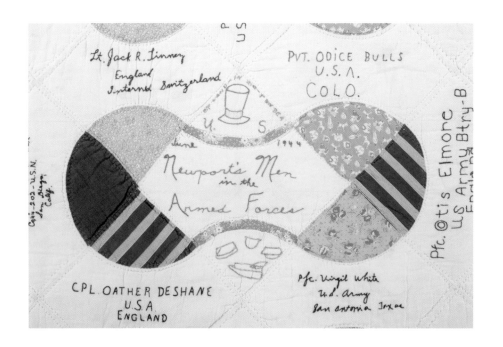

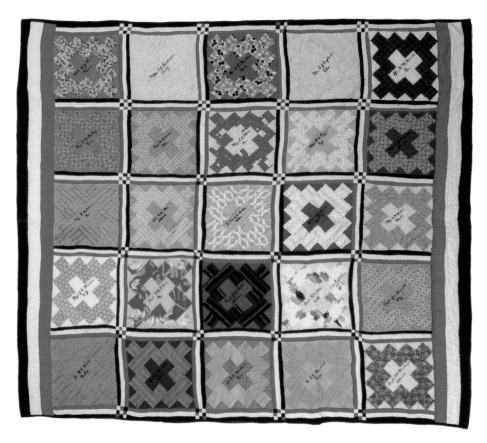

TOP Detail of an Honor Roll / Roll Call quilt from Newport, Texas.

BELOW Post–World War II, Chimney Sweep signature quilt, ca. 1950. Cotton. This quilt was probably made for a reunion of World War II or Korean War soldiers.

embroidery would have been difficult to accomplish at an earlier date without the new embroidery technology of the twenty-first century. The blocks on this well-executed quilt depict iconic symbols of the Vietnam War, including POW-MIAs, the branches of the military, and the Vietnam Wall.

Our country's Bicentennial celebration in 1976 sparked a resurgence in patriotism and the popularity of quiltmaking. Toward the end of the twentieth century, despite military conflicts in the Mideast and the Balkan States, very few quilts were made to honor the men and women in the service of our country in those wars. It was the tragedy of September 11, 2001, that propelled quiltmaking with military themes. As the first war of the twenty-first century began, with our sons and daughters, nieces and nephews, husbands and wives, and brothers and sisters deployed to battlefronts in Afghanistan and Iraq, the needleworkers of our nation once again rallied and used quiltmaking to help vanquish our foes.

Notes

1. *Springfield Republican*, Springfield, Massachusetts, December 14, 1864, p. 2.
2. Rev. A. G. Hibbard, *History of the Town of Goshen, Connecticut* (Hartford, CT: Press of the Case, Lockwood & Brainard, 1897), p. 300.
3. Ibid.
4. Ethel Alice Hurn, *Wisconsin Women in the War between the States* (Madison: Wisconsin History Commission, 1911), pp. 26–27.
5. *Springfield Republican*, Springfield, Massachusetts, December 14, 1864, p. 2.
6. Mary Elizabeth Massey, *Bonnet Brigades* (New York: Alfred A. Knopf, 1966), p. 32.
7. "Civil War Quilt Articles." *Hartford Daily Courant*, Hartford, Connecticut, February 12, 1864, p. 2.
8. "Covering for the Soldiers—A Lady's Suggestion," *Daily Constitutionalist*, Augusta, Georgia, October 15, 1862, p. 4.
9. Virginia Gunn, "Quilts for Union Soldiers in the Civil War" (AQSG, *Uncoverings 1985*), p. 113.
10. *Evansville Courier and Press*, Evansville, Indiana, July 14, 1918, p. 7.

Marine Corps quilt, dated 1993. Cotton. Quiltmaker unknown.
It is uncommon to find a quilt made to honor a Marine. It was possibly made for a Marine with the last name of "Emerson."
Slogans, mottoes, insignia, and the "Marine Corp Hymn" are featured on the quilt.

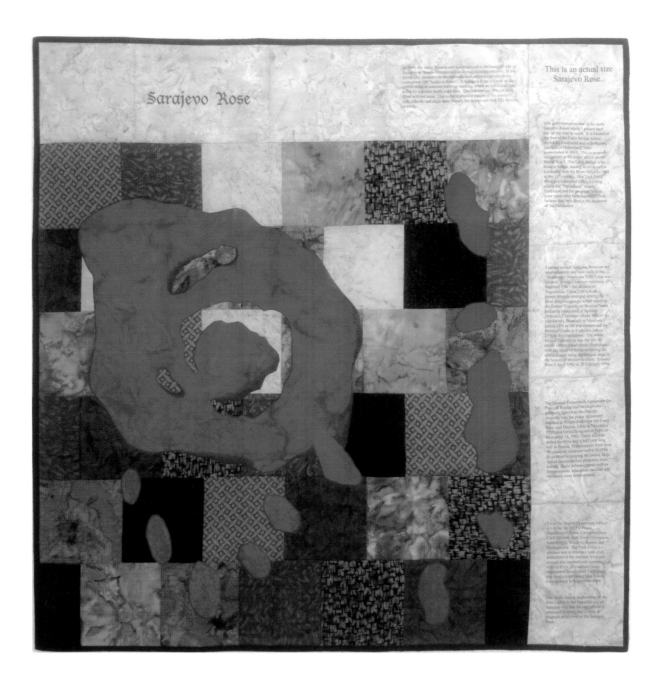

In 1999, Renelda Peldunas-Harter's Army reserve unit was deployed to the beautiful city of Sarajevo, Bosnia-Herzegovina, on a peacekeeping mission. In this lovely city, scattered on the sidewalks and pathways around town, were about 100 "Sarajevo Roses." A Sarajevo Rose is a scar on the cobblestone or concrete walkway marking where an individual was killed by a mortar shell's explosion. The indentations of the scars were filled with red resin. Due to the distinctive pattern of the mortars' size, velocity, and angle upon impact, the impact sites looked like flowers or roses.

This quilt represents one of the many Sarajevo Roses that she passed each day on her way to work. It is located at the foot of the Latin Bridge, where Archduke Ferdinand and wife, Sophie, Duchess of Hohenberg, were assassinated in 1914, which is generally recognized as the event that started World War I.

Made by Colonel Renelda Peldunas-Harter, US Army, Retired.

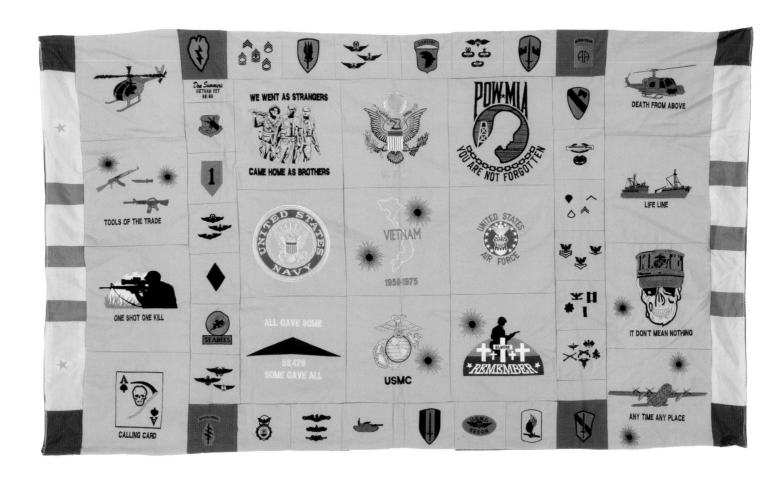

Vietnam Memorial quilt, ca. 2000. Cotton. Quiltmaker unknown.
This twenty-first-century pictorial quilt was executed with an embroidery sewing machine.
It was possibly made for a soldier named "Don Summers." It captures important slogans, insignia, symbols,
and imagery of the Vietnam War and its aftermath.

9-11 Quilt made by Pat Murphy, West Dennis, Massachusetts. Cotton.
After the September 11, 2001, terrorist attacks, Pat Murphy used her creative quiltmaking skills to capture the horrors
of an event that would change America forever. Having served in the US Army, Pat knew the demands and challenges
soon to be placed on our nation's military. This horrific event propelled our country into our current War on Terror,
which inspired Catherine Roberts to begin Quilts of Valor Foundation to "cover military touched by war." *Courtesy of Pat Murphy.*

Quilts of Valor Foundation– Then and Now

Founder Catherine Roberts's Dream

Quilts of Valor Foundation began in 2003 with a dream, literally a dream. Delaware resident Catherine Roberts's son Nat was deployed in Iraq. Catherine remembers:

> The dream was as vivid as real life. I saw a young man sitting on the side of his bed in the middle of the night, hunched over. The permeating feeling was one of utter despair. I could see his war demons clustered around, dragging him down into an emotional gutter. Then, as if viewing a movie, I saw him in the next scene wrapped in a quilt. His whole demeanor changed from one of despair to one of hope and well-being. The quilt had made this dramatic change. The message of my dream was Quilts = Healing.
>
> The model appeared simple: create a volunteer team who would donate their time and materials to make a quilt. One person would piece the top and the other would quilt it. I saw the name for this special quilt. It was a Quilt of Valor, a QOV.

Firecracker quilt. This vintage Stars-and-Squares top, ca. 1940, was donated by Mary Kerr, the wife of a retired US Army lieutenant colonel, who is also an Air Force mom. It was quilted by Doris Bloomer, Army wife, mother of three Army sons and an Air Force daughter, and mother-in-law of an Air Force son-in-law.

This quilt is part of the "Old Glory" quilt collection conceived by Mary Kerr, a career military wife, quilt book author, curator, teacher, and lecturer to raise awareness of Quilts of Valor Foundation. The quilt tops were donated by quilt historians and were quilted by longarm-machine quilters, most with ties to the military.

What Quilts of Valor Are

From the beginning, Catherine Roberts had definite ideas about standards of excellence for Quilts of Valor.

I knew a Quilt of Valor had to be a quality-made quilt. A Quilt of Valor had to be quilted, not tied, which meant hand or machine quilting. Quilts of Valor would be "awarded," not just passed out like magazines or videos. A Quilt of Valor would say unequivocally, "Thank you for your service, sacrifice, and valor in serving our nation in combat."

Humble Beginnings

The first QOV was awarded in November 2003 at Walter Reed Army Medical Center to a young soldier from Minnesota who had lost his leg in Iraq. Catherine recalls:

Chaplain John Kallerson opened the door for us at Walter Reed primarily because his wife, Connie Kallerson, happened to be a quilter. She impressed upon him how comforting quilts can be. John also saw the value of awarding quilts to his wounded because of the message they carried that someone cares.

How the Foundation Grew

From Catherine Roberts's home in Seaford, Delaware, the Quilts of Valor movement spread across the nation and beyond through the power of word of mouth and the Internet.

According to Catherine:

The team consisted of a quilt topper, a person who pieces the top from various fabrics, and a quilter who uses a "longarm" quilting machine to create beautiful machine quilting. Our longarmers immediately played a crucial role in making our quilt tops go from ho-hum to "wow." Two people who helped bring needed exposure at the start of our program to the longarming world were Janet-Lee Santeusanio and Marcia Stevens. I am deeply grateful to them for the faith they showed in a newly formed group.

Other key players on our team who helped our growing community get things done, in addition to those making quilts from coast to coast, were the "longarm coordinator" and "destination coordinator." Our "points of contact" throughout the world identified recipients and often facilitated the actual awards ceremonies.

Our Mission Statement

The organization's original mission statement said its purpose was "to cover all those service members and veterans wounded physically or psychologically with comforting and healing Quilts of Valor." Catherine Roberts recalls:

No one really liked the word "psychologically." Brilliantly, Chaplain Kallerson suggested using the phrase "touched by war" as a replacement for the words "wounded physically or psychologically." This simple phrase was perfect. The group's mission statement was revised to read, "The mission of the Quilts of Valor Foundation is to cover all combat service members and veterans touched by war with

LEFT Catherine Roberts and Chaplain John Kallerson at the 100,000th Quilt of Valor award.

CENTER Award ceremony at the World War II Memorial, Washington, DC, on Pearl Harbor Day, December 7, 2016.

RIGHT Detail of a Quilts of Valor signature quilt called *Expressions of Gratitude* (see page 52).

comforting and healing Quilts of Valor." Later, the words "all" and "combat" were removed, further reflecting our understanding of the true meaning of "touched by war."

The Light of Inclusion

In the early days, the organization's focus was on awarding quilts to service members wounded in the Iraq (Operation Iraqi Freedom, or OIF) and Afghanistan (Operation Enduring Freedom, or OEF) conflicts. Catherine Roberts remembers:

I affectionately referred to these young men as "babies" to distinguish them from veterans of other conflicts. Among us civilians, there were no complaints, as we were in the throes of an ongoing war. However, there were faint rumblings from those who worked at Veterans Administration Medical Centers (VAMCs). They politely pointed out it wasn't fair to award a QOV to one group of wounded and exclude others. The light of inclusiveness began to glimmer.

At an awards ceremony at a VAMC in White River Junction, Vermont, in 2006, we saw wounded veterans from all conflicts being awarded quilts, not our policy at the time. My husband, Chris, "got it" right away, but it took several years for me to really understand. That happened in 2009 in Bellingham, Washington. A group of us had gotten together for a quilting retreat. One of our activities for the weekend was to award quilts at an event called "American Veterans Tribute and Traveling Wall Exhibit" in Bellingham. I could not find a group of OIF/OEF veterans for the QOVs we brought that day. A group of Vietnam veterans were there to perform a "Patriot Guard" ride past the Vietnam traveling memorial wall on their motorcycles. This event changed my whole outlook on who should receive a Quilt of Valor. As we were awarding quilts, the Vietnam vets said over and over again, "Ma'am, this is the first time in forty years anyone has ever thanked me for my service." All of us were thunderstruck. From then on, any warrior who had been touched by war, no matter when his or her service, could receive a Quilt of Valor. No questions asked.

Civilian Awardees

The philosophy of inclusion widened when Catherine became aware of the work that goes on at Air Force Mortuary Affairs Operations (AFMAO), located at Dover Air Force Base, Delaware. She recalls:

I read an essay by Marine Lt. Col. Michael Strobl called "Taking Chance Home." In the essay, Strobl recounts how he escorted the body of Marine Private Chance Phillips to his home in Wyoming for burial. Strobl took the reader through AFMAO, describing who the staff was and what they did to prepare the remains of the fallen for burial. I realized that workers at Dover, though they were stateside, were as touched by war as anyone downrange or "in theater."

We established a relationship with the AFMAO and set a date for an awards ceremony. The day of the ceremony I received a call from the chaplain saying we had a big problem—some of the staff at Dover were civilians. As they all worked as a team, a family, awarding Quilts of Valor only to military service members would not work. The decision was made to award quilts to all working at the Port Mortuary, and this policy has continued ever since.

The Foundation's Name

The first name of the organization was Quilts for Soldiers. Catherine Roberts explains:

Because my son was in the Army, I thought all military service members were "soldiers." I didn't understand that different branches have different names for their members. Fortunately, a Marine straightened me out, and Quilts for Soldiers became Quilts of Valor.

The Foundation's Early Days

Catherine Roberts reminisces:

In the beginning, it was like the "wild, wild West." A few of us handled everything. After we became a national nonprofit in 2005, we created a volunteer board of directors to govern, determining policies and direction. Over the years, a structure of volunteer leadership has evolved.

Without the selflessness of the individuals who have volunteered over the years and who work tirelessly for the foundation now, we would not be the viable group we are today. It's difficult for me to convey to those who may be reading this history the debt I owe these individuals. They have devoted their time, their hearts, and their financial resources to the foundation to keep it afloat, growing, and thriving. I know that many times, many volunteers have felt it was a thankless job, but they have given their service, their sacrifice, and sometimes their valor in service to our mission. I thank you from the bottom of my heart. Without you, we would not be here today.

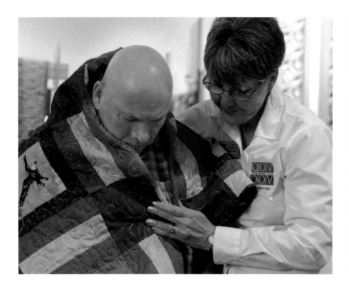

The Foundation Today

The foundation's leadership consists of its board of directors, its executive staff, and its state and area coordinators. The leadership staff, member group leaders, and members are expected to adhere to the mission statement, core values, and policies.

Over the years, standards of excellence have been established that outline size, fabric, and workmanship. A Quilt of Valor must be a generous lap-sized quilt, typically made of 100 percent red, white, and blue cotton. QOVs can be made with any pattern and by individuals or groups. Often the same QOV is pieced, quilted, bound, and awarded by different individuals.

Awards of Quilts of Valor may be made individually or in a group. The mission of Quilts of Valor is "to cover service members and veterans touched by war with comforting and healing Quilts of Valor."

Part of the oath of enlistment into the military states "I do solemnly swear that I will support and defend the Constitution of the United States against all enemies, foreign and domestic."

All enemies, foreign and domestic—these veterans vowed to lay down their lives for you and me, no questions asked. We cannot judge what "being touched by war" means to a veteran. It will be different for each one, no matter where or when they served. A nurse serving in Landstuhl, Walter Reed, or Topeka, Kansas. A general serving in the Pentagon, or an infantry soldier serving in a war zone, in a humanitarian effort, or down the street at the local armory. No judgment, but trust. Quilts of Valor trusts that the awardees have been touched by war, and trusts that veterans will respond if they don't feel they deserve a Quilt of Valor. QOVF is an inclusive, not exclusive, organization, for in reality, who today has not been touched by war, veteran or civilian, abroad or in our own country.

TOP LEFT Ann Rehbein, Executive Director of Quilts of Valor, awarding a Quilt of Valor in Lone Rock, Iowa, January 2017.

TOP RIGHT Marianne Elliott awarding a quilt to a World War II veteran on Pearl Harbor Day, December 7, 2016, at the World War II Memorial, Washington, DC.

BOTTOM State and group leaders plan Quilts of Valor Sew Days throughout the year to fill requests for award ceremonies.

Quotes from Recipients

"I have received many decorations from the US Army for valor;
however, the Quilt of Valor ranks at the top. Thank you very much for the beautiful
and sentimental symbolic quilt."

"Even at age 93, when few things affect him emotionally, you could see the
appreciation through the couple of tears in his eyes. Again, thank you."

"He wanted me to tell all of you that make Quilts of Valor that you saved him."

"My quilt isn't another military medal to be placed in a box and set on a shelf.
I was moved to tears."

"As silly as it might sound from a soldier with over three years in Iraq and Afghanistan
to say, that blanket became a true item of comfort and peace for the road ahead."

"You need to understand what my Quilt of Valor means to me.
Let me tell you some of my story. Before I received my Quilt of Valor, I had nightmares
almost every night. I had to take medication, and I do not like to take meds.
I received my Quilt of Valor and started sleeping with it. I no longer have nightmares,
and I no longer take medication to sleep. What you do matters a lot."

Quilts of Valor Conference, June 2017, Colorado Springs, Colorado.

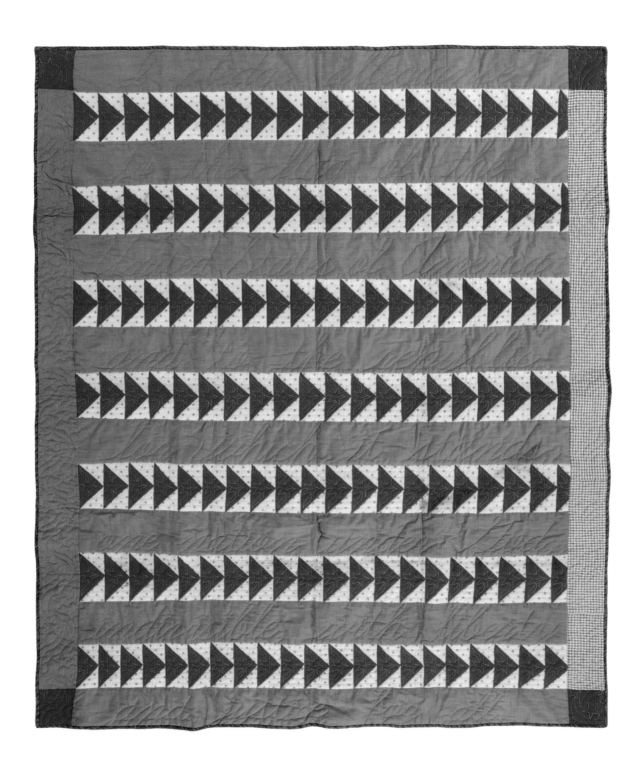

"This I Pledge" quilt. The vintage Flying Geese top, ca. 1900, was donated by Sharon Pinka,
wife of a Naval reservist and daughter of a World War II Merchant Marine. It was quilted in 2017 by Pat Barry,
wife of a Vietnam veteran and daughter of a World War II veteran.

This quilt is part of the "Old Glory" quilt collection conceived by Mary Kerr.

Quilts of Valor from 50 States

In early 2016 the board of directors and the executive staff of the QOVF issued a challenge to the state coordinators and QOVF membership: nominate three to four quilts from your state to be juried for inclusion in a book chronicling the QOVF journey and showcasing the best quilts from your state.

More than 150 quilt pictures were submitted, and the committee chose one quilt from each state for this book. In some instances the quilts clearly reflect the flavor of the state (Hawaii), other quilts reflect the service of the recipient (Missouri), one quilt was a Boy Scout's Eagle project (Kentucky), some used panels, some were simple in design, and some reflected the advanced skill of the quilter and longarm artist.

The Quilts of Valor Foundation story is really two stories. First and foremost is clearly the story of our service members and veterans who are awarded the quilts, the reason Catherine Roberts founded the QOVF. The second story, in many respects, is just as interesting as the first. It is about the quiltmakers—you, the QOVF members.

The quiltmakers comprise an eclectic group, people who cut, piece, sew, quilt, bind, longarm, award, raise money, publicize . . . the list goes on. They, you, are what makes the QOVF work and thrive; you are its heart. In this chapter I have tried to weave the quiltmakers' stories in with the awardees' stories.

As I heard these stories, several themes resonated loudly and clearly: (1) The love of country, the United States of America, is *very* strong in QOVF members, (2) the love of service members and veterans is *very* strong in QOVF members, (3) the love of spouses, parents, siblings, relatives, and children who are veterans and service members is *very* strong in QOVF members, and (4) the willingness to give back to those who have pledged to give all is a *very* strong motivation in QOVF members.

These quilts and stories give me reassurance in our great country and make me proud. As a young service member I served in places that were not always welcoming to Americans and female service members, but I drew strength from the fact that what I was doing, and those I was serving, were making the United States of America a better, stronger place for any future children I would have. My privilege was to serve with outstanding men and women, standing on their shoulders, hoping someday my shoulders would be broad enough for others to stand upon.

For most of us, the QOVF is a very personal calling. I have been privileged to see, handle, and help select the quilts in this book. More than that, I have had the privilege to hear your stories; thank you very much for sharing them with me and, through this book, with everyone who reads them.

Alabama

Joyce's journey with the QOVF started about ten years ago when she witnessed a military honor guard at a quilt show opening, but it wasn't until the Alabama QOVF state coordinator spoke at a quilt guild meeting that Joyce decided this was a great outlet for her talent. She began collecting red, white, and blue fabric and recently became the group leader for the "Stars over Mobile." During the QOVF Award Ceremonies Joyce presides over, she points out that the QOVF has become her community service and her way to say "thank you" to the veterans, thank you for the freedoms she enjoys—the freedoms of religion and of speech, the right to assemble, and the right to bear arms. If you like Joyce's quilt, check out the pattern for this quilt in chapter 4, page 109.

Rockets' Red Glare, 58" × 76". Pieced by Joyce D. Reed and longarm-quilted by Cindy Capell.
Inspiration pattern: Diana Beaubien, Pleasant Valley Creations, Diamond Patch.

Alaska

Judy became involved with the QOVF because of her husband. Tom Morrison was a Vietnam veteran who was never properly recognized for his service to our country upon his return. Judy takes extreme pleasure in participating in the QOVF endeavor.

Let's Fly Away was awarded to Gene I. Horner. Mr. Horner was a bugler for the US Army during Vietnam. He has continued to play at funerals in Alaska for veterans since his honorable discharge. Look for this quilt's pattern on page 112 of chapter 4.

Let's Fly Away, 59" × 77". Pieced by Judy Morrison and longarm-quilted by Ruth Sielaff.
Inspiration: Cutting Corners technique, Missouri Star Quilt Company.

Arizona

Both Terry and her husband, John, are Navy veterans; Terry worked in the intelligence community and John was a career Seabee. Terry, like many veterans who are part of the QOVF family, believes in giving back and doing something for veterans. Look for this quilt's pattern on page 116 of chapter 4.

Constellation, 70" × 83". Pieced by Terry Nesbitt and longarm-quilted by Linda Matteotti.
Inspiration pattern: Alex Anderson, *Simply Stars: Quilts That Sparkle*.

Arkansas

CJ feels that no one in our country is more deserving of our gratitude than our veterans. She loves what the QOVF is doing and wanted to be a part of it by designing and creating a quilt to express her heartfelt gratitude.

Land of the Free, 67" × 85". Original design, pieced and longarm-quilted by C. J. Tinkle.

California

As a mother of a special-forces active-duty Marine, Jerilyn understands what it means to be "touched by war." She says that the hidden impact of military conflict is quite real and that Quilts of Valor are a powerful, tactile, comforting "thank you." Jerilyn is in awe of the healing power the quilts provide as servicemen and women are enveloped in a loving cocoon by the quilt.

Pattye takes a very spiritual journey before and during her process of longarm quilting Jerilyn's quilt tops. She asks God and her Quilting Angels to guide her in her quilting design, and she prays for the awardees, prays that they will feel the peace, comfort, and healing that is sewn into each quilt.

Stellar Propellers, 61" × 72". Pieced by Jerilyn Lightfoot and longarm-quilted by Pattye Austin.
Inspiration pattern: Flowering Snowball.

Colorado

Gina got involved making QOVF quilts in 2006. Her mother and two of her sisters were US Navy WAVES during WWII. Gina makes the quilts in their memory and to honor their service.

The quilt features the September 11 flag raising, using NYFD-themed fabric. Gina's hope is that it will eventually be awarded to a veteran who serves or has served as a firefighter in Colorado.

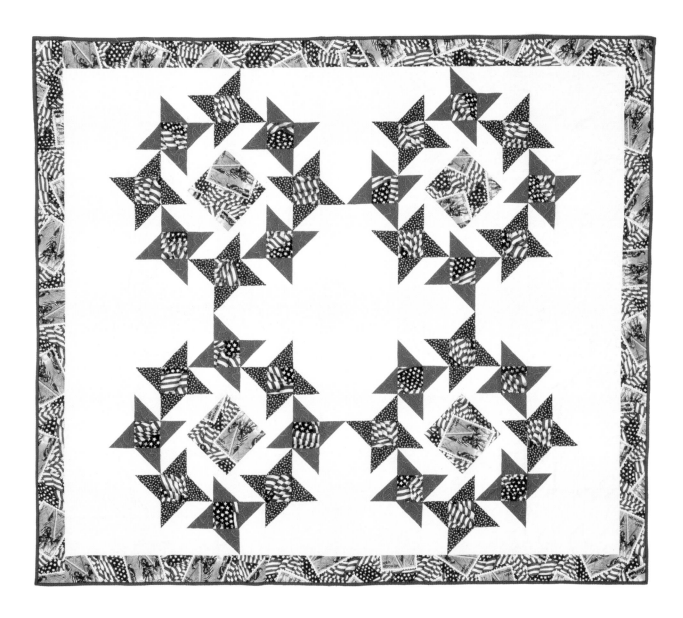

Heroes' Stars, 60" × 70". Pieced and longarm-quilted by Gina Marie Snyder.
Inspiration pattern: Camille Roskelley, Thimble Blossoms, *Round & Round*.

Connecticut

Lauren says that her talent and passion for quilting come from her mother, who also introduced Lauren to the QOVF. In 2012, Lauren and her mother started a Quilts of Valor group, Sew Thankful Quilters, as a new church ministry.

Lauren's father served in the Army during Vietnam, so supporting and honoring those who serve has always been important to Lauren. Look for this quilt's pattern on page 101 of chapter 4.

The Brave, 64" × 74". Original design, pieced and longarm-quilted by Lauren Elliott.

Delaware

Lenny Truitt and Laurel Braunstein are the Delaware state co-coordinators for QOVF. Both remember the nonexistent welcome home for Vietnam-era veterans and wanted to make certain our service members received a warmer welcome home than those returning from Vietnam did. They joined forces with their friend, Catherine Roberts, founder of QOVF, to help support her mission.

This quilt is inspired by Al Lind. Al was a self-taught quilter who loved his military brothers and sisters. This was the design he created to honor them. It is a simple pattern almost anyone can learn.

The Serendipity QOV Stars & Stripes Sew Group meets every other month throughout the year. Members from the Dover Air Force Base Port Mortuary attend almost every sew day. The young men and women often have no sewing experience when they arrive but are eager to learn. They are provided with sewing machines and a quick lesson, and they spend the rest of their day sewing and enjoying the company of the other regulars and guests. They all will receive their own Quilt of Valor at the end of their rotation at the Port Mortuary, and this is their way of paying it forward.

Dover Air Force Base is the nation's point of return to the United States for fallen armed-service members. The care and consideration these mortuary members provide the fallen is professional and dignified.

Al Lind QOV Strings, 62" × 69". Pieced by the Serendipity QOV Stars & Stripes Sew Group, Serendipity Quilt Shop. Longarm-quilted by I. Chandler. Inspiration pattern: Al Lind, a strong QOVF supporter.

Florida

Terry says that she loves to paper piece and was confident this Judy Niemeyer design would make a beautiful QOV quilt. The quilt is made from batiks, with each square including eighteen different batik fabrics. Terry appreciates what our service members and veterans do every day, defending our freedom, and says that making QOVF quilts is her way of saying "thank you" to all who serve.

Japanese Fan, 69" × 69". Pieced by Terry Burtchell and longarm-quilted by Seamstress HollyAnn.
Inspiration pattern: Judy Niemeyer, Japanese Fan.

Georgia

Fran is the group leader of the QOV Belles of Georgia, a group that makes and awards quilts for Georgia, Alabama, and Tennessee. Fran's reason for being a QOVF participant is a familiar story: she comes from a family of veterans and wanted to give back to those who have given so much. After making all the quilts that she and her family could possibly use, but still wanting to continue her love and obsession of quilting, she chose to focus her energies with the QOVF.

Fran says that she is always looking for new designs and different patterns to make into a QOV quilt. During one sew-in at her house, one of her guests had an interlocking quilt with multiple colors, totally scrappy with yellow, green, and blue fabrics. Fran transformed the design into this QOVF quilt with interlocking rings of red and blue. Look for this quilt's pattern on page 124 of chapter 4.

Interlocking Rings of Freedom, 65" × 79". Pieced and longarm-quilted by Fran Randolph,
QOV Belles. Inspiration pattern: Cathy Busch, Nine Patch Chain.

Hawaii

Like many QOVF quilters and longarm quilters, Linda has lived in multiple places as military obligations change. She started her QOVF journey on the small island of Molokai in 2007. Looking for a charity, specifically a quilting charity, she saw information on the QOVF. Linda then moved to Tennessee in 2011 to help her daughter with her first baby.

Both Linda's daughter and son-in-law are in the Army, and she found a quilting group in Trenton, Kentucky.

When Linda saw this pattern in the Missouri Quilt Star Company Block, she knew it would make a great QOV quilt. In all of her QOV quilts, Linda tries to include some Hawaiian fabric. Mahalo, Linda.

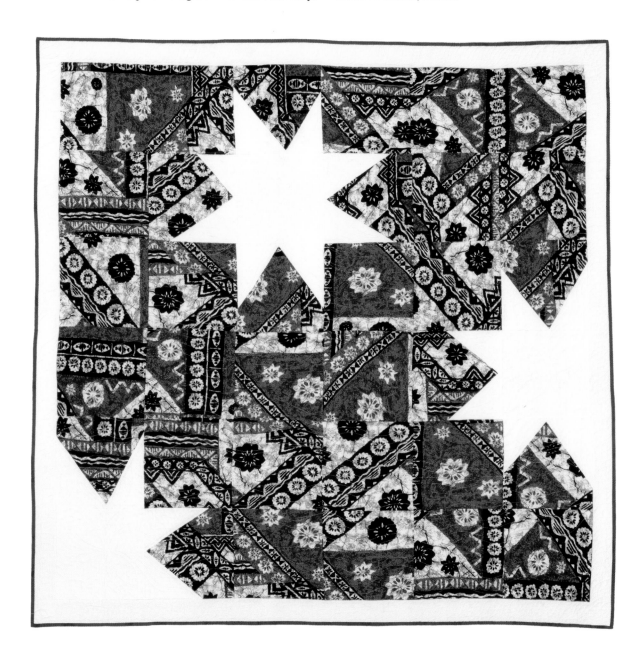

Wonky Quilt, 59" × 59". Pieced by Linda DeGraw and longarm-quilted by Denise Coulter.
Inspiration pattern: from Missouri Quilt Star Company's *BLOCK Magazine*, Vol. 1.5 (Fall 2014).

Idaho

Sharon Ledbetter is a legend within the QOVF family. After learning about the QOVF, she went on to form the Lewis Clark QOV Group, to serve as the Idaho state coordinator, and to serve as the QOVF's Assistant Executive Director. Sharon has awarded well over 2,000 QOVF quilts. Both her husband, Grover W. (Bill) Ledbetter Jr., and her brother-in-law, Kenneth (Ken) Ledbetter, are Vietnam veterans. Bill served in a ground crew on a KC135 and Ken was based in DaNang. Sharon lost a cousin, Donald C. Hart, an Air Force medic in Vietnam.

Sharon thinks that the eagles in the quilt center are the perfect symbol of America, representing the ultimate in freedom. The quilt was awarded to Jeffery Steinwand in 2017. Jeffery, a US Marine Corp veteran, has been deployed throughout the world in service to his country.

Eagles Pass, 60" × 80". Original design and pieced by Sharon Ledbetter.
Longarm-quilted by Experience Quilts of Odessa, Washington. Center is a Northcott panel.

Illinois

Kelly belongs to a group that started to make QOVF quilts after seeing the pattern Old Glory by Yellow Creek Quilt Designs. The quilt uses all 6½" blocks, so the group made extra blocks to piece into a QOFV-sized quilt. However, it wasn't until one of the members won the center Ohio star blocks in a block lotto that this unique design took shape. The group has made three quilts using this design.

Two of them have been awarded. One was awarded to Terry Grant, a Vietnam veteran and group member's husband. Terry is also a quilter and makes QOV quilts for others. The second was awarded to Zach Ziegel, who was deployed to Iraq and Afghanistan. After leaving the Marines, Zach learned that an average of twenty-two veterans a day commit suicide. Zach launched Buddy Check 22, which simply asks people—military and civilian—to contact a veteran on the 22nd of each month and ask how things are going. This way we can help curb the suicide rate among veterans, by reaching out and making sure veterans know that someone is thinking about them.

Stars & Stripes, 69" × 71". Pieced and longarm-quilted by Kelly Harvey.
Original design by Kelly Harvey and Patty Gallmeyer.

Indiana

Joan started to make quilts for the QOVF as a way to give back and to give thanks for those who served our country. To see a service member or veteran wrapped in a quilt of thanks is the only encouragement she needs to keep making more quilts.

Joan belongs to the String-A-Long Stars & Stripes QOV group, which meets monthly and makes precut quilt kits for the members to work on. Joan was presented with a "lonely" bag of scraps, a bag overlooked at several meetings. She decided to make one of her favorite traditional quilt blocks,

the Dresden Plate. After the process of strip piecing the strips together, cutting the wedges, and sewing them together to create those colorful arcs, the Dresdens were hand appliquéd onto the background fabric, and the quilt top was quilted by Joan's friend and fellow QOVF member Judy Holden. The quilt was then bound with a scrappy binding. Joan named it *With Great Fanfare* because the winding wedges remind her of fans and because all soldiers (service members), both current and retired, should be welcomed home "with great fanfare."

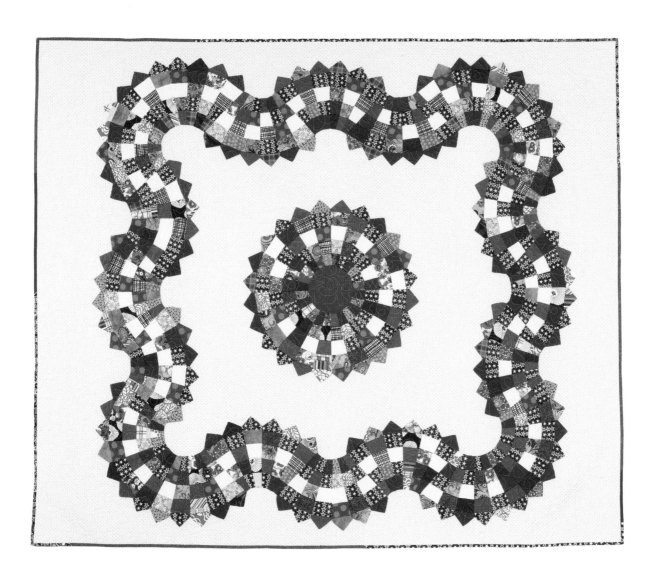

With Great Fanfare, 75" × 83". Original design and pieced by Joan Crookston.
Longarm-quilted by Judy Holden.

Iowa

Doreen, a civilian, knows what it means to be "touched by war." When she was sixteen years old, her mother explained to her why she had divorced Doreen's father. He had been in the US Army during WWII, and after his discharge, one day he tried to kill Doreen, her mother, and her older brother. She left him when Doreen was a baby, and moved across the country. He was in a veterans hospital for more than seventeen years for "shell shock." Doreen never knew her father, and when she read about the QOVF in a quilting magazine, she was moved by the mission statement to award quilts to those veterans who had been "touched by war." She decided to support the QOVF in her retirement years because she too was "touched by war."

Doreen found a unique blue Iowa border print and set it aside for just the right quilt. Two years later, when she saw a chevron quilt on the front cover of a magazine, Doreen knew this was the pattern for her special Iowa fabric. Look for this quilt's pattern on page 128 of chapter 4.

The veteran chosen for this quilt is a native of Fredericksburg, Iowa, as is Doreen. Fredericksburg is a small town with a population of under 1,000. Mick Urness served in the US Navy for thirty years, retiring as a Master Chief. He served on the USS *Andrew Jackson*, a nuclear submarine, as well as other ships. When Mick retired from the Navy he came back to his hometown, and he still resides in Fredericksburg. Doreen feels that Mick is perfect for the quilt, since Mick represents Iowa's Bravest well.

Military service touches the military families as well as the service member, and we need to recognize their sacrifices as well as the veteran's sacrifices. With that being said: Welcome home, Doreen.

Iowa's Bravest, 60" × 75". Pieced by Doreen A. Cook and longarm-quilted by Lynn L. LeBeck.
Inspiration pattern: Scott Flanagan, Sand and Sea, *Quiltmakers Magazine*, March–April 2017.

Kansas

During a meeting of the Prairie Quilt Guild, one of the members appealed for help to make more than 500 QOV quilts for soldiers at Fort Riley, Kansas, and Betty says that she has been a QOVF member ever since.

Ad Astra, 57" × 82". Original design and pieced by Betty G. Blundon.
Longarm-quilted by Leon Puetz.

Kentucky

Nancy, like many of us, has struggled to use printed text in quilt blocks because it seemed to distract from the overall design. Her frustration was overcome when she received a panel of motivating phrases and patriotic symbols. After a series of starts and stops with Log Cabin and two-sided Log Cabin designs, she discovered this Winter Wonderland design. After modifying the block size to accommodate her design elements, Nancy was happy with the outcome. The pattern for this quilt is on page 133 in chapter 4.

Welcome Home, 60" × 74". Pieced and longarm-quilted by Nancy Cann.
Inspiration pattern: Doug Leko, Antler Quilt Design, Memory Lane.

Louisiana

The inspiration for this quilt was the QOVF National Sew Day in 2017, when several QOVF groups met to sew as many tops as possible. Look for a pattern inspired by this quilt on page 137 of chapter 4.

Jacob's Ladder, 64" × 78". Pieced by Lynn McDonald and longarm-quilted by Roxanne Brown.
Inspiration pattern: Donna Robertson, Fabric Café, Jacob's Ladder from *Modern Views with 3-Yard Quilts*.

Maine

Along with being the owner of Village Quilt Shop in Berwick, Maine, Lisa and her husband are members of American Legion Post 47 in Rollinsford, New Hampshire, and the American Legion Riders Chapter 47. While spending time with the veterans at the post, she realized that many of the local veterans had never been thanked or recognized for serving our country. Quite a few of them wouldn't even talk about their time spent serving.

Lisa researched QOVF and decided to ask the local veterans' organizations to nominate local veterans to be recipients of quilts She received a list of thirty-one that first year, and with the help of local quilters they made thirty-one quilts.

Lisa asked her group of Legion Riders if they would help her put together a presentation to honor those thirty-one veterans. Invitations were sent out to the veterans and their families. All the veterans were interviewed in advance, and a short biography was read as the veteran walked up to be awarded their quilt. The hall was decorated with red, white, and blue, and dinner was provided. More than 300 people showed up that day to honor those veterans and awarded them quilts. Lisa says, "There were so many smiles and tears . . . it was truly a wonderful day. We continue to do this once a year and have awarded a total of 177 quilts."

Robert "Bob" Lyons served in the US Navy during WWII and was awarded *Let Freedom Ring* in 2017. Mr. Lyons served aboard the USS *Howorth* in the Pacific theater, seeing action at the Battle of Ormac, the Battle of Mindoro, the Battle of Lingayen Gulf, and the invasion of Iwo Jima, and he was off the coast of Okinawa when a kamikaze airplane struck the *Howorth*, killing nine sailors and injuring Mr. Lyons. He suffered second- and third-degree burns and received an honorable discharge in 1945.

LEFT American Legion Riders, Chapter 47. Left to right: Neal Heon, Mike Gaudette, Bob Lyons, Bubba Duke, and Myke Cole. *Photo courtesy of Lisa Lapierre.*

RIGHT Detail of *Let Freedom Ring*.

Let Freedom Ring, 74" × 77". Pieced by Lisa Lapierre, appliquéd by Vivian Carignan,
and longarm-quilted by Sheryl Rose. Inspiration pattern: Jackie Robinson & Kay Wright-Handy.

Maryland

Marianne is a one-in-a-million lady! Her love of quilting, the QOVF, and service to others are just a few of her many great qualities. She learned to sew from her mother when she was nine years old, using cardboard templates that her dad made. Sewing was put on hold when Marianne entered the US Navy.

She reconnected with a childhood friend who rekindled her love of quilting and introduced her to the QOVF. Her first QOVF experience was a twelve-hour quilting marathon held by the Southern Tier QOV group in the Finger Lakes region of New York on Veterans Day in 2012. After that, there was no question where her energy would be devoted—to giving back by making quilts for those who were touched by war.

What started out as just Marianne quickly spread throughout her entire family. Her husband, Bill, a veteran himself and member of the Scottish American Military Society (SAMS), dons his kilted uniform for award ceremonies.

Expressions of Gratitude, 55" × 77". Pieced by Marianne Elliott and longarm-quilted by Les Page, "the Leatherneck Kilted Quilter."
Inspiration pattern: Barbara Thurman Butler's quilt from the Indian Hatchet Block featured in
Memory Quilts in the Making, compiled by Rhonda Richards.

This quilt, *Expressions of Gratitude*, is unusual in that it is a signature quilt. Marianne explains:

"I have always thought that handwritten notes or signatures on a quilt added to the personal connection between the quilter and the recipient. These messages also preserve the quilt's story. Because QOV quilts honor and comfort, what better a way to communicate the heartfelt appreciation from those who enjoy freedom today by reading the words of thanks and gratefulness on the QOV itself.

"After an award ceremony that concluded a three-month QOV Exhibit on wartime quilting at the Defense Health Headquarters (DHHQ), we invited those attending, military and civilian alike, to write an 'expression of gratitude' on a quilt block. When we were asked multiple times, 'Who will be awarded this quilt?,' it was clear this QOV had to be awarded to someone at DHHQ. Over the next year or so, we returned several times to finally collect the 96 blocks needed."

Along with the quilt, there is a photo album with a picture of each block, so that the messages are preserved even if the ink fades on the quilt though washing and use.

Look for this quilt's pattern on page 140 of chapter 4.

This QOV quilt actually represents the combined efforts of three different QOV groups in three different states to which Marianne belongs. The Southern Tier QOV (NY) group provided all the precut fabric from the group's stash. The longarm quilting was done by Les Page (USMC) from Not Forgotten QOV in Virginia Beach, Virginia. The quilt block collecting was provided with the cooperation of Jeff Thorne at DHHQ. The quilt construction came from the MSP Quilting Angels from Gaithersburg, Maryland, Marianne's home state.

Along with Marianne and Bill, Jeff (QOVF Public Relations) and Kathy Thorne are active members of the QOVF in the northern Virginia / Maryland / District of Columbia area, awarding and documenting numerous QOVF award ceremonies to include awarding twenty-eight Pearl Harbor survivors and WWII veterans QOVF quilts at the 75th-anniversary commemoration at the WWII Memorial in Washington, DC, in December 2016.

TOP LEFT Bill and Marianne Elliott preparing to award a quilt. *Photo courtesy of the QOVF.*

TOP RIGHT Pearl Harbor survivors and World War II veterans being awarded QOVF quilts during the 75th-anniversary commemoration at the World War II Monument in Washington, DC, December 2016. *Photo courtesy of the QOVF.*

BOTTOM Close-up of *Expressions of Gratitude*.

Massachusetts

Theresa says that the Disappearing Nine Patch is a delightful pattern to make and to teach, and it always brings a surprise and smile each time it is finished.

Disappearing Nine Patch, 61" × 73". Pieced by Theresa Perreault and longarm-quilted by Carol Coffin.

Michigan

Susan became involved with QOVF when her son was deployed to Iraq the first time. She felt like there was so little she could do, so she makes QOVF quilts to honor her son, First Sergeant (E-8) Dennis Morton, US Army. He served two deployments to Iraq, one with the 25th Infantry and one with the 10th Mountain Division. Dennis is a career soldier who has been in the Army for seventeen years. He has served with the Old Guard, and at the Pentagon, where he worked search and rescue after 9/11.

Katy longarm-quilted for Susan's quilt, and she has a similar story. Her daughter, Annie Sweigart, just completed six years of honorable service in the USAF. She left the military as Staff Sergeant (E-5) and served in the 56th Security Forces Squadron with two deployments, one to Saudi Arabia and one to Iraq. Katy said Annie "is strong, capable, smart, and fierce." Katy started making quilts for the QOVF during Annie's first deployment and decided to make one for each month she was gone as a way of coping with the "mom worries."

Katy never stopped making QOV quilts and eventually bought a longarm machine so she could help finish more QOV quilts. To date, Katy has made more than fifty QOV quilts on her own and has quilted more than 100 additional quilts for Stitching Sisters QOV group, based in Clawson, Michigan.

Both Susan and Katy say how proud of Dennis and Annie they are, and how proud they are of their children's service to our great nation.

Hero's Tribute, 55" × 70". Pieced by Susan Mullen and longarm-quilted by Katy Sweigart. Inspiration pattern: Liz Porter.

Minnesota

Minnesota's quilt is a collaboration of the Grateful Hearts Quilters. They have thirty-two members and meet once a month to choose patterns and fabrics for future quilts. All of their quilts are red, white, and blue. The Grateful Hearts Quilters have awarded quilts at the St. Cloud VA hospital and are currently awarding quilts to veterans at the Minneapolis VA hospital.

The Grateful Hearts Quilters are humbled by veterans' reactions when their quilts are awarded, and they feel privileged to honor the local veterans and service members, who often feel undeserving of the attention for their service.

It is easy to see why this quilt design is a group favorite—it makes a dynamic impression with the wavy movement of the red and white stripes. The group says that veterans who have received this quilt are delighted with the flag motif.

"Captain Jack," who was their first WWII recipient and was ninety-five at the time, said in his thank-you letter that he "sleeps under it every night." This quilt has also been awarded to a ninety-two-year-old WWII female veteran who spent her service as a Navy teacher of celestial navigation to military pilots, and to two veterans who bravely served in the Vietnam War.

Stars & Stripes, 66" × 80". Pieced by Janice Hartley and longarm-quilted by Millie P's Quilt Shop, Anoka, Minnesota.
Inspiration pattern: Mark Lipinski, Stars & Stripes, *Fons & Porter's Love of Quilting*, September–October 2012.

Mississippi

Cheryl's first encounter with the QOVF was during a quilt show in Atlanta, where Cheryl and her sister spoke with Marianne Fons, an early and ongoing super-supporter of the QOVF. Marianne told the sisters all they needed to know to join, and they have been making QOVF quilts ever since. Their group is called Gracie's Girls, and they try to get together in January every year to make a QOV quilt as a group.

This quilt was made for Buddy Wilson, a WWII vet who was a seaman on the transport ship *DuPage* in the South Pacific. He is taking care of his wife, who has dementia, so he can't go to the reunions of his shipmates. When a niece asked Cheryl to make him a quilt, she was glad to get to work. She used the colors in the panel as inspiration for the stars and stripes.

Indivisible, 60" × 74". Original design, pieced and longarm-quilted by Cheryl Williamson.

Missouri

Janice became involved with the QOVF in 2009 and formed a group, Patriot Piecers, in 2013. Her father and five uncles served in WWII, and her husband served in the Navy during the Cold War, so veterans have a special place in her heart. Janice feels that it is a great honor to award QOVF quilts to veterans, as a very small token of our nation's appreciation for their service and sacrifice. "The expressions on their faces bring tears to everyone's eyes. During our ceremonies it is so obvious how healing our quilts are."

The story of this QOV awardee led Janice to design his quilt with special touches, embroidering a B-17 bomber with the serial number of his plane as the center block and creating corner blocks representing the Purple Heart he received for his injuries, a military jeep, and two patriotic eagle designs.

"Mr. Rowden's QOV is titled *Sleepy Time Gal*, the name given to his airplane by the crew shortly before they started their bombing missions."

Janice continues, "Wilburn Rowden was just twenty years old when he was drafted to fight in World War II in 1943. He was twenty-two when the war ended. At that young age, Mr. Rowden was lucky enough to live through events that had claimed the lives of thousands of other soldiers.

"After he was drafted, Rowden trained as a radio operator and was assigned to the B-17 bomber "Sleepy Time Gal" in January 1944 with 10 other men. Starting in February 1944, the crew flew various bombing missions over France, Poland, and Germany. On March 8, 1944, "Sleepy Time Gal" was flying over Germany when the plane was shot down by enemy forces. Mr. Rowden and the other crew members bailed out and parachuted to the ground, losing two crew members. As soon as he landed, Rowden and his crew were immediately captured by German soldiers. He was held captive as a prisoner of war for thirteen months and eighteen days. When it became clear that the Germans were going to lose the war in 1945, German forces marched Rowden and hundreds of other POWs 500 miles across Germany in an effort to evade American troops."

On April 26, 1945, Mr. Rowden was finally liberated by American forces. "The best day of my life was the day I saw the German flag go down and the American flag go up," Mr. Rowden said.

After the war ended, Mr. Rowden went on to serve thirty-eight years in the armed forces before retiring from the Missouri National Guard. Look for a pattern inspired by this quilt on page 143 of chapter 4.

Sleepy Time Gal, 73" × 73". Original design, pieced and longarm-quilted by Janice Hobbs.

Montana

Kathy became involved with the QOVF when she and her husband retired and moved to their ranch in Montana, where the winters are long and quilting was a way for her to fill the days. During a patriotic ceremony that Kathy and her husband attended, there was a representative there with flyers about the QOVF. Kathy became hooked! The Coontz family is a proud four-generation Navy family, from her father-in-law, who served in the North Sea prior to WWII and on through the entire Pacific theater during WWII and through the Korean Conflict; to her husband, who was a Navy pilot during the Vietnam years (and is a proud disabled veteran); to their daughter, who served in naval aviation during the first Gulf War engagement; and now to their granddaughter, who is currently serving as an Aviation Ordnanceman for the US Navy, having just completed her second tour in the Persian Gulf.

This quilt pattern reminded Kathy of the jagged mountains and valleys that she sees from her back porch in Montana. The colors not only are patriotic but speak to the blue of the Montana sky, the white of the abundant winter snow, and the red of the spectacular sunsets over the golden grasslands in the fall. Kathy is the lone Montana representative, and this quilt is used for QOV awards and local quilt shows. The veterans are spread out in many out-of-the-way spots and, more often than not, prefer their privacy and solitude. Montana is a place to heal the wounds of war.

Detail of *Montana On My Mind.*

Montana On My Mind, 65" × 82". Pieced by Kathy Coontz and longarm-quilted by Kathy Olkowski.
Inspiration pattern: Ann Lauer and Sandi Conrady, Fire & Ice, *Fons & Porter's Love of Quilting*.

Nebraska

Megann first became involved with the QOVF during the Nebraska 4-H challenge. That QOVF challenge asked 4-Hers to create as many quilts as possible. Within that two-year challenge, Megann made three quilts for the QOVF. The idea behind the QOV quilts really inspired Megann, who did not have any family members or friends who had served, but loved the idea of giving back to the service members for all their hard work and dedication to our country.

"I found this pattern while my mom and I were cleaning out her pattern collection. It had originally been my grandmother's, and she passed it down to my mom. I came across this pattern the summer of my final year in 4-H, and I knew that I needed to make a quilt that would help me end my eleven-year 4-H career with a bang. As soon as I saw this thirty-year-old pattern, I just knew that it would be perfect to make for the county fair. I made some minor adjustments to the pattern, and the whole time I was making the quilt, I knew that it would end up in the hands of someone who really needed it and deserved it."

Megann was personally able to wrap the quilt around the awardee, Nebraska state senator Tom Brewer. On the day that he was awarded the quilt, many other senators and legislative members gathered in the Nebraska Capitol Building Rotunda. There was a short ceremony in front of friends and family.

Tom Brewer is the only member of the Nebraska State Legislature who wears a Purple Heart on his lapel and is also a Native American. While he was deployed to Afghanistan in October 2003, he was shot six times during a spontaneous firefight with the Taliban in a desolate site near Ghar Mountain. He suffered from twelve broken ribs, a broken sternum, a broken nose, and gunshot and shrapnel wounds across his body, and his injuries were compounded by a bumpy ambulance ride in which he bounced face down on the floor, with his hands strapped to his waist. In 2011, he was wounded again during his sixth tour in Afghanistan when shrapnel from a rocket-propelled grenade ripped through his body. Senator Brewer credits leaving the Pine Ridge Reservation, where he grew up as an Oglala Sioux, as "by far the best decision of my life." He retired from the military as a US Army Reserve Colonel, having served thirty-six years in uniform.

LEFT Megann and her quilt *Soaring to New Heights*.

CENTER Megann wrapping Senator Tom Brewer.

RIGHT Ann Freese, Megann Freese, and Senator Tom Brewer.
Photos courtesy of Gordon Harrod Photography.

Soaring to New Heights, 71" × 84". Pieced by Megann Freese and longarm-quilted by Marcia Schmidt at Quilt Finishers. Inspiration pattern: Eagle and Peace Pipe, Missouri Breaks Industries.

Nevada

Diane's inspiration for becoming involved with the QOVF was her association with many friends and relatives who served in the military, especially her husband, her uncle who served in Europe during WWII, and a close friend who served in the Pacific. She has been fortunate enough to walk the beach at Normandy and visit the American cemeteries there and in Cambridge, England. Diane has seen how the small villages in Belgium and France adopt graves of the service members who are buried there, and how they teach their children respect for these men and women who gave their lives to preserve the freedoms that they enjoy today.

Diane makes her QOVF quilts with the Comstock Lode Quilters. They work tirelessly to provide quilts for all the veterans upon their returns from Washington, DC, meeting every Honor Flight into Reno.

Look for this quilt's pattern on page 146 of chapter 4.

In Honor Of . . ., 64" × 77". Pieced by Diane McIntyre and longarm-quilted by Sharon Reader, Sierra Sewing Center, Reno, Nevada. Inspiration pattern: Diane Tomlinson, In Honor Of . . . , *Fons & Porter's Love of Quilting*, January–February 2013.

New Hampshire

My Stars & Stripes, 58" × 76". Pieced by Tammi Marsan and longarm-quilted by Janet Cass.
Inspiration pattern: Al Lind, String Pattern, NHQOV website.

New Jersey

Claudia tells an interesting story about how she learned to quilt. "I began quilting almost fifty years ago when I moved to Lancaster, Pennsylvania. I lived in a new development surrounded by Amish farms. I could look across the cornfields and see quilts hanging on the clothesline. I admired the quilts and wanted to learn to make one.

"One day a cow appeared in our backyard. I assumed it belonged to the farm behind our property, so I got my two young sons and took the cow home. Mike and Ethel were Old Order Amish and didn't want to speak. I asked if she sold her quilts, and told her I would love to learn how to make one.

"Several weeks later in the middle of the night came a knock on the door. It was Mike. I thought there was an emergency, but instead he wanted to get the children because the lambs were being born and he thought they should see that. While we were there, he apologized about the cow,

saying it was an imposition to me, and so Ethel would teach me to quilt at 6:00 a.m. on Fridays. I worked and could not meet then, but we arranged to do it on Saturday mornings.

"Everything was done by hand. We cut templates from cereal boxes, traced the shape onto fabric, drew the quarter-inch line, and cut each piece out with scissors. She taught me how to hand piece and much later how to hand quilt. My first quilt was a log cabin king-sized quilt, and I have had a love affair with that block since then."

The Hunterdon County Quilting Guild is a community service guild, and one of the projects they support is the QOVF. Claudia says that she has a special place in her heart for the men and women who are members of our armed forces. Her father was a Marine, her son served in the Navy, and currently her grandson is serving in the Army. For Claudia, it has been a great pleasure to make quilts for the QOVF.

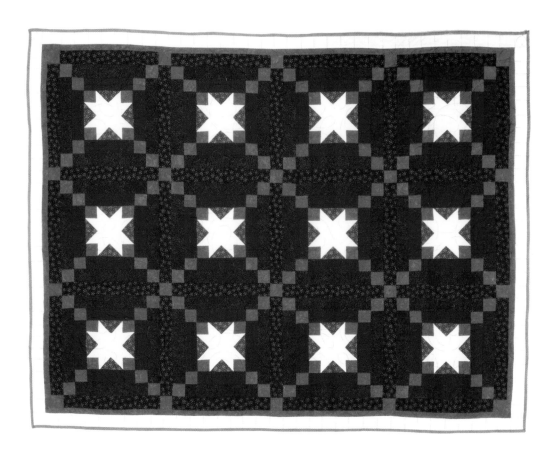

Stairways to the Stars, 59" × 77". Pieced and quilted by Claudia Menendez.

New Mexico

Jean feels military personnel need to be remembered for their commitment to serve and the sacrifices made being away from their families for extended periods of time. Linda has family connections: her father served in WWII, a brother served in Vietnam, and her nephew was a member of US Army Special Forces. She combines her passion for quilting and passion for those who serve in the military for the United States, as a tribute to always remember their sacrifices to keep our freedom.

Eagle Flight, 68" × 70". Pieced by Jean Callaghan and longarm-quilted by Linda Robinson.
Inspiration pattern: Janet Miller, Patriotic Rose, *The City Stitcher Quilt Collection*, #17.

New York

Pat was originally inspired by all the beautiful QOVF quilts that are published monthly in *Fons and Porter's Love of Quilting* magazine. After she attended a QOV marathon, where QOV members gather to cut, piece, sew, press, and construct as many quilt tops as possible during a given time, she decided to join the Southern Tier QOV group. Pat enjoys all the wonderful women she has come to know in the group, and she says it makes her happy to make quilts for very deserving military men and women and veterans. Look for a pattern inspired by this quilt on page 150 of chapter 4.

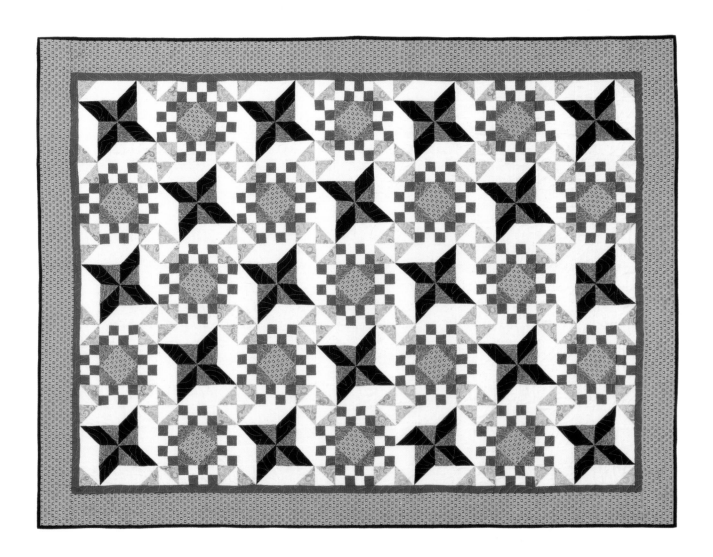

Stars & Checks, 70" × 70". Pieced by Pat Bennett and longarm quilted by Janet Bauter.
Inspiration pattern: Nancy Mahoney, Stars and Checks, *Fons & Porter's Love of Quilting*, September–October 2015.

North Carolina

O'Glory, 60" × 80". Pieced by Mary Hupp and longarm-quilted by Iris Noitalay.
Inspiration pattern: Edie McGinnis, *O'Glory*.

North Dakota

Julie's story is a familiar one: her father and brother were in the Air Force and she has a niece in the Army. The QOVF is her way of giving back. Julie's local QOV group is called Quilters Embrace and is based in Fergus Falls, Minnesota.

Julie's inspiration for this quilt is from a Facebook group block of the month.

Longarm quilter Rosalie Davenport quilts the words "Thank You" into every quilt she does for the QOVF.

Spinning Stars, 60" × 75". Pieced by Julie Meyer and longarm-quilted by Rosalie Davenport.

Ohio

Cindy's three brothers, Mike, Larry, and Fred Blankenship, all served in the military, just as her father, Cecil, did. She remembers thinking as a teenager that she wished she could do something special for them and other veterans as well. Years later she came across an article in a quilt magazine about the QOVF and knew it would be a wonderful way to honor a veteran. Cindy shared her story with three of her high school classmates, and they decided to make a quilt for their 1973 high school classmates who have served.

The Ohio Star Pattern in red, white, and blue was chosen. Cindy, Kim Whitman, Dee Case, and Sandy Genco all pieced, with Cindy finishing up longarm quilting.

The quilt was awarded to Dean Palmer, a Navy veteran and high school classmate of the four. At the presentation,

Cindy summed up the experience by saying, "God bless America, this land that we love!"

Ohio Star, 56" × 68". Pieced by Cindy Lambert, Kim Whitman, Dee Case, and Sandra Genco. Longarm-quilted by Cindy Lambert.

ABOVE Left to right: Kim Whitman, Cindy Lambert, Dean Palmer, Dee Case, and Sandy Genco, August 2017. *Photo courtesy of Cindy Lambert.*

Oklahoma

Donna explains that the center eagle was inspired by a circle wall hanging by Cheryl Phillips at Phillips Fiber Art. Donna didn't want to make a round quilt, so she surrounded the center motif with stars. This quilt is very special to Donna since it was awarded to her husband, Robert McCormack, a 100 percent disabled veteran who did two tours in Vietnam. Robert McCormack received two Purple Hearts and spent fifteen years in the Army before making a career at the Department of Justice.

Donna is the QOVF Oklahoma state coordinator and became interested in the QOVF because of her husband. He told her tales of how he was treated when he returned from Vietnam, and Donna was aghast at the way the Vietnam veterans were treated. Service members put their lives on the line every day to allow us our rights and to protect those who cannot protect themselves. Donna feels that the *very least* we can do is to say thank you to each and every one of them. These quilts are her way of doing that.

American Eagle, 86" × 70". Pieced and longarm-quilted by Donna McCormack.
Center motif by Cheryl Phillips.

Oregon

Sue is a self-taught quilter who likes to try new patterns and techniques and thought it would be a good idea to donate her quilts so that other people could enjoy them as much as she enjoys making them. Sue has a family military connection, with both her father and brother having served in the Army, so she decided that QOVF would be perfect for her.

Sue loves patterns that look intricate and seem to change at every angle. She searches for patterns that challenge her, and reimagines them in red, white, and blue. Snail Tail is one of those patterns that looks very tricky but is simpler than you think! Think the pattern is too difficult? Sue challenges you to check out the pattern on page 154 of chapter 4 and make one for your next QOV award!

Snail Trail, 58" × 80". Pieced and longarm-quilted by Sue Willits.

Pennsylvania

Sarah's son, Ian Scott Campbell, has been in the US Marine Corps since 2001. When he returned from his first deployment in Iraq in 2004, Sarah and her husband flew out to California to greet the bus of returning troops. Some of the young Marines did not have family members there, and her son said not only did they not have family and friends to greet them, but they did not have a place to stay either. The scene was heartbreaking for Sarah. Major Campbell is still on active duty.

Sarah hopes that the QOV that are awarded to veterans and service members show the military that their efforts are appreciated.

Fluttering Flag, 60" × 70". Pieced by Sarah Campbell and longarm-quilted by Nancy King.
Inspiration pattern: Bev Getschel, Fluttering Flag, *McCall's Quilting Magazine*, November–December 2016.

Rhode Island

Ann Marie is a member of the Willoughby Wallace Library Quilters (WWLQ). She has made more than twenty tops for the QOVF, and she loves using striped fabric cut on an angle, and pairing it with floating stars and focus fabric blocks.

Ann Marie's story is another example of the healing power of Quilts of Valor quilts. Her husband, John, served in the Air Force in Vietnam and in the Army during Operation Desert Storm. Ann Marie's QOV Group wrapped John in his quilt during a ceremony in his home three days before he died in 2015.

Rolling Along, 64" × 70". Original design and pieced by Ann Marie Mann Ammann. Longarm-quilted by Jane Dougherty.

TOP Ann Marie is standing beside John's picture; her quilt for the book is on the chair.
Photo courtesy of Ann Marie Mann Ammann.

South Carolina

Sticks & Stones, 60" × 71". Pieced and longarm-quilted by Anne Mixon.
Inspiration pattern: Missouri Star Quilt Company.

South Dakota

Mary describes herself as a lifelong "sewist." She has been designing and making quilts her entire adult life. For this QOV, Mary's inspiration was an antique center-medallion quilt.

Mary also remembers how badly Vietnam veterans were treated when they came home. She wants to honor the service of veterans and service members in her local community.

Thirteen Stars, 67" × 86". Original design and pieced by Mary Steinbach Waller.
Longarm-quilted by RE-CREATIONS Quilting.

Tennessee

Joyce became involved with the QOVF in 2014, when she attended the Starr Mountain QOV sew-in. She enjoyed the process of working with other quilters on a worthwhile project and saw it as an opportunity to enhance her quilting skills while recognizing veterans for their service.

Joyce has requested that this quilt be awarded to a Vietnam Army veteran in honor of her brother, Hubert Meredith, who was killed in Vietnam in 1968.

Stars and Flags, 55" × 69". Pieced by Joyce Craig and longarm-quilted by Jo Bell.
Inspiration pattern: Liz Porter, Hero's Tribute.

Texas

Bridgette's QOVF story started on Thanksgiving Day in 2009, when her brother Thomas "Tommy" Stein Jr., a combat Army Medic, was turning forty and was somewhere in the desert in Iraq. She found the QOVF online and knew she had found a great way to give back to veterans and service members. Bridgette read Executive Director Ann Rehbein's challenge to make a difference every day. It inspired Bridgette to design and make her very first Quilt of Valor, *American Ribbon*.

American Ribbon was awarded to Ruben "Sugar Bear" Johnson, a Vietnam veteran and double amputee. Both Bridgette and Sugar Bear are members of American Legion, and, Bridgette says, Sugar Bear inspires her and is absolutely contagious with his joy for life. Sugar Bear is a preacher now and has a small church in Cleveland, Texas.

Bridgette's brother Tommy is medically retired today after five deployments and is married to a Navy veteran. Bridgette's son, Michael Anderson, is currently on active duty in the Army. Michael and Tommy have a very strong bond, so strong that Tommy rode his motorcycle to Fort Hood to pin on Michael's Sergeant E-5 stripes.

American Ribbon, 56" × 72". Original design, pieced and quilted by Bridgette Stein.

TOP RIGHT Bridgette Stein and Ruben "Sugar Bear" Johnson. *Photo courtesy of Bridgette Stein.*

BOTTOM RIGHT Sergeant Michael Anderson and Tommy Stein, Jr. *Photo courtesy of Bridgette Stein.*

Utah

Waving Freedom, 55" × 67". Pieced and longarm-quilted by Jeena Lugo of J Bear Designs.
Inspiration pattern: Star Spangled Banner Flag, Buggy Barn.

Vermont

Andre was at a quilting demo one evening where a friend was showing how to use pages from old magazines and phone books as foundations to make scrappy quilts. He got hooked on the technique and before long realized he had made enough blocks to create a quilt.

When he moved to Vermont, Andre joined a quilting guild, which started a sewing group to make quilts for veterans in Vermont. That group was named Patriotic Spirits when they registered in the QOVF.

Currently, Andre is making arrangements to award this quilt to a local Vietnam veteran.

Red, White & Blue & Scrappy Too, 66" × 72". Original design, pieced and longarm-quilted by Andre Emmell.

Virginia

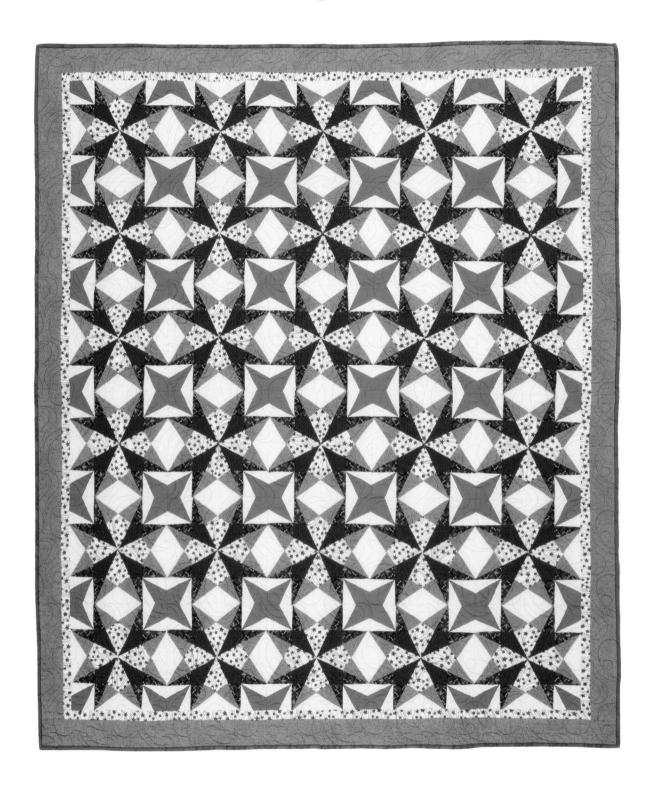

Anna's Starflake, 64" × 74". Pieced by Carrie Johnston and longarm-quilted by Les Page, "the Leatherneck Kilted Quilter."
Inspiration pattern: *Fons & Porter's Love of Quilting*, July–August 2016.

Washington

Kathryn is a military spouse who started sewing by making several red, white, and blue quilts for friends and squadron mates, which left a nice pile of scraps. After moving to Washington in 2013, she found the QOVF and volunteered to use those scraps to stitch binding and make a quilt top.

Since then, she has been making quilt tops for QOV. She has moved to Oklahoma, but she plans on continuing to mail tops back to Washington, since the tiny town she currently lives in doesn't have a local chapter (yet!). This pattern can be found on page 158 of chapter 4.

Chain of Fours, 60" × 80". Pieced and longarm-quilted by Kathryn Starcher.
Inspiration pattern: Jennie Tracy, Porch Swing Quilts, Chain of Fours.

West Virginia

As West Virginia state coordinator, Maribeth Shreve wanted her fellow quilters to create three quilts that uniquely represented West Virginia. She contacted Tresha to design three original quilt patterns. From there, three groups were formed, quilts were made, and *Forever Free* was selected.

Forever Free, 69" × 78". Pieced by Sheila Maxey and longarm-quilted by Sue Papouschek.
Inspiration pattern: Tresha Cottrill.

Wisconsin

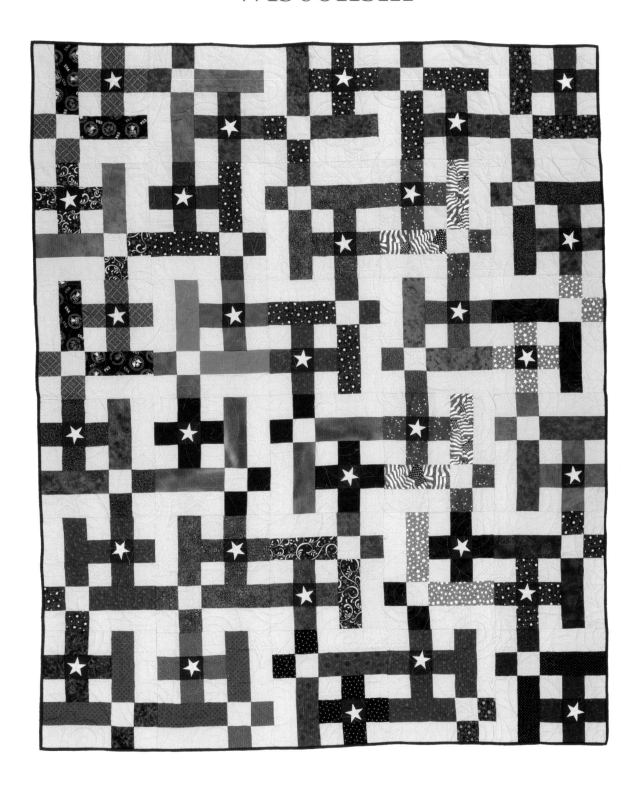

Valor Stars, 61" × 71". Pieced by customers of Hidden Quilts LLC and longarm-quilted by Quilthyme Machine Quilting.

Wyoming

After retiring, Larry expanded a casual interest in embroidery as something to do inside during Wyoming winters. Looking for something else to help him keep a little busier, he discovered the QOVF and made contact with Stephanie Logan, the QOVF state coordinator. He then discovered the association of the QOV group with the local Hunting with Heroes group. As a hunter, Larry felt that the two were a great fit, and he started designing quilts targeted not only to veterans, but veterans who hunt.

After making a few quilts, Betty Cox expressed interest in sewing the blocks together, and now they have formed a team that makes four to five quilts a month. The desire to "keep a little busier" is no longer a problem.

Wyoming Wildlife, 58" × 70". Pieced by Betty Cox. Original design, embroidery and longarm-quilted by Larry Hudson.

RIGHT Detail of *Wyoming Wildlife*.

QOVF Scrapbook

As of summer 2017, the QOVF had two retired military officers on their board, both of whom have been awarded QOV.

Marianne Fons and Walt Davis are holding an Al Lind–inspired quilt that has a special provenance in the QOVF world. It was pieced by Marianne and Catherine Roberts; Marianne has been the most front-and-center QOVF spokesperson and supporter since early QOVF days, and Catherine is, of course, the founder of QOVF.

The quilt was awarded to Major General (Ret.) Walt Davis, an original QOVF board member, who served for more than six years until retiring from the board in 2017. MG Davis retired from active duty in 2012, after serving more than thirty-three years in the US Army as a rotary wing aviator.

Elaine S. Breiner became involved with the QOVF through the Top of the Valley (TOVA) quilters several years ago. Both she and her husband, Chuck, are veterans, and she is very active with the Skyline Quilters of Shenandoah, Virginia, and with the American Legion.

During a talk to the TOVA members in 2016, Renelda Peldunas-Harter mentioned that she had just been selected as a QOVF board member. Much to her surprise, at the end of her talk, TOVA awarded her this QOVF quilt!

TOP Marianne Fons and Major General Walt Davis, US Army, Retired, with his QOVF quilt. *Photo courtesy Marianne Fons.*

BOTTOM *Old Glory*, 49" × 64". Pieced and longarm-quilted by Elaine S. Breiner. From a kit by Simpson and Minnick.

Quilt of Valor Patterns

When I think about those who died protecting our country, my first thought is of the uncle I never met, George Allen Womack. He was only fifteen when he lied about his age and enlisted in the US Navy in June 1943. Imagine a kid from landlocked Oklahoma wanting to go into the Navy. But two of his older brothers had enlisted, so he did, too.

When the Navy discovered that George Allen had lied about his year of birth, they contacted his mother, my great-grandmother. It was up to her to give permission for him to continue to serve or to be discharged. She gave her consent, saying that he was doing what he desired. At one point, she had three sons serving in World War II. She had been through the Great Depression and the Dust Bowl, but this must have been the worst of times for her.

George Allen taught my father how to tie his shoes. He, my father, and I share the gene for great vision. This extraordinary gift of better than 20/20 vision earned him a spot as a gunner on a US Navy Liberator search plane in the South Pacific.

George Allen Womack had just turned seventeen when he died in action near the coast of Palawan in the Philippine Islands on February 17, 1945. When his commanding officer presented the Navy Air Medal to my great-grandmother, he stated, "In the time that your son was serving with our squadron, his performance of duty was at all times outstanding."

The Quilts of Valor program's mission of comforting those who have been touched by war extends beyond veterans. Sometimes, those who are comforted by the giving of quilts are those who made the quilts but were never able to wrap their loved ones.

The patterns that follow are arranged in two sections. The first three patterns were written with the Under Our Wings program in mind. With the guidance of a mentor,

these patterns will guide a community group in the production of a quilt that will be awarded to someone who has served our country.

The remaining patterns are written for quilters of any level of experience.

The "General Directions" explain the techniques and terminology used throughout the patterns.

Enjoy working with your friends and learning from each other as you make these quilts to show your appreciation and gratitude to those who have served.

ABOVE George Allen Womack was born on January 29, 1928, in Sasakwa, Oklahoma. He died on February 17, 1945, just after his seventeenth birthday. This photo was taken in early 1944 at Camp Kearney, California.

GENERAL DIRECTIONS

Throughout the quilt patterns, several techniques are used repeatedly. To save space, the instructions are given here. Even if you are an experienced quilter, take a moment to read through these general directions to become familiar with the types of techniques, methods, and terminology used in the patterns that follow.

BACKING

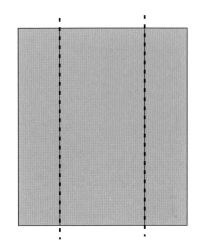

All the quilt backs in these patterns are made from about 5 yards (40" × 180") of fabric. The fabric is cut in half to make two pieces that are approximately 40" × 90". These pieces may be sewn together to make one piece that is approximately 80" × 90".

Another method is to split one of the 40" × 90" pieces lengthwise and attach the two 20" wide strips to either side of the other 40" wide piece to make a wide center with two narrower side strips.

Leftover blocks and scraps can also be pieced together to make interesting backings for quilts.

The dimensions of the backing should be 8" larger than the finished quilt top. For example, a 60" × 80" quilt top will need a backing that measures 68" × 88". Wide backing fabrics are also sold at fabric stores.

BATTING

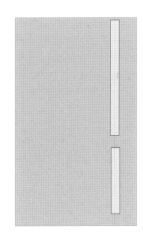

For Quilts of Valor, the following types of batting are recommended: high-quality, low-loft cotton; cotton/polyester blend; or polyester. Packaged twin-size batting is generally the right size for even the largest recommended size of 72" × 90". If you send the top to a longarm quilter, he or she will often supply the right size of batting for the quilt.

If a piece of batting is a little too long on one side and too short on another side, trim off a strip from the too-long side and attach it to the too-short side by butting the batting strips and ironing strips of lightweight, fusible interfacing over the joint. Another way to join batting pieces is to use a zig-zag or other joining stitch by hand or machine.

BINDING

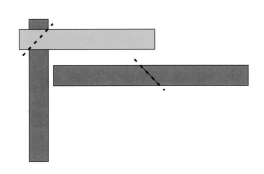

The binding method for these quilts is called "double" or "French fold" binding. The measurement of the finished quilt is used to calculate how many strips measuring 2½" × WOF (width of fabric) will be needed for binding. Attach the strips end to end to make the desired length to go all around the quilt. The ends may be cut off straight and attached to each other with a straight seam.

A less bulky way to join binding strips is to position the strips right sides together at a 90-degree angle and sew them together with a diagonal seam. Trim the seam allowance to ¼" and press open.

The binding is then folded in half, wrong sides together, and pressed. Attach the raw edges to the right side of the quilt with a ¼" seam. Wrap the folded edge of the binding around to the back of the quilt and secure with hand stitching. Another way to attach binding is to stitch it to the back of the quilt, wrap it around to the front, and then neatly machine stitch the binding.

BLOCK STYLES

The following directions tell you how to make all the block styles used in the patterns included in this book.

Chevron

A chevron is a rectangular block (see Flying Goose), where the opposite corners form parallel lines at either end of the center fabric.

Flying Goose Unit (FG)

One of the basic elements of quilt piecing, the Flying Goose consists of three triangles—one large and two small. Traditionally, these triangles are referred to as the "Goose" (large) and the "Sky" (small). Usually, squares or rectangles are used to make the units.

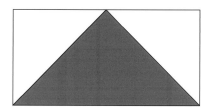

One-at-a-Time FGs with Bonus Half-Square Triangles

A Flying Goose unit (FG) is usually twice as wide as it is high. For example, if a 3" × 6" finished-size FG is called for in a quilt pattern:

Cut (1) 3½" × 6½" rectangle (the "Goose")

Cut (2) 3½" squares (the "Sky")

Place one Sky square, right sides together at one end of the Goose rectangle

Sew a diagonal seam from corner to corner

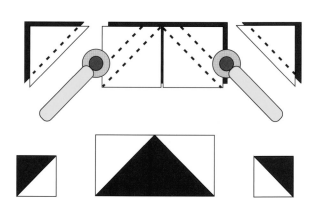

At this point, the excess fabric from the corners could be trimmed off, leaving a ¼" seam allowance, and discarded. Or, to make a bonus half-square triangle (HST):

Sew another seam ½" away from the first seam and cut in between the two

Press the Sky triangle away from the Goose triangle

Repeat with the other Sky square at the other end of the Goose rectangle

Set aside the (2) bonus HSTs for use in another project.

Four-at-a-Time FGs

If many FG units are needed, this is a particularly good method:

> For the Goose part of the unit, cut (1) square finished width + $1\frac{1}{4}$"
>
> For the Sky part of the unit, cut (4) squares finished height + $\frac{7}{8}$"
>
> Place two Sky squares, right sides together, on opposite corners of the Goose square
>
> Draw a line diagonally from corner to corner over the Sky squares.

Sew $\frac{1}{4}$" from each line

Cut on drawn line

Press seam allowance open or toward Sky

Place another Sky square at the corner of one of the units just made

Draw a diagonal line from corner to corner

Sew $\frac{1}{4}$" from each line

Cut on drawn line

Repeat with other side

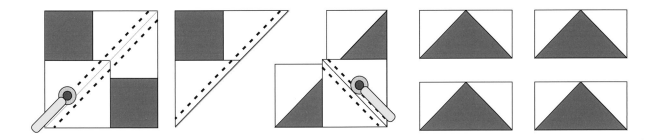

Four-Patch Unit

These units are a good way to use up scrap squares that are left over from other projects. Keep a stack of squares handy for use as thread savers. These units are also a good way to use up bonus HSTs. To make multiple Four-Patch units, see **Strip Sets** on page 95.

To make a single Four-Patch unit:

> Cut four squares the same size
>
> Sew two squares together into pairs RST (right sides together)
>
> Press seam allowance toward the darker fabric
>
> Sew pairs together, positioning the colors diagonally
>
> The seam allowances will nest, making the intersection very accurate

To finish the unit:

> Turn unit to back and finger-press all seam allowances going the same direction
>
> Make a tiny four-patch in the center and make the seam lay flat by pulling the last set of seams at the intersection in opposite directions to release the last 2–3 stitches and allow the seams to "spin" around the center

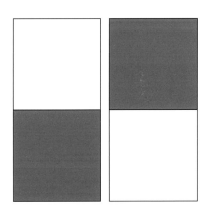

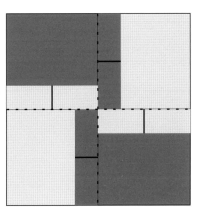

Half-Square Triangle (HST) Unit

The HST unit is probably the most useful patch in all of patchwork.

- Cut squares of two different colors

- Cut them in half on the diagonal

- Switch the triangles

- Sew them back together

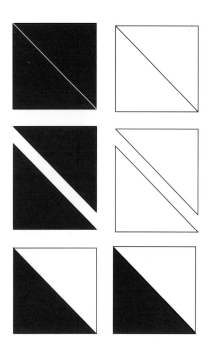

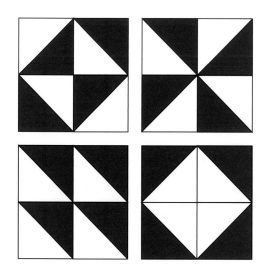

Because these units are so versatile, quilters have come up with many ways to put them together alone or in combination with plain squares or other units.

Making HSTs: Two at a Time

Note that the math is a little different for HSTs than for squares: Finished-size patch + ⅞" = cut size for HST unit squares

Because the bias grain of fabric is stretchy, this is a good way to make a pair of HSTs:

- Cut (1) square from each color

- Place right sides together

- Draw a line diagonally from corner to corner

- Sew ¼" on each side of the drawn line

- Cut on the drawn line

- Press seam allowance toward darker fabric or open

Bonus HSTs

There are many ways to make HST units. One method involves using the extra corners that otherwise would be cut off Square-in-Square units or Flying Goose / Chevron rectangle units and making them into HSTs for later use. Often, these bonus HSTs are useful for sawtooth borders or scrap quilts. See **Flying Goose Units** on page 90.

Four-at-a-Time HSTs

To make blocks stable and avoid the distortion of bias edges, quilters try to keep the straight grain on the outside of both blocks and the units that make them up. Notice that in a regular HST, the outer edge of the unit is on the straight grain, whereas the diagonal seam is on the bias. When used in a larger block, this unit stays very square.

This four-at-a-time HST method leaves bias edges on the outside of the units but, if the fabric is handled carefully, is a quick and easy way to get an interesting result with the units—particularly if striped fabric is used.

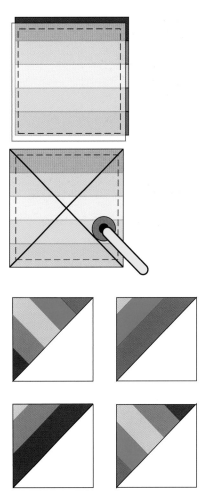

Place two squares right sides together and sew $1/4$" from the edge all around. The effect is most dramatic if one of the squares is either a striped fabric or made from strips that are sewn together.

Press the squares to set the outer seam

Now would be a good time to use a spray starch or starch substitute to minimize stretching on the bias edges

Cut TWICE on the diagonal to make (4) HST units

Open and press toward darker fabric.

The resulting HSTs will be odd sizes, so they must be trimmed to the desired size. For example:

10" starting squares will produce (4) HSTs that can be trimmed to 6 $1/2$" (for 6" finished size) HSTs

7" starting squares will yield 4 $1/2$" cut (4" finished size) HSTS

5" starting squares will yield 3" cut ($2^1/2$" finished size) HSTs

Make a few samples to be sure that the size you need can be cut from the resulting HSTs.

Eight-at-a-Time HSTs

This is the method to use for turning out dozens and dozens of HSTs quickly and accurately. Only two squares are needed from each fabric.

The math is: (Finished HST size × 2) + 1¾".

For example, to make (8) 3" finished-size HSTs, cut the large squares (3" × 2) + 1¾" = 7¾".

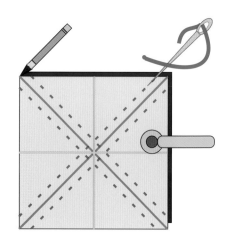

Cut (1) square from each color

Draw diagonal lines from corner to corner on the back of the lighter fabric

Place right sides together

Sew ¼" from drawn lines

Press

First Cut: through the center into (4) squares

Second Cut: from corner to corner into (8) triangles

Press seam allowances open or toward darker fabric

Nine-Patch Unit

Like Four-Patch units, these units are a good way to use up scrap squares. To make multiple Nine-Patch units, see **Strip Sets** on page 95. You will see the Nine-Patch repeatedly in all quilts. The nine squares can consist of plain fabric, HSTs, QSTs, Rail Fence units, and any other square unit.

To make one Nine-Patch unit:

Cut nine squares the same size, usually:
(4 light + 5 dark) or (5 light + 4 dark)

The squares are usually arranged as "light center" or "dark center"

 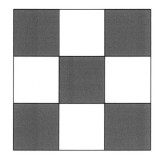

Sew three rows of three squares together

Press seam allowances in opposite directions so that the seam allowances will nest

Quarter-Square Triangle Unit (QST)

Sometimes called the "Hourglass" block, QSTs start out as HSTs. The technique is the same as for making HSTs, but there is an extra step and the measurement is larger to account for the extra seam allowance needed.

For two-at-a-time QSTs: cut (2) squares finished QST size + 1¼"

For eight-at-a-time QSTs: cut (2) squares (finished QST size × 2) + 2½"

Use any method to make HSTs from (2) squares of fabric

Place (2) HSTs right sides together with alternate colors facing each other

Nest the seam allowances

Draw a line diagonally across the seamline from corner to corner

Sew $\frac{1}{4}$" on each side of the drawn line

Cut on the drawn line

Press final seam open

Trim QST unit to finished size $+ \frac{1}{2}$", if necessary

Rail Fence

A square block made from strips of fabric—usually 3–5 strips. The size of the strips is determined by the desired finished block size. Strip measurements must be multiples of $\frac{1}{8}$" so that rotary cutters and rulers can be used.

For example, a 9" finished-size block could be made of (3) 3" finished-size strips, cut $3\frac{1}{2}$" wide by $9\frac{1}{2}$".

An 8" finished-size block would have to be cut from (3) 3.166" wide strips, which doesn't work with rotary cutting.

However, an 8" block could be made from (4) 2" finished-size strips, cut $2\frac{1}{2}$" × $8\frac{1}{2}$".

The reason that 12" blocks are so popular is that they can be evenly divided by 1.5, 2, 3, 4, or 6 to calculate the size of the units that make up the block.

To calculate the size of the strips to cut:

Strip width = (finished size of block divided by number of strips) + $\frac{1}{2}$"

Strip length = finished size of block + $\frac{1}{2}$"

Strip Sets and Sub-cutting

To make a Nine-Patch or a Rail Fence block unit quickly, cut WOF strips and sew together on the long edges.

Subcut these strip sets into segments the same width as the original strips. For example, to make a 9" finished-size Nine-Patch block, cut strips $3\frac{1}{2}$" wide × WOF.

Cut (2) $3\frac{1}{2}$" × WOF from fabric for Corners

Cut (3) $3\frac{1}{2}$" × WOF from fabric for Sides

Cut (1) $3\frac{1}{2}$" × WOF from fabric for Center (might be the same color as sides or corners)

Attach strips in two sets of three:

Corner + Side + Corner and press seam allowances away from center

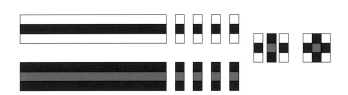

Side + Center + Side and press seam allowances toward center

Subcut the strip sets into $3\frac{1}{2}$" segments

Attach the units to make the Nine-Patch block

Notice that twice as many Corner + Side + Corner strip sets are needed to form the Nine-Patch

BORDERS

All patterns in this book that have a border (some don't) use the "long horizontal" method: strips for the left/right sides of the quilt top are added first; next, the top/bottom borders are added. Continue adding borders in this manner for however many borders are required.

Strips of plain fabric borders for quilts are generally cut one of two ways: **pieced** or **unpieced**.

For unpieced borders, cut the border strips from one long piece of fabric that has been cut or ripped lengthwise.

For pieced borders, cut strips across the width of the fabric and attach them end to end or with diagonal seams, as with binding strips.

An adjusting border is added to a panel to bring the panel to the correct size for the pattern being used. For example, a printed panel might be 8" × 8" square, but to be used in a quilt that is made of 12" blocks, a 2" border might need to be added to all sides of the panel to "adjust" the size to 12". Also, large panels are sometimes used as the central medallion of a quilt. In this case, the size of the panel might need to be adjusted with added borders to make the math work out with other blocks or pieced borders.

About Border Measurement: When to Cut

The worst way to add a border is to cut a much-too-long strip and just start sewing it onto the edge of the quilt top. This is where wavy "potato chip edge" quilts come from! There are two good ways to cut borders:

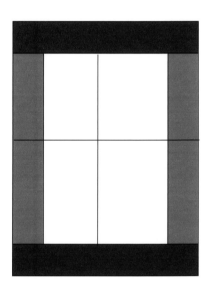

A better way is to cut the border strips to the exact length required by the pattern (which assumes that all cutting and sewing will be completely accurate).

The best way is to wait until the main part of the quilt is made, and then measure the quilt so they will have actual or average measurements. Measure through the center (which is more stable than the edge) of the quilt top.

Whether you cut the borders before or after the top is assembled, keep in mind that there are very few people whose piecing is completely accurate, and that fabric does have some give to it. Borders are your opportunity to "square up" a slightly wonky quilt top.

ENDER OR THREAD SAVER

Keep a stack of extra pairs of squares or triangles next to your sewing machine. At the end of a seam, instead of pulling out a long length of thread to snip and then separate the piece from the sewing machine, immediately sew onto a pair of scrap squares. Snip between the first and second units to save thread and to create Four-Patch units for later use.

FABRIC

Quilting fabric for a Quilt of Valor should be 100 percent cotton, first quality, 40+" wide, and is purchased by the yard (36"). Precut fabric is also available in collections of 2½" strips, 5" squares, 10" squares, and other sizes. Avoid juvenile prints. Also, unless the recipient is known, avoid prints that are branch specific (such as Army or Navy). Quilts of Valor can be made in any colors; however, red, white, and blue are the most popular both with male and female recipients.

Fussy-Cutting

When you isolate a printed motif in a piece of fabric and then cut it out in such a way as to fit into a particular size patch, this is called fussy-cutting. A piece of fabric that has been fussy-cut resembles Swiss cheese.

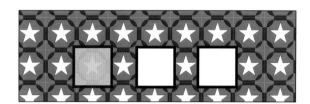

Washing Fabric

Some people prewash fabric yardage before cutting out the quilt pieces. After the fabric is washed and dried, it must be pressed. Be aware that fabric is sometimes folded unevenly before being wrapped onto a bolt. Refold the fabric after washing and drying, being sure that the folded edges match straight across the grain. Width of fabric (WOF) strips that are cut from crookedly folded fabric will be "V" shaped and the printed motifs will be misaligned.

Snip and Rip

Good-quality cotton fabric can be torn lengthwise or crosswise to make absolutely straight strips. Some people don't like the torn edges, but ripping is a good way to remove selvages and to split the yardage lengthwise for borders and backings.

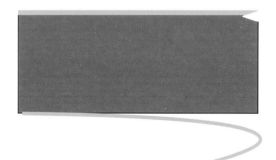

MEASUREMENTS:
"CUT" VS. "FINISHED" VS. "UNFINISHED" VS. "TRIM"

See the "Seam Allowance" section for an explanation of the importance of ¼" seams in quilting.

Generally, quilts are made from blocks, which are made from patches of various sizes.

Cut Size: The size of a patch before it is added to a block. Because patches in a block are attached to each other by using a ¼" seam, this measurement must be added to all sides of a patch to determine the "cut" size of a patch. For example, if a patch is to measure 4" square in a block, it must be cut 4½" square.

Finished Size: The size of a patch or block as measured in an assembled block or quilt. For example, (9) 4½" cut-size patches will form 4" finished-size squares in a 12" finished-size Nine-Patch block.

Unfinished Size: The size of a block before it is sewn into a quilt. The 12" finished-size block will measure 12 ½" before it is attached to the other blocks in a quilt.

Trimmed Size: In some cases, blocks or units are made larger than needed and then cut down to the correct size. For example, HSTs and QSTs are often made too big and then trimmed down to the correct size for the sake of precision. With HSTs, many people would cut 5" squares instead of 4⅞" squares and then trim the finished unit to 4½". This method is very accurate but requires the extra step of trimming all the units.

QUILT BLOCK SETTINGS

Setting Squares
Side-Setting Triangles
Corner Triangles

Quilt blocks are most frequently attached in horizontal rows, which are then attached to each other to complete the quilt top.

Blocks that are rotated 45 degrees are set on-point. Often, **Setting Squares** are used to leave plain squares between pieced blocks so that appliqué or quilting motifs can be featured.

If the edges of the quilt are to be straight, **Side-Setting Triangles** must be placed at the end of rows.

Corner Triangles complete the square or rectangular top.

Considering the grain of the fabric is particularly important when cutting these squares and triangles, so that the straight grain, not the stretchy bias, will fall at the outer edge of the quilt.

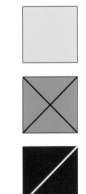

Cut the square in half on the diagonal TWICE to make (4) side-setting triangles

Cut enough additional squares, depending on the number of rows in the quilt

A. Setting Squares

Cut the same size as finished blocks + ½"

B. Side-Setting Triangles

Multiply the finished block size by 1.414

Round up to the next ⅛" measurement

Add 1¼" for seam allowance

Cut (1) square

C. Corner Triangles

Divide the finished block size by 1.414

Round up to the next ⅛" measurement

Add ⅞" for seam allowance

Cut (2) squares this size

Cut each square in half ONCE on the diagonal

QUILT WASHING

Opinions vary about the best way to wash a quilt, but new quilts (not antique quilts) that are well made, machine quilted, and neatly bound are intended to be used. A quilt that will be used will need to be washed periodically. Also, quilts may pick up dust and pet hair in the process of being made, so washing before presenting may be necessary.

Wash these quilts in a washing machine. Dry them on a cool or damp dry setting in the dryer and lay them out flat to finish drying, if necessary. Avoid scented detergents and fabric softeners.

SEAM ALLOWANCE

The distance from the edge of the fabric to the seamline is critical for accuracy in pieced blocks. Quilting patterns always use $\frac{1}{4}$" seams to attach the patches in a block, to attach borders, and to attach blocks together into a quilt top. That seam allowance amount is included in the measurements you see in the pattern. Because an accurate seam allowance is so important, a good idea is to test accuracy by making a sample.

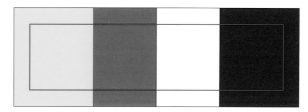

$$2\frac{1}{4}" + 2" + 2" + 2\frac{1}{4}" = 8\frac{1}{2}"$$

Cut (4) 2½" squares and sew them together with your best, most accurate $\frac{1}{4}$" seam

Press to flatten the strip

Measure from end to end

The total length should be 8½"

The two interior squares should measure exactly 2" across

Practice with different techniques or machine attachments and guides until an accurate $\frac{1}{4}$" seam is achieved.

SIZES FOR QUILTS

The recommended size for Quilts of Valor is 60" × 80" (minimum 55" × 65" to maximum 72" × 90"). All quilt patterns in this book fall within the recommended size ranges. Sometimes, if a pattern is slightly too small to meet these requirements, borders can be added to increase the size and to add an extra design element.

LET'S GET STARTED

Enjoy working with your friends and learning from each other as you make these quilts to show your appreciation and gratitude to those who have served.

Patterns for the Under Our Wings Program

The Under Our Wings (UOW) program was created and launched by Quilts of Valor Foundation Board of Directors member Marianne Fons. It is an exciting and important initiative offering young people and civic organizations the opportunity to perform community service, to learn about veterans and service members touched by war, and to introduce them to the art of quilting.

The program focuses on America's youth through Girl Scouts, Boy Scouts, 4-H, 4-H Military Partnership, and any other youth group participating in a community service project. The UOW program also serves adult civic organizations that seek to participate in a national service project.

These three patterns were written with the Under Our Wings program in mind. They are simple and set up for groups of nonquilters to follow easily.

UOW program groups can use these patterns to learn to quilt by making a Quilt of Valor, and to experience the joy of awarding the quilt to a deserving veteran! Enjoy the process.

WWW.QOVF.ORG/WINGS

GENERAL DIRECTIONS: PP. 89–99

The "General Directions" starting on page 89 explain the techniques and terminology used throughout the patterns.

LEFT Nebraska 4-H member Bailee Remmers honors Vietnam veteran Douglas Smith with her Quilt of Valor during an American Legion Rider event.

CENTER Nebraska 4-H member Carter O'Neel loves to study history, the military, and aeronautics. His Marine veteran cousin was deeply moved when wrapped with Carter's Quilt of Valor.

RIGHT Nebraska 4-H member Grace O'Neel was born in New York City and created the "Lady Liberty" Quilt of Valor as a personal tribute to honor the bravery of a US veteran.

The Brave

An Under Our Wings Pattern

Photo on page 38
Traditional quilt design by Lauren Elliott
Finished size 68" × 76"

This project should be led by a mentor, an experienced quilter, who will guide the group through the process of making a Quilt of Valor for the Under Our Wings program. Under the mentor's leadership, the group should be able to make the blocks and put them together to create a quilt top in one day.

HELPFUL HINTS

Read through all instructions before you begin

WOF = width of fabric

RST = right sides together

Sew with ¼" seams

FABRIC REQUIREMENTS

Notes

You can buy precut charm packs of 5" squares, or you can cut your own 5" squares of fabric. Please note that the mentor will need to use the rotary cutter until the mentor is sure that a member of the group is familiar with the use of the rotary cutter, to avoid accidents.

Using a variety of fabrics will enhance the look of the finished quilt top. When cutting 5" squares from a single fat quarter (18" × 22"), you will be able to cut (12). From one-half yard of fabric (18" × 40"), you will get (24) squares.

In all, you will need:

(72) 5" squares of assorted red, white, and blue fabrics (or fabrics of your choice)

(51) 2½" × WOF strips of assorted red, white, and blue fabrics (or fabrics of your choice)

Backing: 5 yards

Binding: ¾ yard

CUTTING

From the (51) 2½" × WOF strips cut:

(72) 2½" × 5" strips

(144) 2½" × 7" strips

(72) 2½" × 9" strips

PREPARING TO SEW

Sort the cut fabric into (72) **Block Sets**.
Each set should contain:

- (1) 5" square
- (1) 2½" × 5" strip
- (2) 2½" × 7" strips
- (1) 2½" × 9" strip

Once the squares and strips are sorted, pin each Block Set together. Now you are ready to sew.

MAKING THE BLOCKS

There are at least two ways to arrange the fabric square and the rectangles to form a square block

Attach the pieces with a ¼" seam in the order indicated

Make (72) **Log Cabin Variation Blocks**

Press the blocks and, if necessary, trim to 9" square

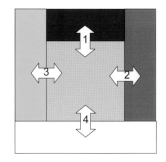 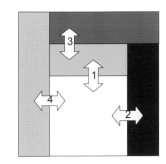

ASSEMBLING THE QUILT TOP
Attaching Blocks into Rows

Attach the (72) blocks into (9) rows of (8) blocks each

Turn the blocks in random directions—there is no right way to position the blocks, which is part of the beauty of this quilt design

Attaching the Rows

Attach the (9) rows together to complete the quilt top

Pin the raw edges at the beginning, the end, and at the seamline intersections where the blocks line up with the previous row

Press long, row-joining seams open to avoid bulk

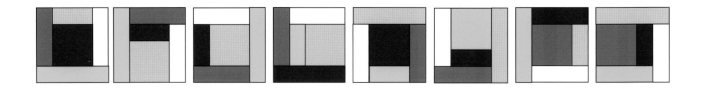

FINISHING THE QUILT

The quilt top should now measure 68½" × 77"

Refer to the "General Directions" (page 89) for preparing **Backing** and **Binding**

Backing for this quilt should measure 76" × 85"

For **Binding**, cut (8) 2½" × WOF strips

GENERAL DIRECTIONS: PP. 89–99

Journey to Eagle: On My Honor

An Under Our Wings Pattern

Traditional quilt design by Nancy Cann
Finished size 60" × 80"

This project should be led by a mentor, an experienced quilter, who will guide the group through the process of making a Quilt of Valor for the Under Our Wings program. Under the mentor's leadership, the group should be able to make the blocks and put them together to create a quilt top in one day.

HELPFUL HINTS

Read through all instructions before you begin

WOF = width of fabric

RST = right sides together

HST = half-square triangle

Sew with ¼" seams

NOTES

This quilt top is made from two blocks:
Rail Fence and **Corner Star**

Journey to Eagle: On My Honor, 60" × 80". Original design and longarm-quilted by Nancy Cann.
Pieced by Nancy Cann and the Boy Scouts and leaders of BSA Troop 473.

FABRIC REQUIREMENTS

Select fabric that is at least 42" wide when the selvages are removed

Red: 2 yards

Blue: 2 yards

White: 1 1/4 yards

Backing: 5 yards

Binding: 3/4 yard

CUTTING

Rail Fence Blocks

Reminder: remove selvage before cutting

WOF strips must be at least 42" long

Cut (22) red 2 1/2" × WOF strips

Cut (22) blue 2 1/2" × WOF strips

Cut (11) white 2 1/2" × WOF strips

Corner Star Blocks

Reminder: remove selvage before cutting

WOF strips must be at least 42" long

Cut (48) red 2 1/2" squares

Cut (4) blue 2 1/2" × 8 1/2" rectangles

Cut (4) blue 2 1/2" × 10 1/2" rectangles

Cut (48) white 2 1/2" squares

PREPARING TO SEW

Rail Fence Blocks

Group together and pin (11) **5-Strip Set**s, each containing:

(2) blue strips

(2) red strips

(1) white strip

Corner Star Blocks

Group together and pin (4) **Star Block Sets**, each containing:

(12) white 2 1/2" squares

(12) red 2 1/2" squares

(1) blue 2 1/2" × 8 1/2" rectangle

(1) blue 2 1/2" × 10 1/2" rectangle

SEWING THE BLOCKS

Make (44) Rail Fence Blocks

Sew the **5-Strip Strip Sets** together with 1/4" seams, as shown

Make (11) strip sets with strips in this order: blue + red + white + red + blue

Press the strip sets with seam allowances going in the same direction

Cut (4) 10 1/2" segments from each strip set

10 1/2"

10 1/2"

GENERAL DIRECTIONS: PP. 89–99

Make (4) Corner Star Blocks

First, make the red + white HSTs for each block

Place (8) white and (8) red 2½" squares RST in (8) pairs

Draw a diagonal line from one corner to the opposite corner on the back of the white squares

Sew on the drawn line

Cut off the corner as shown, leaving ¼" seam allowance

Discard the extra corners

Press seam allowance toward darker fabric

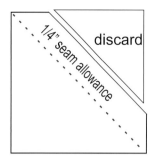

For each **Corner Star Block**

Attach the (4) remaining **White Square**s, (4) remaining **Red Squares**, and (8) **Red + White HSTs** as shown

Add **Blue Rectangle**s as shown, starting with the 8½" rectangle on one side.

Repeat for all four **Corner Star Blocks**

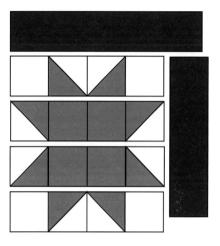

ASSEMBLING THE QUILT TOP

Make (8) rows of (6) blocks each, attaching the blocks together with ¼" seam

The first and last rows have **Corner Star Blocks** at each end

Notice that the **Blue Rectangles** form an outer corner for the quilt, so be sure to turn them the right way

Refer to the illustration of the whole quilt to turn the **Rail Fence Block**s in the correct direction to achieve the woven effect

After joining the blocks into a row, press the seam allowances going in opposite directions from one row to the next row so that the seams will nest when the rows are attached to each other. For example, press the seam allowances to the left in row 1. Press seam allowances to the right in row 2

Attach rows and press the long seams open after attaching the rows together

FINISHING THE QUILT

The quilt top should now measure 60½" × 80½"

Refer to the "General Directions" (page 89) for preparing **Backing** and **Binding**

Backing for this quilt should measure 68" × 88"

For **Binding**, cut (8) 2½" × WOF strips

A Hero's Weave

An Under Our Wings Pattern

Original design by Dennis L. Taylor
Finished size 60½" × 80" including borders

This project should be led by a mentor, an experienced quilter, who will guide the group through the process of making a Quilt of Valor for the Under Our Wings program. Under the mentor's leadership, the group should be able to make the blocks and put them together to create a quilt top in one day.

HELPFUL HINTS

Read through all instructions before you begin

WOF = width of fabric

RST = right sides together

Sew with ¼" seams

FABRIC REQUIREMENTS

Red: 2 yards

White: 2 yards

Blue: 1½ yards

Backing: 5 yards

Binding: ¾ yard

A Hero's Weave. Longarm quilted by Doyleen W. Taylor.

CUTTING

Except for the borders, all fabric for this quilt can be cut from 4½" × WOF strips. A good idea is to cut and set aside the strips for the borders first.

Borders

Cut and attach 3½" × WOF strips as follows to make long border strips (see page 96):

(7) white 3½" × WOF

(4) red 3½" × WOF

(3) blue 3½" × WOF Because you will save these borders for later, pin a **label** to each set of borders to remind you where they go. From these long strips, cut:

(2) white 3½" × 68½" for **Left/Right Inner Borders**

(2) white 3½" × 55" for **Top/Bottom Inner Borders**

(2) red 3½" × 74½" for **Left/Right Outer Borders**

(2) blue 3½" × 61" for **Top/Bottom Outer Borders**

Blocks

After the borders are cut, all remaining fabric is cut into 4½" × WOF strips.

The mentor can cut and **label** the squares and rectangles beforehand, as noted below:

Red: (48) 4½" × 6½" rectangles marked **R1**

Red: (8) 4½" squares marked **R2 END**

Blue: (63) 4½" squares marked **B1**

White: (71) 4½" × 3½" rectangles marked **W1**

White: (48) 4½" × 1½" rectangles marked **W2**

- -

PREPARING TO SEW

There are no "blocks" in this quilt, only rows of rectangles. Make sets of the pieces needed for each row. For each **Row Set**, you will need:

(9) **Blue + White Row Sets**, each containing:

(7) B1 squares

(7) W1 rectangles

(8) **Red + White Row Sets**, each containing:

(6) R1 rectangles

(6) W1 rectangles

(1) R2 square (marked as "R2 end")

(1) W1 rectangle (marked "W1 end")

Pin the row sets together

- -

ATTACHING THE ROWS

As you attach the pieces for each row, notice that each row has a 4½" × 3½" white rectangle marked "W1" at one end

In addition, the red rows have a 4½" square (marked "R2 end") at the opposite end from the W1 rectangle

These "end" units are important for aligning the rows to each other

The other important task: after each row is assembled, to cut off ½" from the white W1 end pieces that fall at the beginning or end of the rows

ASSEMBLING THE QUILT

Attach the rows, starting and ending with a blue + white row and alternating with the red + white rows

The spacing of the rows depends on having cut off ½" from each white rectangle that falls at the end or beginning of a row

If the rows don't seem symmetrical this might be the problem

ADDING BORDERS
Attaching Borders

Press the completed quilt top and attach the borders in the following order, pressing after each pair is attached:

White **Left/Right Inner**

White **Top/Bottom Inner**

Red **Left/Right Outer**

Blue **Top/Bottom Outer**

COMPLETING THE QUILT

The quilt top should now measure 61" × 80½"

Refer to the "General Directions" (page 89) for preparing **Backing** and **Binding**

Backing for this quilt should measure 68" × 88"

For **Binding**, cut and attach (8) 2½" × WOF strips

The rest of the quilt patterns in this book range from easy to challenging but are within reach of most quilters.

GENERAL
DIRECTIONS:
PP. 89–99

Rockets' Red Glare

Photo on page 32
Inspiration pattern: Diana Beaubien, Diamond Patch
Finished size 61" × 78" including borders

There are (24) 6" **Nine-Patch Blocks** and (59) 6" **Plain Blocks** set on-point in this quilt. The Nine-Patch blocks are quickly made from strip sets, making this an easy quilt to put together. Notice that there are two arrangements of Nine-Patch blocks and that they are turned in different directions to make the design very lively. A 2" inner border and a 3" outer border finish the design

FABRIC REQUIREMENTS

For Blocks
White: 2 yards
Blue: 1 yard
Red: 1 yard

For Borders
White: ³/₄ yard
Blue: ³/₄ yard

For Setting and Corner Triangles
Red: 1 yard

For Backing
5 yards

For Binding
³/₄ yard

CUTTING INSTRUCTIONS

Cutting and Organizing the Block Parts

Cut plain square blocks
White: cut (35) 6¹/₂" squares from (6) 6¹/₂" × WOF strips

Red: cut (12) 6¹/₂" squares from (2) 6¹/₂" × WOF strips

Blue: cut (12) 6¹/₂" squares from (2) 6¹/₂" × WOF strips

Cut and Organize Strip Sets for Nine-Patch Blocks

White: cut (7) 2 1/2" × WOF strips

Red: cut (4) 2 1/2" × WOF strips

Blue: cut (4) 2 1/2" × WOF strips

Pin together sets of strips as follows and set aside to be sewn later:

(1) Red + white + blue strip set

(1) White + blue + white strip set

(1) White + red + white strip set

Cut Setting Triangles
Side Triangles (see page 98)

Red: cut (6) 9 3/4" squares from (2) 9 3/4" × WOF strips

Cut squares in half TWICE on the diagonal to make (24) quarter-square triangles

Label "side triangles" and set aside

Cut Corner Half-Square Triangles

Red: cut (2) 5 1/8" squares from (1) 5 1/8" × WOF strip

Cut squares in half ONCE on the diagonal

Label "corner triangles" and set aside

Cutting the Borders

Refer to the "General Directions" (page 96) about deciding to cut the borders before or after the main part of the quilt top is complete. **Labeling** the strips is a good idea. These are the specific cut sizes for the borders on this quilt:

Inner Border

White: cut and attach (7) 2 1/2" × WOF strips

From the long strip:

Cut (2) 2 1/2" × 68 1/2" for **Left/Right Inner Borders**

Cut (2) 2 1/2" × 55 1/2" for **Top/Bottom Inner Borders**

Outer Border

Blue: cut and attach (7) 3 1/2" × WOF strips

From the long strip:

Cut (2) 3 1/2" × 72 1/2" for **Left/Right Outer Borders**

Cut (2) 3 1/2" × 61 1/2" for **Top/Bottom Outer Borders**

MAKING THE NINE-PATCH BLOCKS
Make the Strip Sets (see page 95)

Make strip sets for Nine-Patch blocks by sewing the long strips together:

Make (1) red + white + blue strip set

Make (1) white + blue + white strip set

Make (1) white + red + white strip set

Press seam allowances away from white strips

Cut strip sets crossways into 2 1/2" segments

Cut (48) red + white + blue segments

Cut (12) white + blue + white segments

Cut (12) white + red + white segments

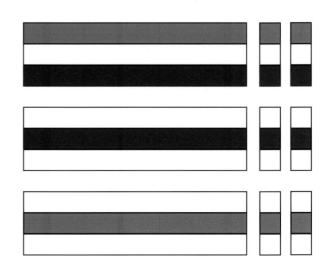

Assemble Nine-Patch Blocks

Assemble the (24) Nine-Patch blocks as shown

(12) with red center so that red squares form a diagonal

(12) with blue center so that blue squares form a diagonal

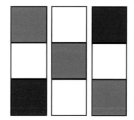 

ASSEMBLING THE QUILT TOP

Attach the corner triangles, plain squares, Nine-Patch blocks, and setting triangles in (15) diagonal rows, as shown

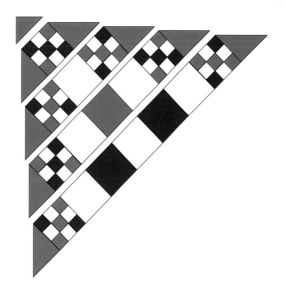

ADDING BORDERS (see page 96)

Attach borders in the following order:

2¹/₂" white **Left/Right Inner Borders**

2¹/₂" white **Top/Bottom Inner Borders**

3¹/₂" blue **Left/Right Outer Borders**

3¹/₂" blue **Top/Bottom Outer Borders**

FINISHING THE QUILT

The quilt top should now measure 61¹/₂" × 78¹/₂"

Refer to the "General Directions" (page 89) for preparing **Backing** and **Binding**

Backing for this quilt should measure 69" × 86"

For **Binding**, cut (8) 2¹/₂" × WOF strips

Let's Fly Away

Photo on page 33
Inspiration pattern: Cutting Corners,
Missouri Star Quilt Company
Finished size 60" × 78"

There are so many panels available that have a patriotic theme and would be perfect for a Quilts of Valor project. Panels are found in many different sizes, but once you have added borders to the **Center Panel** to bring it to the right size, the rest of the quilt is just a matter of adding more borders until the desired overall size is achieved. The pieced-block border for this quilt is made from (60) 6" finished-size **Half-Square Triangle Blocks**. These HSTs can be made from many different methods; however, you might enjoy using a different method for making these blocks with strip-pieced squares instead, as shown in the original quilt on page 33. In addition to the HST borders, there are 2" and 4" borders.

FABRIC REQUIREMENTS
For Center Panel

Select a printed panel up to 24½" × 42½". If the chosen panel is smaller, use coordinating fabrics to add borders to adjust the unfinished size to 24½" × 42½". If the center panel is larger than this size, it will need to be cut down to the size specified for this pattern, so be sure to look at the design carefully to see if you will lose important elements of the design when it is cut down.

For Border HST Blocks

White: 1¼ yards
(10–15) assorted red 2½" × WOF strips
(10–15) assorted blue 2½" × WOF strips

For Borders

Inner border (gold): ½ yard
Outer border (blue): ⅝ yard

For Backing

5 yards

For Binding

¾ yard

CUTTING INSTRUCTIONS

Center Panel

For this pattern, the size of the HSTs determines the size of the **Center Panel**. The center panel, ideally, should measure 24½" × 42½" unfinished size (24" × 42" finished size) for the double HST border to work out evenly. If the panel you are using is smaller, simply subtract the measurement of the smaller panel from these dimensions and adjust the size to 24½" × 42½" total. If the panel is too large, cut it down to 24½" × 42½". Do the math with finished-size measurements and then add the ½" seam allowance before you cut.

Cutting and Organizing the HST Border Blocks

White: cut (16) 10" squares

Assorted red: cut at least (10) 2½" × WOF strips

Assorted blue: cut at least (10) 2½" × WOF strips

Pin together sets of strips as follows and set aside to be sewn later:

(2) sets of (5) red strips each

(2) sets of (5) blue strips each

Cutting the Borders

Refer to the "General Directions" (page 96) about deciding to cut the borders before or after the main part of the quilt top is complete. **Labeling** the strips is a good idea. These are the specific cut sizes for the borders on this quilt.

Inner Border

Gold: cut and attach (7) 2½" × WOF strips

From the long strip:

Cut (2) 2½" × 66½" strips for **Left/Right Inner Border**

Cut (2) 2½" × 52½" strips for **Top/Bottom Inner Border**

Outer Border

Blue: cut and attach (8) 4½" × WOF strips
From the long strip:

Cut (2) 4½" × 70½" strips for **Left/Right Outer Border**

Cut (2) 4½" × 60½" strips for **Top/Bottom Outer Border**

SEWING THE HST BLOCKS

Make Strip Sets (see page 93)

Sew the assorted red 2½" × WOF strips together to make (2) **Red 5-Strip Sets**

Repeat with the assorted blue 2½" × WOF strips to make (2) **Blue 5-Strip Sets**

Press seam allowances all in same direction

Cut each strip set into (4) 10" **Strip Set Squares**

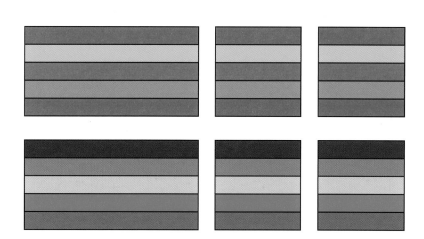

GENERAL DIRECTIONS: PP. 89–99

Make Four-at-a-Time HSTs

Pair (8) 10" **White Squares** with (8) 10"
Blue Strip Set Squares

Align the two squares and sew ¼" from the edge
all around the square

Use a spray starch or starch substitute to
minimize the stretching on the bias edges when
pressing the unit

Cut the square TWICE on the diagonal to make
(4) HST units

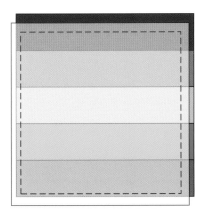

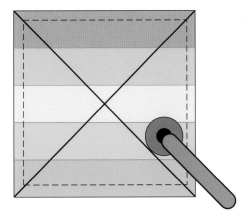

Open HST unit and press seam allowance toward
dark fabric or press seam open

Carefully trim HSTs to 6½" square, placing the ruler's
45-degree line on the seamline

Repeat with remaining (8) 10" **White Squares** and
(8) 10" **Red Strip Set Squares**

Notice that the strips run parallel to the seam in half of the
blocks. In the other half, the strips run perpendicular to
the seam. You could achieve a similar effect with striped
fabric. You should now have:

(32) red + white HSTs

(32) blue + white HSTs (there will be two left over
from each color grouping).

ASSEMBLING THE QUILT TOP

Adding the HST Border

Keep in mind that all the HSTs should be oriented in the same direction. Alternate the red and blue HSTs units, while also alternating the parallel/perpendicular strip orientation.

- Make (2) columns of (7) pairs of red + white and blue + white HSTs
- Attach to left/right sides of center panel
- Make (2) rows of (8) alternating red + white and blue + white HSTs
- Attach to top/bottom of center panel

Adding the Remaining Borders

Attach the inner and outer borders in the following order:

- 2½" gold **Left/Right Inner Border**
- 2½" gold **Top/Bottom Inner Border**
- 4½" blue **Left/Right Outer Border**
- 4½" blue **Top/Bottom Outer Border**

FINISHING THE QUILT

The quilt top should now measure 60½" × 78½"

Refer to the "General Directions" (page 89) for preparing **Backing** and **Binding**

Backing for this quilt should measure 68" × 86"

For **Binding**, cut (8) 2½" × WOF strips

Constellation

Photo on page 34
Inspiration pattern: *Simply Stars:*
Quilts That Sparkle, Alex Anderson, C&T Publishing
Finished size 72" × 84"

This design is wonderful because when you look at the quilt you think, "It looks so difficult! All those different block sizes!" But, look again. There are (27) 12" finished-size **Star Blocks** and there are (12) 6" finished-size Star blocks, but only (12) different block designs. There are three things that make the quilt look complicated:

1. The blocks are made from four different grid scales, 1½", 2", 3", and 4"
2. The blocks are set into columns, instead of rows
3. Every other column substitutes two side-by-side 6" blocks at the top and bottom in place of (1) 12" block, which causes the column to visually "drop" by six inches compared to its neighboring columns

The 12" grid is perfect for making blocks that are 3 × 3, 4 × 4, and 6 × 6 arrangements of plain squares, HSTs, QSTs, Flying Goose units, and Checkerboards. Easy units to make, but a spectacular collection of Star blocks.

FABRIC REQUIREMENTS

For Blocks

Instead of trying to exactly duplicate the coloring in this illustration or in the original quilt, select various fabrics for the blocks but use a consistent background throughout the quilt top. For example, select:

12–15 fat quarters from an assortment of light, medium, and dark blues

2–3 fat quarters from an assortment of reds

3½ yards light background

For Border

For unpieced borders: 2¼ yards, and fabric will be left over to use in the quilt blocks or binding

For pieced borders: 1½ yards

For Backing

5 yards

For Binding

3/4 yard (or, see "Border" yardage, above)

CUTTING INSTRUCTIONS

Cutting directions are given for each block, with the background fabric indicated. Choose fabrics for the other block units as desired for each individual block. Block A is 6" finished-size square (6½" unfinished size); all the other blocks are 12" finished-size square (12½" unfinished size).

After cutting the pieces for each block, group them into a **labeled** bag, for example:

"For making (12) A blocks"

"For making (2) B blocks"

If the pieces for a block are small or similar in size, pin the individual pieces together and **label** them, too. For example:

"FG-G" (shorthand for Flying Goose unit–Goose fabric)

"HST color #1" (half-square triangle color #1)

Refer to "General Directions" (pages 90–94) for illustrations for making the different block units:

Half-square triangles (**HST**s): Can be made two- or eight-at-a-time method, always from two fabrics

(/) means, "Cut square in half on the diagonal ONCE."

Quarter-square triangles (**QST**s): can be made two- or eight-at-a-time method, always from two fabrics

(X) means, "Cut square in half on the diagonal TWICE."

Flying Goose (**FG**): Can be made one at a time with bonus HSTs or by using the four-at-a-time method

(**FG-G**) means, "the Goose (larger triangle) of the FG unit."

(**FG-S**) means, "the Sky (smaller triangles) of the FG unit."

Notes:

Usually, the Flying Goose Sky (FG-S) starts as a plain square; however, in one pattern (Block D), the FG-S starts as a HST!

In many of the block designs, the Flying Goose units form the points of the star

Four-Patch: Can be made from four plain squares or can include HSTs, QSTs, or both

---

Cutting and Organizing the Block Parts

Again, **labeling** as you cut is a critical part of making this quilt.

Block A, the only 6" finished size blocks: (see page 93)

For (12) A Blocks

Background: cut (48) 2" **Squares for Corners**

Background: cut (12) 4¼" **Goose Squares** for four-at-a-time Flying Goose method

Flying Goose Sky squares: Cut (48) 2⅜" **Sky Squares**

Center: cut (12) 3½" **Center Squares**

Block B and all remaining blocks are 12" finished size. (see page 93)

For (2) B Blocks

Background: cut (8) 3½" **Squares for Corners**

Background: cut (2) 7¼" **Goose Squares** for four-at-a-time Flying Goose method

Flying Goose Sky squares: cut (8) 3⅞" **Sky Squares**

Center checkerboard: cut (18) 2½" **Checkerboard Squares**

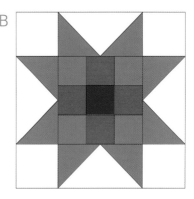

A

B

Block C (see page 93)

For (4) C Blocks

Background: cut (16) 4^1/$_2$" **Squares for Corners**

Background: cut (2) 9^3/$_4$" squares for eight-at-a-time QST method **QST (color #1)**

Star Points (color #2): cut (2) 9^3/$_4$" squares for eight-at-a-time QST method **QST (color #2)**

Center square: cut (4) 4^1/$_2$" **Center Squares**

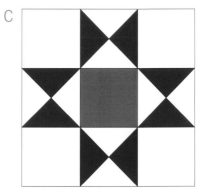

Block D (see page 90)

For (2) D Blocks

Background: cut (8) 3^1/$_2$" **Squares for Corners**

Background: cut (8) 3^1/$_2$" × 6^1/$_2$" **Goose rectangles** for one-at-a-time Flying Goose method

Half of Flying Goose "Sky" HSTs: cut (8) 3^7/$_8$" squares **FG-S (color #1)**

For other half of Flying Goose "Sky" HSTs: cut (8) 3^7/$_8$" squares **FG-S (color #2)**

Center square: cut (2) 6^1/$_2$" **Center Squares**

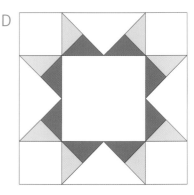

Block E (see page 91)

For (3) E Blocks

Background: cut (6) 4^7/$_8$" **Squares for Corner HSTs (color #1)**

Background: cut (3) 5^1/$_4$" **Goose Squares** for four-at-a-time Flying Goose method

Corner HSTs: cut (6) 4^7/$_8$" **Squares for Corner HSTs (color #2)**

Flying Goose Sky: cut (12) 2^7/$_8$" **Sky Squares** for four-at-a-time FG method

Center square: cut (3) 4^1/$_2$" **Center Squares**

Block F (see page 91)

For (2) F Blocks

Background: cut (8) 2^1/$_2$" × 4^1/$_2$" **Rectangles for Corners**

Background: cut (8) 2^1/$_2$" squares

Background: cut (2) 5^1/$_4$" **Goose Squares** for four-at-a-time FG method

Flying Goose Sky: cut (8) 2^7/$_8$" **Sky Squares** for four-at-a-time FG method

Center squares: cut (2) 4^1/$_2$" **Center Squares** (red)

Central block corners: cut (8) 2^1/$_2$" **Central Block Squares** (medium)

Center block sides: cut (8) 2^1/$_2$" × 4^1/$_2$" **Center Block Rectangles** (light)

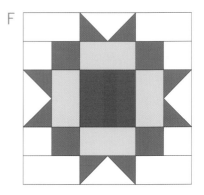

Block G (see pages 91–92)

For (4) G Blocks

Background: cut (16) 3½" **Squares for Corners**

Background: cut (4) 7¼" **Goose Squares** for four-at-a-time FG method

Flying Goose Sky: cut (16) 3⅞" **Sky Squares** for four-at-a-time FG method

Central Four-Patch: cut (8) 3½" **Central Four-Patch Squares**

Central Four-Patch HSTs: cut (4) 3⅞" **Central Four-Patch HSTs (color #1)**

Central Four-Patch HSTs: cut (4) 3⅞" **Central Four-Patch HSTs (color #2)**

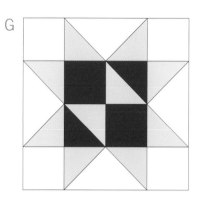

Block H (see page 91)

For (2) H Blocks

Background: cut (8) 3½" **Squares for Corners**

Background: cut (2) 7¼" **Goose Squares** for four-at-a-time FG method

Flying Goose Sky: cut (8) 3⅞" **Sky Squares** for four-at-a-time FG method

Center Star corners: cut (8) 2" **Center Star Squares**

Center Star FG: cut (2) 4¼" **Goose Squares** for four-at-a-time FG method

Center Star FG: cut (8) 2⅜" **Sky Squares** for four-at-a-time FG method

Center square: cut (2) 3½" **Center Squares**

Block I (see page 94)

For (2) I Blocks

All squares are cut for use in eight-at-a-time HST method

Background: cut (3) 7¾" squares

From medium fabric: cut (3) 7¾" squares

From light fabric: cut (2) 7¾" squares

Pair up for HSTs: (2) background + medium, (1) background + light, (1) light + medium

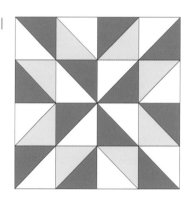

Block J (see pages 91–92)

For (2) J Blocks

Background: cut (8) 3½" **Squares for Corners**

Background: cut (2) 7¼" **Goose Squares** for four-at-a-time FG method

Flying Goose Sky: cut (8) 3⅞" **Sky Squares** for four-at-a-time FG method

Center Pinwheel: cut (4) 3⅞" squares for two-at-a-time **HSTS (color #1)**

Center Pinwheel: cut (4) 3⅞" squares for two-at-a-time **HSTS (color #2)**

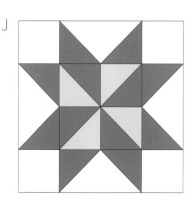

Block K (see page 92)

For (2) K Blocks

Background: cut (8) 4½" **Squares for Corners**

Background: cut (4) 4⅞" squares for Pinwheel **HSTs (color #1)**

Pinwheel blades: cut (4) 4⅞" squares for Pinwheel **HSTs (color #2)**

Center square: cut (2) 4½" **Squares for Center**

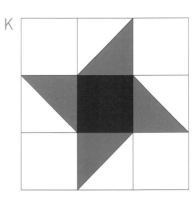

Block L (see page 94)

For (2) L Blocks

Background: cut (8) 3½" **Squares for Corners**

Background: cut (2) 7¼" **Goose Squares** for four-at-a-time FG method

Flying Goose: cut (8) 3⅞" **Sky Squares** for four-at-a-time FG method

Center square triangle corners: cut (4) 3⅞" squares (/) for **Triangle Corners**

Center Pinwheel: Cut (1) 6" square for eight-at-a-time **HSTs (color #1)**

Center Pinwheel: Cut (1) 6" square for eight-at-a-time **HSTs (color #2)**

Cutting the Borders

Refer to the "General Directions" (page 96) about deciding to cut the borders before or after the main part of the quilt top is complete. **Labeling** the strips is a good idea. These are the specific cut sizes for the borders on this quilt.

Pieced Borders

Cut and attach (8) 6½" × WOF strips

From the long strip: cut (4) 6½" × 72½" **Border Strips**

SEWING THE BLOCK PARTS TOGETHER

Refer to the "General Directions" for making the Flying Goose units and half-square triangles for each block. Keep these block elements together with the other pieces in the **labeled** bags until you are ready to assemble the blocks.

Because this quilt has so many pieces and kinds of blocks, a good idea is to lay out the pieces for the block you're working with onto a miniature design wall (such as a piece of flannel or the back of a square of vinyl tablecloth). You should be able to follow the block illustrations on page 121 to assemble the blocks.

GENERAL DIRECTIONS: PP. 89–99

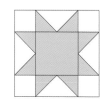

Block A: Make (12)

Block E: Make (3)

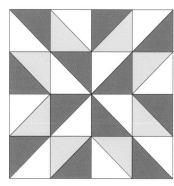

Block I: Make (2)

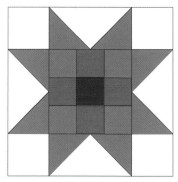

Block B: Make (2)

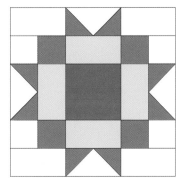

Block F: Make (2)

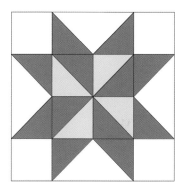

Block J: Make (2)

Block C: Make (4)

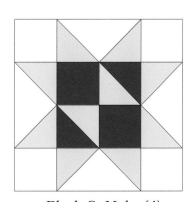

Block G: Make (4)

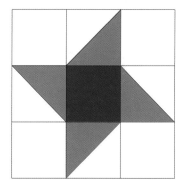

Block K: Make (2)

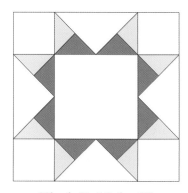

Block D: Make (2)

Block H: Make (2)

Block L: Make (2)

ASSEMBLING THE QUILT TOP

If space allows, lay out the 12" blocks on a large surface. While the **Block A Stars** are still unattached, place them at the top and bottom of columns 1, 3, and 5 to decide on color placement. When you like the arrangement, attach them together to make the drop blocks. Refer to the key below when arranging the blocks. However, feel free to reorganize the blocks in any way you choose.

ADDING BORDERS

All borders are the same length of 72½". Start by attaching borders to the left and right sides of the quilt top. Then, add the top and bottom borders. Because there are so many seams in this quilt, the borders will help square up the quilt for finishing.

FINISHING THE QUILT

With the borders attached, the quilt top should now measure 72½" × 84½"

Refer to the "General Directions" (page 89) for preparing **Backing** and **Binding**

Backing for this quilt should measure 80" × 92"

For **Binding**, cut (9) 2½" × WOF strips

GENERAL
DIRECTIONS:
PP. 89–99

Interlocking Rings of Freedom

Photo on page 41
Inspiration pattern: Nine Patch Chain by Cathy Busch
Finished size 65" × 79"

In addition to (12) 7" **Plain Squares**, there are only two pieced blocks in this dynamic quilt. The other two blocks (the **X-block** and the **Bar Block**) are made from pieced squares. There are two borders: the 2" inner border matches the background fabric, and the 6" outer border is a flag print. The flag print is also used in the center of the X-blocks.

FABRIC REQUIREMENTS

For Blocks

White (or other light background): 2½ yards

Red: 1¼ yards assorted

Blue: 1¼ yards assorted

X Block

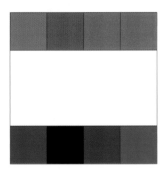

Bar Block

For Border

2 yards Print

Note: If you plan to use the same print fabric for the **Outer Border** and for the **Binding**, split the print fabric lengthwise into (4) 6½" wide strips and (4) 2½" wide strips. The **X-block Center Squares** can be cut from the remainder.

For Backing

5 yards

For Binding

³/₄ yard, or the border print fabric can be used.
See note under "Cutting the Borders," above.

CUTTING INSTRUCTIONS

A good idea is to cut, **label**, and set aside the borders
before cutting the individual block parts.

Cutting the Borders

Refer to the "General Directions" (page 96) about
deciding to cut the borders to the final size before or
after the main part of the quilt top is complete. These
are the specific cut sizes for the borders on this quilt.

Inner Border

White: cut and attach (7) 2¹/₂" × WOF strips

From the long strip:

Cut (2) 2¹/₂" × 63¹/₂" for **Left/Right Inner Borders**

Cut (2) 2¹/₂" × 53¹/₂" for **Top/Bottom Inner Borders**

Outer border

Print: cut and attach (7) 6¹/₂" × WOF strips

OR, from the 6 ¹/₂" lengthwise strips (see Note)

Either way, here are the sizes:

Cut (2) 6¹/₂" × 67¹/₂" for **Left/Right Outer Borders**

Cut (2) 6¹/₂" × 65¹/₂" for **Top/Bottom Outer Borders**

Cutting and Organizing the Block Parts

To avoid confusion, cut, separate, and **label**
before you begin to sew.

For Plain Squares

White: cut (6) 7¹/₂" × WOF strips

Then, cut (12) 7¹/₂" squares from (2) of the strips
and part of a third strip

Remainder of this strip will be used in bar blocks

For Bar Blocks

White: cut remaining 7¹/₂" × WOF strips into (31)
7¹/₂" × 4" rectangles

Red (assorted): cut (8) 2¹/₄" × WOF strips and set
aside for **4-Strip Sets** (See "Sewing")

OR, cut (124) 2¹/₄" squares from assorted red fabrics to
be pieced individually

Blue (assorted): cut (8) 2¹/₄" × WOF strips and set
aside for **4-Strip Sets** (See "Sewing")

OR, cut (124) 2¹/₄" squares from assorted blue fabrics
to be pieced individually

For X-blocks

Print (remaining from cutting outer border): cut (20)
3" squares for **X-block Centers**

White: cut (7) 3" × WOF strips, then cut strips into
(80) 3" squares

Red (assorted): cut (7) 3" × WOF strips, then cut
strips into (80) 3" squares

Blue (assorted): Cut (7) 3" × WOF strips, then cut
strips into (80) 3" squares

SEWING THE BLOCK PARTS TOGETHER

Bar Blocks: Make (31)

There are two ways to make these units:

Sew individual 2¹/₄" assorted red and blue squares together into sets of four (A)

Make (31) **Red 4-Square Units** and (31) **Blue 4-Square Units**

Another way to make these units is to:

Attach (4) 2¹/₄" × WOF strips into strip sets

Cut the sets into (31) red segments and (31) blue 2¹/₄" segments (B)

Assemble the bar blocks

Attach the **Red and Blue 4-Square Units** to either side of the (31) **White Rectangles** (C)

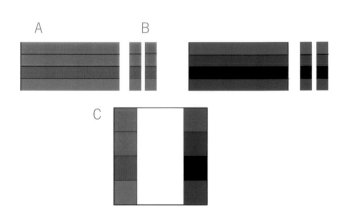

Press seam allowances toward white rectangle

The bar block should measure 7¹/₂" square at this point

X-blocks: Make (20)

For each block, start by making a Nine-Patch block from 3" squares as shown

(4) white corners

(2) red squares on opposite sides

(2) blue squares on opposite sides

(1) print center

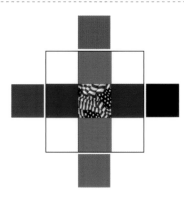

Complete the unit

Add (2) more **Red Squares** and (2) more **Blue Squares** to the **Nine-Patch**, attaching red to red and blue to blue

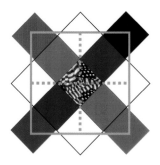

Trim to 7¹/₂" square

Be sure that the $3^3/_4$" lines on the ruler pass through the center of the block AND that you have at least $^1/_4$" seam allowance outside the intersections

ASSEMBLING THE QUILT TOP

Note: pay attention to the orientation of the red and blue in the blocks as you sew them together in both types of rows

Make (5) rows, alternating the **X-block** with a **Horizontal Bar Block**

Make (4) rows, alternating the **Vertical Bar Block** with a **Plain Square**

Join the rows and press seams open

The quilt top should now measure $49^1/_2$" × $63^1/_2$"

ADDING BORDERS

Inner Borders

Attach inner borders in the following order:

$2^1/_2$" × $63^1/_2$" white **Left and Right Inner Borders**

$2^1/_2$" × $53^1/_2$" white **Top and Bottom Inner Borders**

Outer Borders

Attach outer borders in the following order:

$6^1/_2$" × $67^1/_2$" print **Left and Right Outer Borders**

$6^1/_2$" × $65^1/_2$" print **Top and Bottom Outer Borders**

FINISHING THE QUILT

The quilt top should now measure $65^1/_2$" × $79^1/_2$"

Refer to the "General Directions" (page 89) for preparing **Backing** and **Binding**

Backing for this quilt should measure 73" × 87"

For **Binding**, cut (8) $2^1/_2$" × WOF strips

Iowa's Bravest

Photo on page 46
Inspiration pattern: Scott Flanagan, Sand and Sea,
Quiltmaker Magazine, 2017
Finished size 63" × 75" with borders

The 4" × 10" **Chevron Units** are made from 2½" strips and would be a good way to use a jelly roll collection or strips cut from an assortment of yardage. Two Chevron units are combined to make each of the (36) 8" × 10" finished-size **Chevron Blocks**. The method used for making the Chevron units will produce (144) **Bonus HSTs**, which can be used in another quilt or in a border. A **Bonus Pattern** is included for these HSTs.

FABRIC REQUIREMENTS

Important note about fabric: The usable width of the fabric strips must be **AT LEAST 42"** for this pattern. "Usable width" refers to the measurement from edge to edge of the fabric WITHOUT SELVAGES.

For Blocks

(36) 2½" × 42+" **WOF strips** in assorted prints and colors

Background: 2½ yards

For Borders

Note that if you choose to use a border print and you plan to miter the corners, allow extra fabric for matching border designs and mitering, depending on the repeat of the printed design on the fabric.*

Inner border: ½ yard

Outer border: 2 yards unpieced or 1½ yards pieced

For Backing

5 yards

For Binding

¾ yard

CUTTING INSTRUCTIONS

Cutting the Borders

Refer to the "General Directions" (page 96) about deciding to cut the borders before or after the main part of the quilt top is complete. **Labeling** the strips is a good idea. These are the specific cut sizes for the borders on this quilt.

Inner Border

Cut and attach (7) 2" × WOF strips

From the long strip:

Cut (2) 2" × 60$\frac{1}{2}$" for **Left/Right Inner Borders**

Cut (2) 2" × 51$\frac{1}{2}$" for **Top/Bottom Inner Borders**

Outer border

From length of fabric:

Cut (4) 6$\frac{1}{2}$" × 63$\frac{1}{2}$" strips if you will use the long-horizontal method pictured

*These strips will need to be longer if you use a border print and plan to miter the corners

OR

From pieced WOF strips: cut and attach (7) 6$\frac{1}{2}$" × WOF strips

From the long strip: cut (4) 6$\frac{1}{2}$" × 63$\frac{1}{2}$" strips

Cutting and Organizing the Block Parts
Background Squares

Cut (144) 4$\frac{1}{2}$" squares

On the wrong side of each square, mark a diagonal line from corner to corner. This will be the stitching line for Chevrons

Mark another line $\frac{1}{2}$" away from the first line. This will be the stitching line for Bonus HSTs

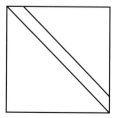

Strip Sets for Chevrons (see page 90)

Reminder: the WOF strips must be **at least 42" without selvages**

Sort the (36) 2$\frac{1}{2}$ × WOF strips into pairs

Sew the strips together and press seam toward darker fabric or open

You now have (18) **Two-Strip Strip Sets**

Cut the strip sets into (72) 10$\frac{1}{2}$" segments

You now have (72) 4$\frac{1}{2}$" × 10$\frac{1}{2}$" two-strip segments

Divide the segments into (2) piles of (36) each

Label one pile **Left Angle Cut** and label the other pile **Right Angle Cut**

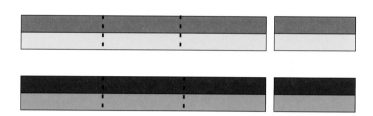

SEWING THE CHEVRON UNITS AND MAKING BONUS HSTS

Note that half of the **Chevron Units** are angled one way, and the other half are angled the other way

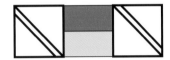

Starting with the **Left Angle Cut** pile of (36) segments:

Place one marked 4¹/₂" **Background Square** at each end of the 4¹/₂"x 10 ¹/₂" rectangle, right sides together

Turn the background squares so that the second drawn line is closer to the corner

AND

The background squares are angled toward the left end of the rectangle (see illustration)

Pin square in place

Sew on the first diagonal lines

Sew on the second lines

Repeat for remaining **Left Angle Cut** segments

Chain piecing is an efficient way to make these units

Repeat the process for the other pile of **Right Angle Cut** 10½" segments, but this time angle the 4½"

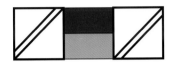

Background Squares toward the right (see illustration). **Caution: Do not** make all (72) Chevron units the same way! Remember that half of the units slant to the left, and the other half slant to the right.

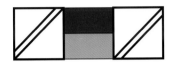

Cutting the Chevrons and Bonus HSTs

Press the sewn units to set the seams

Cut between the sewn lines

Press seams away toward the background corners

The (72) **Chevron Units** should measure 4¹/₂" × 10¹/₂"

The (144) **Bonus HSTs** should measure about 3³/₄" square—trim them down to 3¹/₂" square and set aside

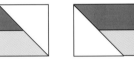 

SEWING THE BLOCK PARTS TOGETHER

Attach Left and Right Angle **Chevron Units** to make (36) **Chevron Blocks**

The blocks should measure 8½" × 10½" at this point

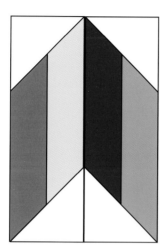

ASSEMBLING THE QUILT TOP

Attach the **Chevron Blocks** into (6) rows of (6) blocks each

All blocks point the same direction, but the row appears as a zigzag

Attach the rows together

The quilt top should now measure 48½" × 60½"

ADDING BORDERS

Attach borders in the following order:

2" **Left and Right Inner Borders**

2" **Top and Bottom Inner Borders**

6½" **Left and Right Outer Borders**

6½" **Top and Bottom Outer Borders**

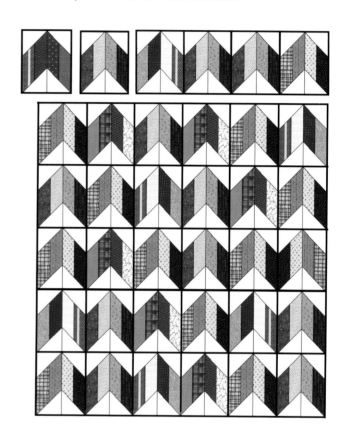

FINISHING THE QUILT

The quilt top should now measure 63½" × 75½"

Refer to the "General Directions" (page 89) for preparing **Backing** and **Binding**

Backing for this quilt should measure 71" × 83"

For **Binding**, cut (8) 2½" × WOF strips

GENERAL DIRECTIONS: PP. 89–99

SCRAPPY BONUS QUILT WITH BONUS HSTS
Finished size 66" × 66" with 2" borders

You should have (144) **Bonus HSTs** that were cut from the corners of the **Chevron Units**.

They might have been roughly 3¾" square when they were cut, but should be trimmed to 3½".

Here is a way to make another quilt top from additional 2½" strips of fabric, either leftover strips or strips cut from 2¾ yards fabric:

First, cut (12) WOF strips into (132) 2½" × 3½" rectangles for **Block Sashing** (A)

Next, from lengthwise of remaining fabric, cut (13) 2½" × 58½" strips for **Row Sashing** and **Left/Right Inner Borders** (B)

Also, cut (2) 2½" × 62½" strips for **Top/Bottom Inner Borders** (C)

Sew a row of (12) 3½" bonus HSTs, alternating with 2½" × 3½" rectangles, beginning and ending with HSTs

Attach 2½" × 58½" strips for **Row Sashing** and **Left/Right Inner Borders**

The quilt top will now measure 58" square

To bring the quilt to 66" square, add (2) more borders from randomly pieced 2½" × WOF strips

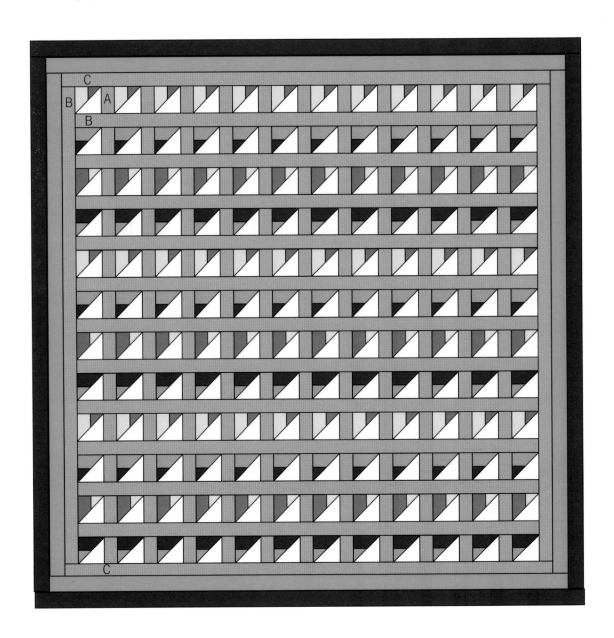

Welcome Home

Photo on page 48
Inspiration pattern: Doug Leko,
Antler Quilt, Memory Lane
Finished size 60" × 74" with border

The 6" and 4" squares in this quilt design are the perfect holding places for motifs that have been fussy-cut from an inspiration fabric, from panels, or from custom-embroidered designs. If you know who the recipient will be, you can personalize this quilt easily. The (20) 14" finished-size **Log Cabin Variation Blocks** are made with 2½" strips and squares in addition to the 6" and 4" squares. The key to an effective finished quilt will be keeping the motifs or text oriented in the same direction.

FABRIC REQUIREMENTS

For Blocks

Approximately (40) assorted medium/dark 2½" × WOF strips

(20) 6½" squares and (20) 4½" squares containing motifs from panels, fussy-cuts, or embroidery

Note: These squares could also be cut from plain fabric or from the light background.

Light background: ¾ yard

For Border

¾ yard

For Backing

4½ yards

For Binding

¾ yard

CUTTING INSTRUCTIONS
Cutting the Block Parts
Motif Blocks

Cut (20) 6½" motif blocks
(See Note, above)

Light Background

Cut (20) 4½" squares

Cut (40) 2½" squares

Assorted Medium/Dark Strips

Cut (40) 2½" × 6½" strips

Cut (80) 2½" × 8½" strips

Cut (40) 2½" × 12½" strips

Note: You could get the pieces needed from (31 to 32) strips, but for maximum variety, cut (1) 6½" segment, (2) 8½" segments, and (1) 12½" segment from each of (40) strips. There will be a scrap piece left from the end of each strip.

Cutting the Borders

Refer to the "General Directions" (page 96) about deciding to cut the borders before or after the main part of the quilt top is complete. **Labeling** the strips is a good idea. These are the specific cut sizes for the borders on this quilt.

Border fabric: cut and attach (8)
2½" × WOF strips

From the long strip:

Cut (2) 70½" strips for **Left/Right Borders**

Cut (2) 60½" strips for **Top/Bottom Borders**

ASSEMBLING THE BLOCKS AND ORIENTING THE MOTIF SQUARES

Refer to the illustration to lay out the parts of each block

Starting from the motif square, add the rectangles and squares as shown

Be sure that the motif square is oriented correctly

Labeling each block A, B, C, or D will also help keep you organized:

Make (6) A Blocks

Make (6) B Blocks

Make (4) C Blocks

Make (4) D Blocks

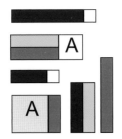
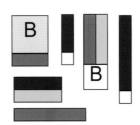
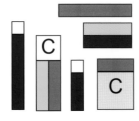
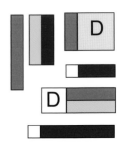

ASSEMBLING THE QUILT TOP

Attach the blocks into rows as shown in the illustration:

Rows 1, 3, and 5: A + B + A + B

Rows 2 and 4: C + D + C + D

Press seams joining blocks open or in alternating directions

Attach the rows together and press seams open

Quilt top should now measure 56½" × 70½"

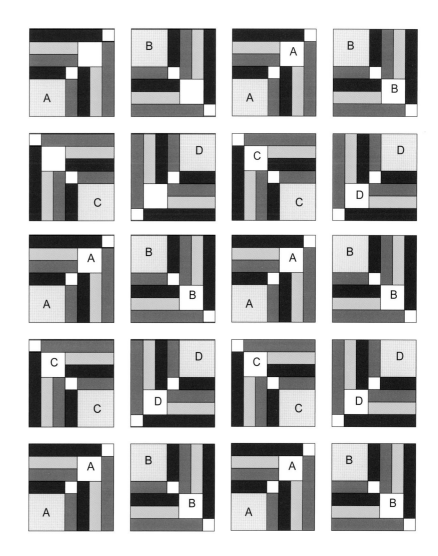

GENERAL DIRECTIONS: PP. 89–99

ADDING BORDERS

Attach borders in the following order:

$2^1/_2" \times 70^1/_2"$ strips for **Left and Right Borders**

$2^1/_2" \times 60^1/_2"$ strips for **Top/Bottom Borders**

FINISHING THE QUILT

The quilt top should now measure 60½" × 74½"

Refer to the "General Directions" (page 89) for preparing **Backing** and **Binding**

Backing for this quilt should measure 68" × 82"

For **Binding**, cut (8) 2½" × WOF strips

Jacob's Ladder

Photo on page 49
Inspiration pattern: Donna Robertson, Jacob's Ladder
Finished size 64" × 78" with three borders

With only two blocks and three colors, this quilt has the distinction of being both stunning and easy. There are (32) **Four-Patch Blocks** and (31) **HST Blocks**. All blocks are 7" finished size. Three borders of 2," 3", and 2½" complete and frame the top.

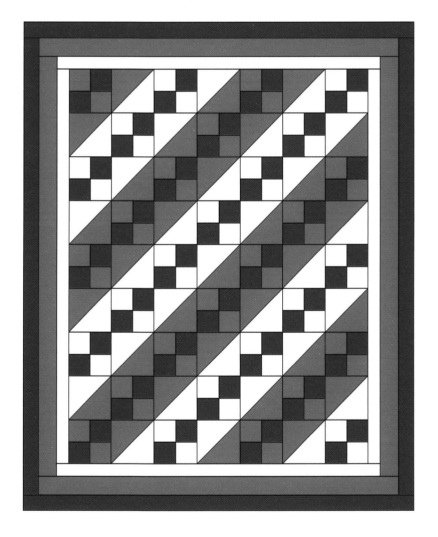

FABRIC REQUIREMENTS

For Blocks
Red: 2 yards
White: 1½ yards
Blue: 1½ yards

For Borders
First (inner) border: ⅝ yard
Second (middle) border: 1 yard
Third (outer) border: 1 yard

For Backing
5 yards

For Binding
¾ yard

CUTTING AND PIECING INSTRUCTIONS

For Four-Patch Blocks

Red: cut (4) 4" × WOF strips

White: cut (4) 4" × WOF strips

Blue: cut (8) 4" × WOF strips

Seam together (4) **Red + Blue Strip Sets** (A)

Seam together (4) **White + Blue Strip Sets** (B)

Cut each **Strip Set** into (10) 4" segments (C)

Pair the segments of the same color and sew, being sure to place colors opposite each other and to nest the seams (D)

Press and trim to 7½" square, if necessary

You should have (16) **Red + Blue Four-Patch Blocks** and (16) **White + Blue Four-Patch Blocks** (there will be leftovers).

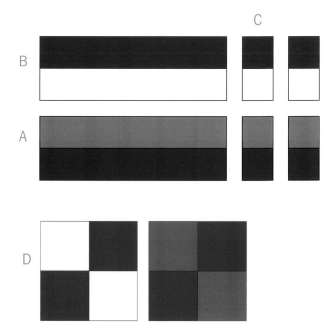

For Half-Square Triangles (see page 92)

Red: cut (4) 8" × WOF strips

White: cut (4) 8" × WOF strips

Cut strips into (16) **Red 8" Squares** and (16) **White 8" Squares**

Pair red + white squares right sides together

Refer to "General Directions" for making two-at-a-time HSTs

Hint: Draw diagonal line on back of white square. Sew ¼" on either side with red + white squares RST. Cut on drawn line.

Press seam allowance toward darker fabric

Trim to 7½" square, if necessary

You should have (31) **Red + White HSTs** (plus one leftover)

Cutting the Borders

Refer to the "General Directions" (page 96) about deciding to cut the borders before or after the main part of the quilt top is complete. **Labeling** the strips is a good idea. These are the specific cut sizes for the borders on this quilt.

First (Inner) Border

White: cut and attach (7) 2½" × WOF strips

From the long strip:

Cut (2) 2½" × 63½" strips for **Left/Right Inner Borders**

Cut (2) 2½" × 53½" strips **Top/Bottom Inner Borders**

Second (Middle) Border

Red: cut and attach (8) 3½" × WOF strips

From the long strip:

Cut (2) 3½" × 67½" strips for **Left/Right Middle Borders**

Cut (2) 3½" × 59½" strips for **Top/Bottom Middle Borders**

Third (Outer) Border

Blue: cut and attach (8) 3" × WOF strips

From the long strip:

Cut (2) 3" × 73½" strips for **Left/Right Outer Borders**

Cut (2) 3" × 64½" strips for **Top/Bottom Outer Borders**

SEWING THE BLOCKS INTO ROWS

You should now have:

(16) red + blue Four-Patch blocks

(16) white + blue Four-Patch blocks

(31) red + white HST blocks

Attach these blocks into (9) rows, as shown

Be sure to turn the blocks in the right direction for each row

Press seam allowances to opposite side in every other row, or press seams open

Again, **labeling** the rows will help keep them organized

ASSEMBLING THE QUILT TOP

Attach the rows together, again being sure to attach the rows in the right order

The seams should nest together

Press long, joining seams open

The quilt top should now measure 49½" × 63½"

ADDING BORDERS

Attach borders in the following order:

2½" white left and right inner borders

2½" white top and bottom inner borders

3½" red left and right middle borders

3½" red top and bottom middle borders

3" blue left and right outer borders

3" blue top and bottom outer borders

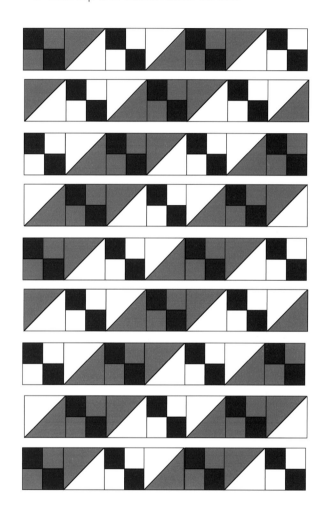

FINISHING THE QUILT

The quilt top should now measure 64½" × 78½"

Refer to the "General Directions" (page 89) for preparing backing and binding

Backing for this quilt should measure 72" × 86"

For **Binding**, cut (8) 2½" × WOF strips

Expressions of Gratitude

Photo on page 52
Inspiration pattern: Barbara Thurman Butler, Butler Family Quilt
with Indian Hatchet Blocks from *Memory Quilts in the
Making*, Rhonda Richards (Oxmoor House, 1999)
Finished size 60½" × 82½" with three borders

Quilters have a long history of making signature quilts. These quilts commemorate events and serve as expressions of remembrance and gratitude. The (96) 5½" finished-size **Indian Hatchet Blocks** in this quilt contain sentiments penned by a variety of people. When you look at the photo on page 52, you will notice that a different border has been used from the pattern you find here. When Marianne Elliott made that

quilt, she had lots of red and blue 4" squares left over, and she decided to use them in the border. However, the technique used in this pattern for making the signature blocks produces lots of **Bonus HSTs** with very little additional effort. It would be a shame to waste them, so while you can of course add whatever kind of border you want to this quilt, this pattern features a bonus HST border instead of squares.

FABRIC REQUIREMENTS
For Blocks
White: 2³/₄ yards

Red: 1¹/₄ yards

Blue: 1¹/₄ yards

For Borders
The second border (middle) will be made from bonus HSTs

White (inner) border: ³/₄ yard

Blue (outer): 1 yard

For Backing
5 yards

For Binding
³/₄ yard

CUTTING INSTRUCTIONS

For Blocks

White: cut (16) 6" × WOF strips into (96) squares

Red: cut (10) 4" × WOF strips into (96) squares

Blue: cut (10) 4" × WOF strips into (96) squares

Cutting the Borders

Refer to the "General Directions" (page 96) about deciding to cut the borders before or after the main part of the quilt top is complete. **Labeling** the strips is a good idea. These are the specific cut sizes for the borders on this quilt.

Inner Border

White (inner) border: cut and attach (7) $3\frac{1}{4}$" × WOF strips

From the long strip:

Cut (2) $3\frac{1}{4}$" × $66\frac{1}{2}$" strips for **Left/Right Inner Borders**

Cut (2) $3\frac{1}{4}$" × 50" strips for **Top/Bottom Inner Borders**

Middle (HST) Border:

White: cut (4) $3\frac{1}{4}$" squares for corners

HST units will be made along with blocks

Outer Border

Blue (outer) border: cut and attach (8) $3\frac{1}{4}$" × WOF strips

From the long strip:

Cut (2) $3\frac{1}{4}$" × $77\frac{1}{2}$" strips for **Left/Right Outer Borders**

Cut (2) $3\frac{1}{4}$" × 61" strips for **Top/Bottom Outer Borders**

SEWING THE BLOCKS TOGETHER AND MAKING BONUS HSTS

Draw a line from corner to corner on the backs of all the **Red and Blue 4" Squares**

Draw another line $\frac{1}{2}$" from the first line, as shown, on all red and blue squares (A)

Place a **Blue 4" Square** in the corner of a **6" White Square**, right sides together

Orient the square so that the second line is closest to the corner of the white square

Sew ON both lines then cut apart between the two lines

Press seam allowance toward darker fabric (B)

Repeat for all (96) blue 4" squares

Repeat the process for the **4" Red Squares**, placing them on the opposite corner (C)

Trim the signature block, if necessary, to 6" square

Trim the bonus HSTs to $3\frac{1}{4}$" square

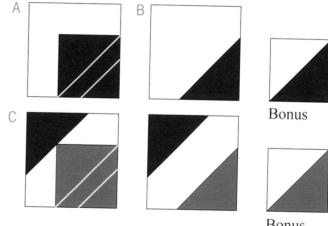

Bonus

Bonus

GATHERING SIGNATURES OR MESSAGES

At this point, you will decide whether to gather the signatures or other messages on the blocks individually (maybe they must be mailed to people), or have people sign the blocks at an event (such as a ceremony). Either way, encourage people to use archival-quality, permanent pens (such as Pigma) for the signatures. Avoid other felt pens or ballpoint pens.

ASSEMBLING THE QUILT TOP

Assemble the (96) **Indian Hatchet Blocks** into (12) rows of (8) blocks, carefully following the quilt illustration for orienting the signature blocks.

Another way to assemble the quilt top is to attach the blocks into four quarters, as shown in the illustration. Notice that:

Upper-left and lower-right quarters are the same

Upper-right and lower-left quarters are the same

The quilt top should now measure 44½" × 66½"

ASSEMBLING THE HST PIECED BORDER (SECOND OR MIDDLE BORDER)

Refer to the illustration to attach alternating **Red and Blue Bonus HSTs** to prepare the second border as follows:

Attach (26) HSTs for each of the **Left and Right Borders**

Attach (18) HSTs for each of the **Top and Bottom Borders** PLUS add a **3¼" White Square** to each end

ADDING BORDERS

Attach borders in the following order:

3¼" × 66½" white left and right inner borders

3¼" × 50" white top and bottom inner borders

Pieced HST left and right middle borders

Pieced HST top and bottom middle borders

3¼" × 77½" left and right outer borders

3¼" × 61" top and bottom outer borders

FINISHING THE QUILT

The quilt top should now measure 61" × 83"

Refer to the "General Directions" (page 89) for preparing **Backing** and **Binding**

Backing for this quilt should measure 69" × 91"

For **Binding**, cut (8) 2½" × WOF strips

GENERAL DIRECTIONS: PP. 89–99

Red, White, and Blue Forever

Photo of *Sleepy Time Gal* on page 59
is designed by Janice Hobbs.
Based on traditional Carpenter's Wheel.
Finished size 73" × 73" including borders

This quilt is made from only 5" finished-size squares and half-square triangles (HSTs). Four identical blocks are stitched together to make the body of the quilt. The center and corners are good places to add personalized embroidery.

FABRIC REQUIREMENTS

For Blocks

White: 2¼ yards

Red: 1¼ yards

Blue: 1¼ yards

For Borders

Inner (blue): ½ yard

Outer (red): 1¼ yards

For Backing

5 yards

For Binding

¾ yard

CUTTING INSTRUCTIONS

From White Fabric
For Plain Squares

Cut (4) 5½" × WOF strips into (24) 5½" squares

For HSTs

Cut (9) 6" × WOF strips into (52) 6" squares

From Red Fabric
For HSTs

Cut (6) 6" × WOF strips into (34) 6" squares

From Blue Fabric

For HSTs (see page 96)

Cut (6) 6" × WOF strips into (34) 6" squares

Note: Refer to the "General Directions" about deciding to cut the borders before or after the main part of the quilt top is complete. **Labeling** the strips is a good idea. These are the specific cut sizes for the borders on this quilt.

From Inner Border Fabric (Blue)

Cut and attach (7) 2" × WOF strips

From the long strip:

Cut (2) 2" × 60½" strips for **Left/Right Inner Borders**

Cut (2) 2" × 63½" strips for **Top/Bottom Inner Borders**

From Outer Border Fabric (Red)

Cut and attach (7) 5½" × WOF strips

From the long strip:

Cut (4) 5½" × 63½" strips **for Outer Borders**

From Scraps (Red and Blue)

Cut (4) 5½" squares

OR, make (4) 5" finished-size QSTs from scraps for **Corner Blocks in Outer Border**

MAKING AND ORGANIZING THE BLOCKS

Refer to "General Directions" for making two-at-a-time HSTs, which will need to be trimmed slightly to 5½" square for this pattern.

Make HSTs

Pair together 6" squares and mark a diagonal line on the back of the lighter of the two:

(26) white + (26) red squares

(26) white + (26) blue squares

(8) red + (8) blue squares

Sew ¼" on each side of the drawn line

Cut apart on drawn line

Press seam allowance to darker fabric

Trim to 5½" square

Organize Block Sets

Make a set of squares and HSTs for each of the quadrants containing:

(6) white squares

(13) white + red HSTs

(13) white + blue HSTs

(4) red + blue HSTs

Make the (4) Large Blocks

Lay the **Squares** and **HSTs** out into rows for assembly

Sew units together (being sure to orient the **HSTs** correctly)

Press seam allowances in alternating directions for each row

Attach the rows and press the seam allowances open

Repeat for other three quadrants

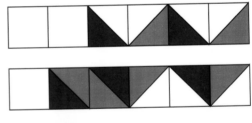

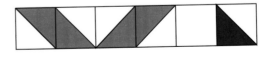

ASSEMBLING THE QUILT TOP

Attach the Quadrants

Attach the four, identical quadrants, rotating to bring the center squares together as shown

Press seam allowances open

The quilt top should now measure $60\frac{1}{2}$" square

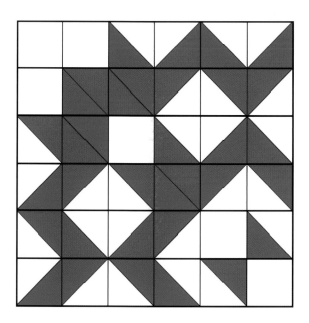

Attach the Borders

Attach borders in the following order:

2" × $60\frac{1}{2}$" blue **Left and Right Inner Borders**

2" × $63\frac{1}{2}$" blue **Top and Bottom Inner Borders**

$5\frac{1}{2}$" × $63\frac{1}{2}$" red **Left and Right Outer Borders**

Attach corner blocks to $5\frac{1}{2}$" × $63\frac{1}{2}$" **Top and Bottom Outer Borders**

Attach to quilt top

FINISHING THE QUILT

The quilt top should now measure $73\frac{1}{2}$" square

Refer to the "General Directions" (page 89) for preparing **Backing** and **Binding**

Backing for this quilt should measure 81" × 81"

For **Binding**, cut and attach (9) $2\frac{1}{2}$" × WOF strips

GENERAL
DIRECTIONS:
PP. 89–99

In Honor of . . .

Photo on page 64
Inspiration pattern: Diane Tomlinson, In Honor Of . . .
Finished size 64" × 77"

To achieve the dramatic effect of the stripes in the (30) 9" finished-size **HST Stripe + Solid Blocks**, you will need to find a strong striped fabric and cut very precisely so that a stripe is centered on the diagonal from one corner of the square to the other. The (20) 9" finished-size **Variable Star Blocks** contain QST units that will be made by using the eight-at-a-time HST and QST Methods found in the "General Directions."

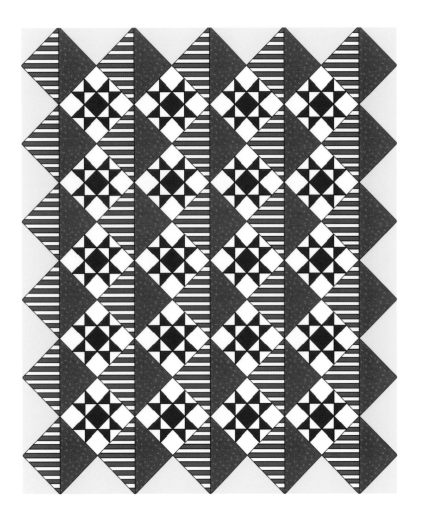

FABRIC REQUIREMENTS

For Blocks

For Variable Star Blocks

White: 1³/₄ yards

Blue #1: 1 yard

For HST Stripe + Solid Blocks

Blue #2: 1¹/₄ yards

Red + white stripe: 1³/₄ to 3¹/₄ yards (See Note, below)

Note: The squares of red + white striped fabric for the **HST Stripe + Solid Blocks** will be fussy-cut so that the stripe runs from point to point across the square; therefore, it is difficult to estimate yardage. This estimate is based on a fabric with even, approximately 1" wide red and white lengthwise stripes. The usable width of the fabric is assumed to be 40", but it may be more than that on the particular fabric that you choose.

To estimate the amount of yardage needed:

Cut (2) 9⁷/₈" squares from paper or template plastic

Cut the end of the fabric at a 45-degree angle (or just fold it under if you are at a fabric store!)

Use the paper/plastic squares to calculate how many squares can you cut across a 9⁷/₈" diagonal strip with a stripe running evenly through the square?

Multiply the number of diagonal strips you will need by 14.5" to calculate approximate yardage

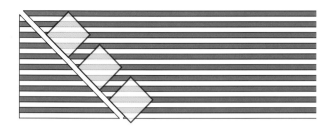

For example:

If you can get (2) squares across one diagonal cut, you will need 8 strips × 14½" = about 116" (3¼ yards)

If you can get (3) squares across one diagonal cut, you will need 5 strips × 14½" = about 72" (2 yards)

If you can get (4) squares across one diagonal cut, you will need 4 strips × 14½" = about 58" (1¾ yards)

For Side-Setting Triangles and Corners

1½ yards

For Backing

5 yards

For Binding

¾ yard

●----------------------------------●

CUTTING INSTRUCTIONS

From White Fabric

Cut (3) 8½" × WOF strips into (10) 8½" squares for **Star Block QSTs**

Cut (8) 3½" × WOF strips into (80) 3½" squares for **Star Block Corners**

From Blue Fabric #1 for Variable Star Block

Cut (3) 8½" × WOF strips into (10) 8½" squares for **Star Block QSTs**

Cut (2) 3½" × WOF strips into (20) 3½" squares for **Star Block Centers**

From Blue Fabric #2 for **HST Stripe+Solid Blocks**

Cut (4) 9⅞" × WOF Strips into (15) 9⅞" squares

From Striped Fabric **HST Stripe+Solid Blocks**

Fussy-cut (15) 9⅞" squares, as described above

Be sure to have the same stripe running from corner to corner on each square

From Setting Triangle Fabric (see page 98)

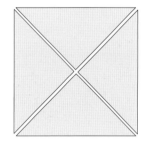 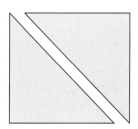

Cut (3) 14" × WOF strips into (5) 14" squares

Cut the 14" squares in half on the diagonal TWICE to make (20) **Side-Setting Quarter-Square Triangles**

Cut (1) 7¼" × WOF strip into (2) 7¼" squares

Cut the 7¼" squares in half ONCE on the diagonal to make (4) **Corner Half-Square Triangles**

MAKING AND ORGANIZING
THE BLOCKS

Make the (20) Variable Star Blocks
(see page 94)

Using the eight-at-a-time HST method

Make (80) blue #1 + white HSTs from the (10) 8½" blue #1 + white squares

After you make the (80) HSTs, you are ready to make (80) QSTs

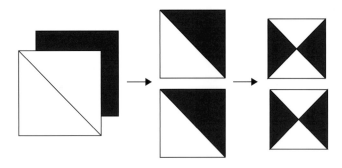

- -

Using the eight-at-a-time QST method

Make (80) blue #1 + white QSTs from the (80) HSTs from the previous step

If necessary, trim the blue + white QSTs to 3½"

Be sure to center the unit when trimming

Complete the Nine-Patch **Variable Star Blocks** with the 3½" white and blue squares

Make the (30) Stripe + Solid HST Blocks

Place (1) 9⅞" blue #2 square and (1) 9⅞" red + white striped square right sides together

Draw a diagonal line from corner to corner ACROSS the back of the red + white striped fabric

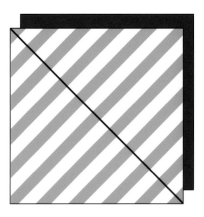

Sew ¼" on each sided of the drawn line

Cut on the drawn line

Press seam allowance toward the blue #2 fabric

Trim to 9½" square, if necessary

ASSEMBLING THE QUILT TOP

Attach the Diagonal Block Rows

Attach blocks, corners, and setting squares in diagonal rows, as shown

Be sure to keep the red + white striped half of the HST blocks oriented in the correct direction

Press seam allowances toward the HST blocks

Attach the rows, nesting the seams

Press the long seam allowances open

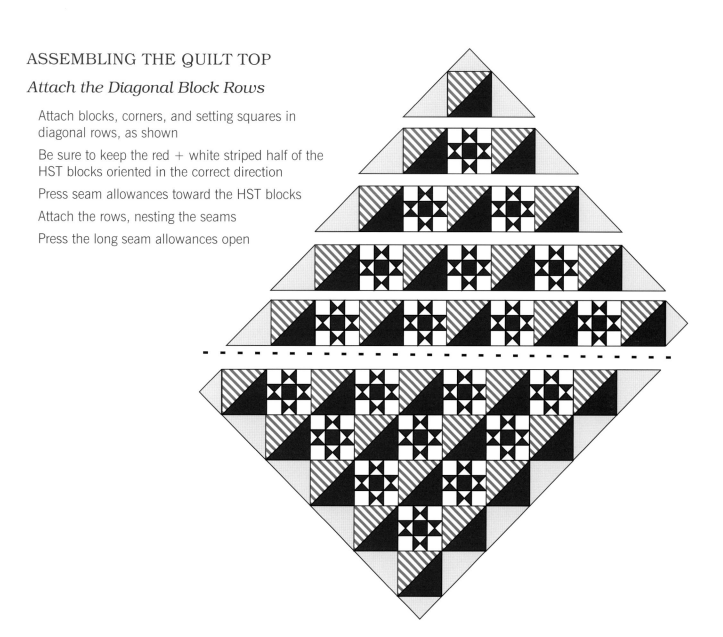

FINISHING THE QUILT

The quilt top should now measure 64½" × 77½"

Refer to the "General Directions" (page 89) for preparing **Backing** and **Binding**

Backing for this quilt should measure 72" × 85"

For **Binding** cut and attach (8) 2½" × WOF strips

GENERAL DIRECTIONS: PP. 89–99

Stars and Checks

Photo on page 68
Inspiration pattern: Nancy Mahoney, Love of
Quilting, Stars and Checks
Finished size: 60" × 80" with 1" and 4" borders

You will use simple techniques to make a stunning quilt. The (18) 10"
finished-size **Star Blocks** are made from plain squares and HSTs that
are made by using the eight-at-a-time method. The (17) 10" **Checks
Blocks** are made up of **Checkerboards** made from **Strip Sets**, **HST
Units** made with the eight-at-a-time method, and **Square-in-a-Square
Units** that are made by using a method that also produces **Bonus HSTs**.

FABRIC REQUIREMENTS

If you select a print for the **Outer Border**
and for the **Square-in-a-Square Centers**,
also use that fabric to coordinate the other
fabrics: white, red, light blue, medium blue,
and dark blue.

For Blocks

Print: 1½ yards for **Outer Border** and
Checks Block Center

Red: 1⅛ yards for **Checks Blocks** and
Inner Border

Dark blue: ¾ yard for **Star Blocks**

Medium blue: 1 yard for **Star Blocks** and
Checks Blocks

Light blue: 1 yard for **Star Blocks** and
Checks Blocks

White: 2¼ yards for **Star Blocks** and
Checks Blocks

For Backing

5 yards

For Binding

¾ yard

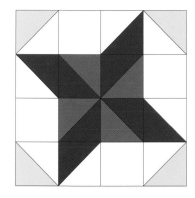

CUTTING INSTRUCTIONS

As always, it is a good idea to **label** the units as you cut.

From Print Fabric

Cut (3) 5½" × WOF strips into (17) 5½" **Squares for Checks Block Center**

Cut and join (7) 4½" × WOF strips for **Outer Border**

From the long strip:

Cut (2) 4½" × 72½" for **Right/Left Outer Borders**

Cut (2) 4½" × 60½" for **Top/Bottom Outer Borders**

From Red Fabric

Cut (14) 1¾" × WOF strips for **Strip Sets for Checks Blocks**

Cut and join (7) 1½" × WOF strips for **Inner Border**

From long strip:

Cut (2) 1½" × 70½" for **Left/Right Inner Borders**

Cut (2) 1½" × 52½" for **Top/Bottom Inner Borders**

From Dark Blue Fabric

Cut (3) 6¾" × WOF strips into (18) 6¾" squares for **Star Block HSTs**

From Medium Blue Fabric

Cut (2) 6¾" × WOF strips into (9) 6¾" squares for **Star Block HSTs**

Cut (6) 3" × WOF strips into (68) 3" squares for **Checks Blocks**

From Light Blue Fabric

Cut (2) 6¾" × WOF strips into (9) 6¾" squares for **Star Block HSTs**

Cut (2) 6¾" × WOF strips into (9) 6¾" squares for **Checks Blocks Corner HSTs**

From White Fabric

Cut (3) 6¾" × WOF strips into (18) 6¾" squares for **Star Block HSTs**

Cut (6) 3" × WOF strips into (72) 3" squares for **Star Block Plain Squares**

Cut (2) 6¾" × WOF strips into (9) 6¾" squares for **Checks Block HSTs**

Cut (14) 1¾" × WOF strips for **Strip Sets** for **Checks Blocks Checkerboard**

MAKING THE BLOCK PARTS AND ASSEMBLING THE BLOCKS (see page 94)

Make (18) Star Blocks

Use eight-at-a-time method to make HSTs. Pair the 6¾" squares, right sides together, as follows:

(9) light-blue + (9) white 6¾" squares

(9) Dark-blue + (9) white 6¾" squares

(9) Dark-blue + (9) medium-blue 6¾ 4" squares

After making the HSTs, you should have:

(72) light-blue + white HSTs

(72) dark-blue + white HSTs

(72) dark-blue + medium-blue HSTs

Combine HSTs with plain squares to make (18) **Star Blocks.** Be sure to turn the HSTs in the correct direction. For each **Star Block** you need:

- (4) light-blue + white HSTs
- (4) plain white squares
- (4) dark-blue + white HSTs
- (4) dark-blue + light-blue HSTs

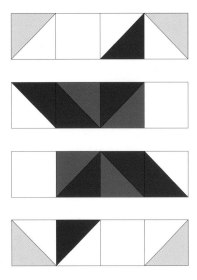

Make (17) Checks Blocks
Make (17) Square-in-Square Units and (68) Bonus HSTs

Mark the backs of the 3" medium-blue squares with a diagonal line from corner to corner (A)

Mark a second line $^{1}/_{2}$" from the first line

Sew on both drawn lines

Cut between the lines; set aside Bonus HST

Press seam allowances toward the darker fabric

Repeat the process of adding blue corners to the center squares and making bonus HSTs (B)

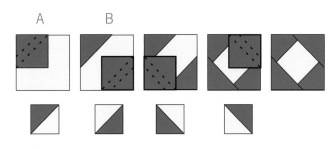

Bonus HSTs

Make (68) Checkerboard Units (see page 95)

Attach (2) red + white segments that were cut from the **Strip Sets** to make each **Checkerboard Unit**

Be sure to reverse the ends and nest the seams

Press seam allowance open

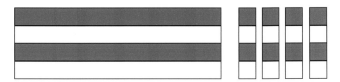

Make (72) Light Blue + White Checkerboard Block HST Units (see page 94)

Pair together (9) light-blue and (9) white $6^{3}/_{4}$" squares right sides together

Use eight-at-a-time method to make (72) light-blue + white **Checkerboard Block HSTs**

Press seam allowance toward darker fabric

Assemble (17) Checks Blocks

Be sure to turn the HSTs in the correct direction. For each **Checks Block** you need:

- (1) center Square-in-Square unit
- (4) Checkerboard units
- (4) corner HSTs

ASSEMBLING THE QUILT TOP

Attach Blocks and Rows

Attach blocks, alternating Star blocks and
Checks blocks as shown

Press seams one direction in one row, then
the other direction in the next row

Attach rows, nesting the seamlines

Press long seams open

Attach the Borders

Attach the borders in the following order:

$1\frac{1}{2}" \times 70\frac{1}{2}"$ strips for left/right
inner borders

$1\frac{1}{2}" \times 52\frac{1}{2}"$ strips for top/bottom
inner borders

$4\frac{1}{2}" \times 72\frac{1}{2}"$ strips for left/right
outer borders

$4\frac{1}{2}" \times 60\frac{1}{2}"$ strips for top/bottom
outer borders

FINISHING THE QUILT

The quilt top should now measure $60\frac{1}{2}" \times 80\frac{1}{2}"$

Refer to the "General Directions" (page 89) for preparing **Backing** and **Binding**

Backing for this quilt should measure 68" × 88"

For **Binding**, cut and attach (8) $2\frac{1}{2}"$ × WOF strips

GENERAL
DIRECTIONS:
PP. 89–99

Snail Trail

Photo on page 73
Traditional design
Finished size 60" × 80"

The **Snail Trail Block** has been around since at least 1935, perhaps longer. It looks devilishly complicated, but it is only a Square-in-a-Square block with a Four-Patch in the center. The design is made by arranging the colors of the triangles, setting four blocks together, and turning each of them so that the same color meets in the center. There are (48) identical 10" blocks in this quilt, arranged six across and eight down

FABRIC REQUIREMENTS

For Blocks

White: 3¼ yards

Red: 2 yards

Blue: 2 yards

For Backing

5 yards

For Binding

¾ yard

CUTTING INSTRUCTIONS

Cut the 2¼" strips for the **Center Four-Patch Strip Sets** first and set them aside. All the rest of the fabric will be cut into squares and then recut into half-square triangles (/) in small, medium, and large from the red, white, and blue fabrics. You will have twice as many white squares and triangles as red and blue.

From White Fabric

Cut (6) 2¼" × WOF strips for **Center Four-Patch Strip Sets**

Cut (5) 3⅜" × WOF strips into (48) 3⅜" squares (/) for **Round 1 (Small)**

Cut (6) 4⅜" × WOF strips into (48) 4⅜" squares (/) for **Round 2 (Medium)**

Cut (8) 5⅞" × WOF strips into (48) 5⅞" squares (/) for **Round 3 (Large)**

From Blue Fabric

Cut (3) 2¼" × WOF strips for **Center Four-Patch Strip Sets**

Cut (3) 3⅜" × WOF strips into (24) 3⅜" squares (/) for **Round 1 (Small)**

Cut (3) 4⅜" × WOF strips into (24) 4⅜" squares (/) for **Round 2 (Medium)**

Cut (4) 5⅞" × WOF strips into (24) 5⅞" squares (/) for **Round 3 (Large)**

From Red Fabric

Cut (3) 2¼" × WOF strips for **Center Four-Patch Strip Sets**

Cut (3) 3⅜" × WOF strips into (24) 3⅜" squares (/) for **Round 1 (Small)**

Cut (3) 4⅜" × WOF strips into (24) 4⅜" squares (/) for **Round 2 (Medium)**

Cut (4) 5⅞" × WOF strips into (24) 5⅞" squares (/) for **Round 3 (Large)**

MAKING AND ORGANIZING THE BLOCKS (see page 95)

Make (48) Center Four-Patch Units

Make **Strip Sets** from 2¼" × WOF strips

Make (3) red + white two-strip strip sets (A)

Make (3) blue + white two-strip strip sets (B)

Press seam allowance away from white strip

Cut the strip sets into 2¼" segments (C)

Attach segments, alternating the blue + white and red + white to make (48) **Center Four-Patch Units** (D)

Trim to 4", if necessary

Add Triangles to Center Four-Patch Units

This is a project that was made for chain piecing. Organize the piecing into three piles of triangles:

Round 1: small red, white, and blue triangles

Round 2: medium red, white, and blue triangles

Round 3: large red, white, and blue triangles

Round 1 (Small Triangles)

Set aside the medium and large triangles for now

Keep all the **Center Four-Patch Units** oriented in the same direction as you begin round 1

Notice in illustration that the **Red Square** is at the **Upper Right** of the **Four-Patch**

Add a **Small Red Triangle** to the **Right Side** of the Four-Patch as shown (A)

Add a **Small Blue Triangle** to the side opposite the small red triangle (B)

Press seam allowances away from center

Add **Small White Triangles** to the other two sides (C)

Press seam allowances away from center

Repeat for all the center Four-Patch units

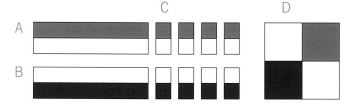

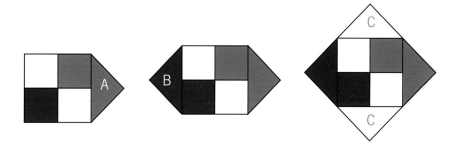

Round 2 (Medium Triangles)

Work with only the medium triangles for this round

- Keep all the **Center Four-Patch Units** oriented in the same direction in round 1
- Add a **Medium Red Triangle** to the **Lower Right Side** of the Four-Patch as shown
- Add a **Medium Blue Triangle** to the opposite side
- Press seam allowances away from center
- Add **Medium White Triangles** to the other two sides
- Press seam allowances away from center
- Repeat for all the remaining units

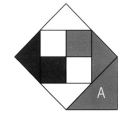 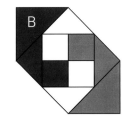 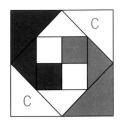

Round 3

All that are left are the large triangles

- Keep all the **Center Four-Patch Units** oriented in the same direction in rounds 1 and 2
- Add a **Large Red Triangle** to the **Bottom Side** as shown
- Add a **Large Blue Triangle** to the opposite side
- Press seam allowances away from center
- Add **Large White Triangles** to the other two sides
- Press seam allowances away from center
- Repeat for all the remaining units

 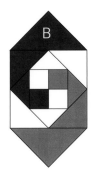 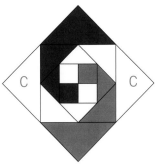

ASSEMBLING THE QUILT TOP

Make (12) Four-Block Sets

Turn each block so that the large red triangles meet in the middle of the block

Attach (4) Snail Trail blocks into (1) larger block

Repeat for remaining blocks

Press seam allowances open or all in same direction

Attach the (4) Rows of Four-Block Sets

Sew the Four-Block rows together

Press the long seam open

Finishing the Quilt

The quilt top should now measure 60½" × 80½"

Refer to the "General Directions" (page 89) for preparing **Backing** and **Binding**

Backing for this quilt should measure 68" × 88"

For **Binding**, cut and attach (8) 2½" × WOF strips

GENERAL
DIRECTIONS:
PP. 89–99

Chain of Fours

Photo on page 83
Inspiration pattern: Jennie Tracy, Chain of Fours
Finished size 60" × 80"

There are (12) 20" finished-size blocks in this easy, yet impressive, quilt. Directions are given for using assorted red and blue fabrics along with one white background. However, the quilt would be equally exciting in multicolor scraps.

FABRIC REQUIREMENTS

The greater the range of red and blue shades and prints, the more interesting the quilt will be. However, for this pattern, directions are given for (2) shades of blue, (1) red, and (1) white.

For Blocks

Light blue: ³/₄ yard

Dark blue: ³/₄ yard

Red: 2 yard

White: 3¹/₂ yards

For Backing

5 yards

For Binding

³/₄ yard

- -

CUTTING INSTRUCTIONS

Label the fabric as you cut to avoid confusion

From Light-Blue Fabric

Cut (8) 2¹/₂" × WOF strips for **Four-Patch Strip Sets**

From Dark-Blue Fabric

Cut (8) 2¹/₂" × WOF strips for **Four-Patch Strip Sets**

From Red Fabric

Cut (6) 4⅞" × WOF strips into (48) 4⅞" squares for **Red+White HST Units**

Cut (5) 3⅜" × WOF strips into (48) 3⅜" squares for **Square-on-Point Units**

From White Fabric

Note on cutting white fabric: to avoid confusion later while you are assembling the block units, please be sure to **label** the units as you cut.

Cut (12) 2½" × WOF strips for **Four-Patch Strip Sets**

Cut (6) 4⅞" × WOF strips into (48) 4⅞" squares for **Red + White HST Units** (keep as squares)

Cut (6) 4⅞" × WOF strips into (48) 4⅞" squares (/) for **HSTs for Square-on-Point Units** (cut in half on diagonal)

Cut (4) 5¼" × WOF strips into (24) 5¼" squares (X) for **QSTs for Square-on-Point Units** (cut in quarters on diagonal)

MAKING AND ORGANIZING THE BLOCK PARTS

(see page 95)

Make (108) Four Patch Units from Strip Sets

Make **Two-Strip Strip Sets** from 2½" × WOF strips as follows:

(6) light blue + (6) white (A)

(6) dark blue + (6) white (B)

(2) dark blue + (2) light blue (C)

Cut strip sets into 2½" segments (D):

Cut (96) 2½" segments from **Light Blue + White Strip Sets**

Cut (96) 2½" segments from **Dark Blue + White Strip Sets**

Cut (24) 2½" segments from **Light Blue + Dark Blue Strip Sets**

Attach 2½" segments to make Four-Patch units (E) as follows:

Make (48) light-blue + white **Four-Patch Units**

Make (48) dark-blue + white **Four-Patch Units**

Make (12) light-blue + dark-blue **Four-Patch Units**

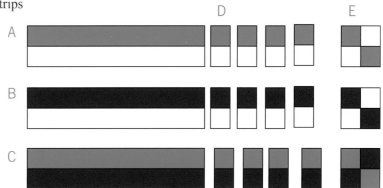

Make (96) Red + White HSTs (see page 92)

Pair together (48) red $4^7/_8$" squares with (48) white $4^7/_8$" squares, right sides together (A)

Draw a diagonal line on the back of the white square

Sew $1/_4$" on either side of the drawn line

Cut on the drawn line

Press seam allowance toward the red fabric (B)

Trim to $4^1/_2$" square, if necessary

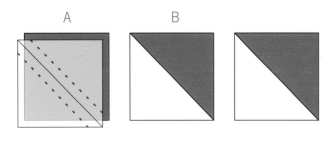

Make (48) Square-on-Point Units

For these units, you will need:

A. (96) white HSTS that were cut from $4^7/_8$" squares (/)

B. (96) white QSTs that were cut from $5^1/_4$" squares (X)

(48) red $3^3/_8$" squares

Attach **White** (B) **QSTs** to two sides of red square, as shown

Attach **White** (A) **HSTs** to the other sides of the red square

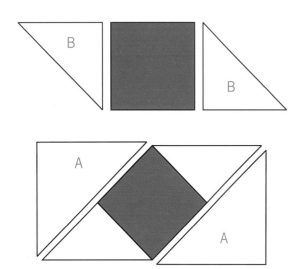

ASSEMBLING THE BLOCKS

You should now have all the units needed to make the blocks:

(48) light-blue + white **Four-Patch Units**

(48) dark-blue + white **Four-Patch Units**

(12) light-blue + dark-blue **Four-Patch Units**

(96) red + white **HSTs**

(48) **Square-on-Point Units**

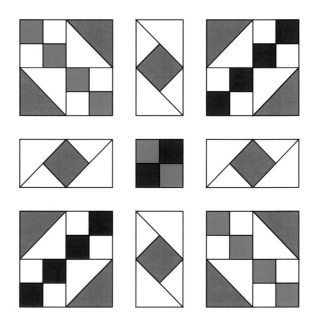

Assemble the corner units by combining the **Four-Patch Unit**s with the **Red + White HSTs**

Attach the units as shown, being sure to orient the units correctly.

ASSEMBLING THE QUILT TOP

Attach the (12) completed Chain of Four blocks into (4) rows of (3) blocks

FINISHING THE QUILT

The quilt top should now measure 60½" × 80½"

Refer to the "General Directions" (page 89) for preparing **Backing** and **Binding**

Backing for this quilt should measure 68" × 88"

For **Binding**, cut and attach (8) 2½" × WOF strips

GENERAL
DIRECTIONS:
PP. 89–99

How to Request a Quilt of Valor

To request a Quilt of Valor, go to the website www.qovf.org.
Click on "How to Request a Quilt of Valor" on the home page, fill in the form, and submit.

ABOVE Theresa Gouker and Diane Ernst of the Myrtle Beach Shore Birds of Myrtle Beach, South Carolina, awarded Dennis Cole USAF 1973–1983 with a Quilt of Valor in May 2018.

Quilts of Valor awardees at the 2018 QOVF Conference in Myrtle Beach, South Carolina.

Memory Pages

In keeping with the mission of the Quilts of Valor Foundation to cover service members and veterans touched by war with comforting and healing Quilts of Valor, these pages are provided as a place to tell a personal story. Record information about the recipient, add photographs, share memories, and provide reference information for future generations.

Quilts of Valor has nearly 8,000 members nationwide, who have awarded nearly 200,000 Quilts of Valor to military members. Quilting experts Ann Parsons Holte, Renelda Peldunas-Harter, Ann Rehbein, and Sue Reich are dedicated to the QOVF mission to "cover military touched by war" with a quilt.

Marianne Fons is the cofounder of Fons & Porter and its *Love of Quilting* television show and magazine. She consults, teaches, and supports quilting education and is a longtime QOVF board member.